Level 1

MENTORING GUIDEBOOK

For information:

 Corwin Press
A Sage Publications Company
2455 Teller Road
Thousand Oaks, California 91320
www.corwinpress.com

Sage Publications Ltd.
1 Oliver's Yard
55 City Road
London EC1Y 1SP
United Kingdom

Sage Publications India Pvt. Ltd.
B-42, Panchsheel Enclave
New Delhi 110 017   India

Printed in the United States of America

LCCN 2002104353
ISBN 1-5751-7846-X

This book is printed on acid-free paper.

06 07 08 09 10 9 8 7 6 5 4 3 2 1

Level 1

MENTORING GUIDEBOOK

Starting the Journey
2nd Edition

Kay Burke
Editor

CORWIN PRESS
A SAGE Publications Company
Thousand Oaks, California

Dedication

In honor of the sisterhood—To my sister and friend, Carol Brown and my sisters by marriage—Pauline, Sharon, Kathy, Annalisa, and Merrill. We mentor the rest of the family!

Contents

Acknowledgments

My mentoring journey began in January 2001 when Julie Sausen, Vikki Myers, Karen Evans, and I met to discuss the essential skills we thought new teachers needed in order to succeed in the educational profession. The conversations continued as we worked with Carol Luitjens, John Nolan, and others.

Under the thoughtful editorial leadership of Chris Jaeggi and Anne Kaske, we selected key chapters from books that we thought would help new teachers become more confident in designing curriculum, delivering instruction, managing the classroom, and assessing student work. We also included articles to help schools and districts organize a mentoring program and help mentors develop trust with their proteges and learn how to communicate effectively during pre- and post-observation conferences.

Contributors include Barry Sweeny, Debra Pitton, Julie Sausen, Jan Skowron, David Lazear, James Bellanca, and Robin Fogarty. I also selected chapters from my assessment and classroom management books that beginning teachers said helped them survive the first critical months of teaching.

I would like to thank Bruce Leckie, David Stockman, Bob Crump, Donna Ramirez, and Carrie Straka in the Publishing Department for their cooperation, creativity, and commitment throughout the mentoring projects and all the other books and manuals we worked on together over the past 12 years.

I would especially like to thank Julie Sausen, my friend and Mentoring Project Manager, for her tireless and enthusiastic commitment to helping new teachers. Julie inspires all of us to "try harder" to help both mentors and their proteges feel more confident in their roles. A special thanks to Susan Gray, Lois Brown, Frank Burke and all my family members who helped me survive the many "Mentor Madness Months."

Finally, I would like to thank mentors throughout the world for their willingness to share their time, expertise, and enthusiasm with the ever-increasing number of beginning teachers. Their commitment to support and nurture new teachers not only improves the quality of their teaching, but most importantly, improves the quality of our students' learning.

—Kay Burke
May 2002

Introduction

Beginning teachers who do not participate in an Induction Program are twice as likely to leave as those who do participate. (NEA Today, Vol. 19, No. 8, May 2001)

he journey new teachers embark upon when they enter the educational profession offers exciting challenges that stimulate personal growth. The adrenaline flows when a first-year teacher encounters her first group of students without being under the watchful eyes of the supervising teacher sitting quietly in the back of the room. New teachers quickly realize, however, that they must take control of the classroom and make hundreds of decisions affecting the lives of the children entrusted to their care. Even though many first-year teachers have observed other teachers and experienced student teaching in college, the academic and classroom management challenges faced by first-year educators can be overwhelming. According to statistics from the National Education Association (NEA), 30 percent of new teachers leave within the first five years! In big cities, the percentage leaving within the first five years is even higher: 50 percent.

In some schools new teachers are assigned a "buddy" teacher to show them around the school and help them get their books and supplies. Often, the buddies teach the same grade level or content area so they also help the new teachers plan their curriculum. Usually the arrangement is informal and neither party receives any official training. A more formal type of mentoring program may be required, however, because of the retirement of so many Baby Boomer generation educators and the subsequent need to recruit and train new teachers to fill growing numbers of vacancies. Statisticians predict a need to hire between 0.5 million and 2.5 million new teachers over the next decade. In addition to teacher retirements, the demand for so many new teachers is the result of the increasing numbers of students and the call for class-size reduction programs (Schultz as cited in Scherer 1999, p. 99). Recruiting, training, and retaining qualified teachers are important priorities in many cities as districts struggle to hire certified teachers and to attract people from business and overseas to fill teaching vacancies. Schools and districts across the country are creating or expanding formal mentoring programs to help new educators become committed, competent, and confident professionals who enjoy teaching.

The term *mentoring* comes from classical literature. In the Greek epic, the *Odyssey,* the poet Homer describes how the young hero Odysseus gave the responsibility of raising his son, Telemachus, to Mentor, his trusted friend and advisor, before he sailed to Troy to fight in the Trojan War. Mentor guided Telemachus while Odysseus was away by educating him in all of the physical, social, and intellectual facets of life. When Odysseus returned to Ithaca after ten years of fighting the Trojan war and ten years of wandering in search of his homeland, Telemachus had grown into an independent thinker who readily helped his father reclaim his property and rescue his wife from ambitious suitors.

The term *mentor* today usually refers to someone with more experience who teaches someone with less experience. The person with less experience could be called a *mentee, a beginning teacher,* a *novice,* or a *protégé.* Protégé is derived from a French term and means "one who is protected . . . by a person with experience, prominence, or influence" (Merriam-Webster's Collegiate Dictionary, Tenth ed.).

Just as Mentor assisted young Telemachus on his life's journey, so too do mentor teachers assist new teachers as they begin their teaching careers. The excerpts in this book provide critical components mentors can use to help their protégés gain confidence in their teaching and develop trust in their mentor relationship. This book also provides important concepts and lessons to help educators shape the social and academic lives of their students. Mentoring is a process that requires dedication, commitment, and an openness to a trusting, ongoing relationship on the part of both the mentor and the protégé. One goal of any mentoring program is to empower veteran teachers to become skillful coaches who help beginning educators gain confidence in their abilities to meet the diverse needs of their students. I hope this guidebook will help start the journey toward providing a positive and stimulating learning environment for the mentors, protégés, and students.

REFERENCES

Merriam-Webster's Collegiate® Dictionary, Tenth Edition. 1996. Springfield, MA: Merriam-Webster, Incorporated.

National Education Association. *A better beginning: Helping new teachers survive and thrive.* A guide for NEA local affiliates interested in creating new teacher support systems. A publication of the NEA New Teacher Support Initiative. Washington, DC: National Education Association.

NEA Today. 2001. Young, dedicated—and out the door. *NEA Today.* 19(8). <www.nea.org/neatoday>

Schultz, B. 1999. Combining mentoring and assessment in California. In *A better beginning: Supporting and mentoring new teachers,* edited by M. Scherer. Alexandria, VA: Association for Supervision and Curriculum Development.

Level 1

MENTORING GUIDEBOOK

SECTION I

Defining the Relationship

Teaching is an unusual profession because the first-year teacher in most cases is assigned to the same tasks in and out of the classroom as a long-term veteran.

—Heidkamp and Shapiro 1999

efore embarking on a journey, it is always helpful to meet and get to know one's traveling companions. Schools and school districts engage in a wide variety of formal and informal social activities before school starts to help the seasoned travelers, the mentors, work with the first-time travelers, the protégés, to set the course for the new school year. Sometimes the activities are very structured and form the basis of the first steps in a formal two- to -three-year new teacher induction program. The formal induction program may include an orientation program, professional development training, mentor training, peer support groups, classroom observations, professional development plans, and a professional portfolio.

By working together, mentors and protégés forge a strong foundation.

In Selection 1, **Structures for Induction and Mentoring Programs,** Barry Sweeny shows how all the puzzle pieces of an induction program fit together to form a coherent and integrated long-term development program to initiate new teachers. He defines a common vocabulary for all involved in the process and provides guidance in deciding whether to take an informal approach to mentoring beginning teachers or to establish a formal mentoring program to ensure more accountability.

Sweeny defines the roles of the mentor and the evolving picture of the protégé. He also describes the differences between the traditional one-to-one mentoring relationship and the team approach where a group of teachers shares the mentoring duties and their multiple talents and strengths with the protégé. Based upon his extensive experience working with mentoring programs, he includes checklists to cover many first- and second-week responsibilities of new teachers.

In Selection 2, **The Heart of Mentoring: Trust and Open Communication,** Debra Pitton reviews what she calls the "heart of mentoring"—the necessity of open communications. Both verbal and nonverbal signals should provide nonjudgmental feedback that allows the mentee (i.e., protégé) to discover and solve problems independently whenever possible.

Pitton talks about the importance of "exact language" to help avoid misinterpretation. Non-verbal messages could be sending signals that contradict verbal messages. She also addresses other aspects of communication, such as proximity, turn-taking, eye contact, and use of time-critical components of open communication.

Section I, *Defining the Relationship*, focuses on the initial stages of helping mentors and protégés become familiar and comfortable with the mentoring process. Together the mentors and the new teachers define their respective roles and develop a common vocabulary to help them communicate effectively. Mentors and protégés who take the time to define their responsibilities and share their expectations for the partnership create a strong foundation for future growth. Defining the ground rules for mentoring helps set the course for a positive and mutually beneficial mentoring relationship. Each journey begins with one step and most new teachers look forward to the new adventure. Proactive educators, however, spend time planning the trip in order to avoid unpleasant surprises or unexpected diversions. By working together to define relationships before the first day of school, mentors and protégés forge a strong foundation for building a successful mentoring experience.

> The mentor has to know how to be the "guide on the side" and how to offer suggestions in a supportive way.

REFERENCE

Heidkamp, A. and J. Shapiro. 1999. The elements of a supportive induction program. In *A better beginning: Supporting and mentoring new teachers,* edited by M. Scherer. Alexandria, VA: Association for Supervision and Curriculum Development.

More and more states have mandated mentoring programs for all new teachers. Sweeny reviews the issues leaders should address in order to meet the needs of new teachers, mentors, and the districts.

Structures for Induction and Mentoring Programs

by **Barry Sweeny**

This selection explores some fundamental issues program leaders must consider sooner or later in a mentoring program. Some of the issues discussed regard how leaders intend the individuals in the program to think about mentoring. The other issues concern decisions about program-level strategies that determine how leaders should conduct the program. Figure 1.1 defines the terms used throughout Selection 1. Figure 1.2 outlines the components of a teacher induction program. Although this selection primarily focuses on the mentoring piece of the puzzle, it is helpful to understand how mentoring can fit into a complete induction program.

Informal or Formal Mentoring?

Veteran teachers are usually very helpful and supportive people. However, beginning educators can easily fall through the cracks despite others' informal intentions to be helpful, especially once the school year has started and the pace of activity has accelerated to

Adapted from *Leading the Teacher Induction and Mentoring Program* by Barry Sweeny, pp. xii, xiii, 1–14. © 2001 by Corwin Press. Used with permission.

Structures for Induction and Mentoring Programs

Common Vocabulary for Uncommon Roles

1. **Beginning Educator**—A brand new educator who has little or no previous paid experience as an educator.

2. **New Educator**—An educator with at least two or more years of paid professional education experience, but who is newly hired in the district.

3. **Protégé**—A beginning or new educator who is working with a mentor.

4. **Mentor**—The title and status applied to a person who assumes the primary responsibility to provide mentoring. The mentor is a more experienced and, frequently, more senior person who works in a similar location and role as the protégé.

5. **Mentoring**—The complex developmental process mentors use to support and guide their protégés through the necessary transitions that are a part of learning how to be effective educators and career-long learners.

6. **Team Mentoring**—An approach to mentoring that divides the tasks of mentoring among several veteran educators who share the responsibilities based on their individual strengths. A teacher who has excellent, engaging lessons can help a protégé in a different way than can a teacher whose strength is avoiding and defusing confrontations in the classroom. Each contributes in different ways to the development and support of the protégé.

7. **Induction**—The activities and processes necessary to successfully induct a novice teacher into the profession. An effective induction program should include orientation, mentoring, staff development specific to the protégé's needs, observations of experienced teachers at work, and peer support groups.

8. **Coaching**—The support for learning provided by a colleague who uses observation, data collection, and descriptive, nonjudgmental reporting on specific requested behaviors and technical skills. The goal is to help an individual see his or her own patterns of behavior through someone else's eyes and to prompt reflection, goal-setting, and action to increase the desired results.

Figure 1.1

The Components of an Effective Induction Program

Figuring out the pieces you need to make an effective induction program should not be a puzzle. All you need is the lid for the box of puzzle pieces so you can see how to fit them all together effectively. Once you have the big picture, you can do it!

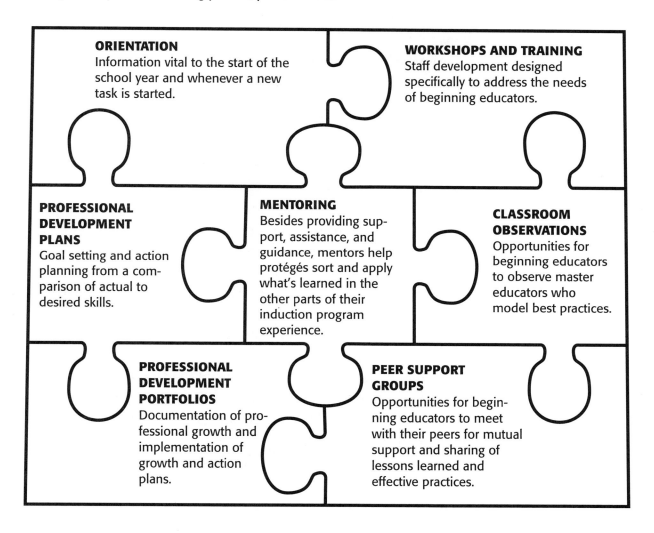

ORIENTATION
Information vital to the start of the school year and whenever a new task is started.

WORKSHOPS AND TRAINING
Staff development designed specifically to address the needs of beginning educators.

PROFESSIONAL DEVELOPMENT PLANS
Goal setting and action planning from a comparison of actual to desired skills.

MENTORING
Besides providing support, assistance, and guidance, mentors help protégés sort and apply what's learned in the other parts of their induction program experience.

CLASSROOM OBSERVATIONS
Opportunities for beginning educators to observe master educators who model best practices.

PROFESSIONAL DEVELOPMENT PORTFOLIOS
Documentation of professional growth and implementation of growth and action plans.

PEER SUPPORT GROUPS
Opportunities for beginning educators to meet with their peers for mutual support and sharing of lessons learned and effective practices.

Figure 1.2

what is typical for September. This can occur because everyone who would like to help the beginning teacher becomes extremely busy with his or her own work, and because some may fear appearing critical of the beginning teacher's work and thus are uncomfortable making suggestions or offering help.

In addition, beginning teachers often have so much to learn and to do immediately at the start of their new jobs, they may find it difficult to take time out from their work to seek out the assistance they need. They frequently believe they are expected to do the same work as a twenty-year veteran, and because of this they often do not want to reveal their concerns and problems for fear of looking incompetent.

Most school districts care about the success of their new employees and the students they serve. Many educational leaders have become dissatisfied with the informal approach to mentoring beginning teachers. Leaders who want to ensure beginning teacher success often find that an informal approach makes it difficult to know whether a given person is receiving the help he or she needs, and which experienced teachers are really helping their new colleagues and therefore deserve support or some form of recognition.

Another factor causing the move to a more formal mentoring approach is the increasing accountability placed on educators today and the greater expectation to provide instruction that ensures all students are successful. The increase in alternative certification routes to teaching, increasing standards for teaching and certification, the retirement of the Baby Boomer generation, and the need to attract a more diverse population to teaching are additional reasons for the surge in use of formal mentoring approaches. Informal approaches to mentoring are no longer viewed as sufficient for the needs of today's beginning educators and schools.

Considering these factors, it is no wonder that by 1998 mentoring of beginning teachers was mandated and funded in twenty-nine states in the United States and required in various forms in a number of others (Sweeny 1998). Mentoring is an investment in the success of both beginning teachers and the thousands of students whose lives those teachers will touch throughout their careers. Mentoring also protects that investment by dramatically increasing the retention of beginning teachers, saving organizations the loss of several thousands of dollars when a teacher leaves.

What Is a Mentor?

The fundamental means for providing beginning teacher support is, of course, the mentor. A mentor is a person who assumes the *primary responsibility* to provide mentoring (see Figure 1.1). The mentor is described this way because there are several approaches for providing the assistance, support, and guidance beginning teachers deserve. Each approach incorporates a different conception of mentoring and purposes for induction. At this point, we need to consider the impact of one's concept of a mentor on the choices one makes about structuring the induction and mentoring program.

Defining a Mentor

At the most fundamental level, the mentor is always a role model. No one disagrees with this statement, because everyone who uses a mentoring strategy is interested in novices learning from experts who are the kind of role models leaders want novices to emulate. Where disagreement sometimes occurs is in answering the question, "What is it a mentor should be modeling?"

The earliest mentoring programs used approaches that at least implied that the mentor was an expert with all the answers, whose job was to provide the answers to the novice and to ensure that the novice eventually became someone who had all the answers too. I call that approach to mentoring the mentor cloning model. I know the label exaggerates this position a bit, but I urge leaders to examine their concept of the mentor to be sure it does not look like this exaggerated cloning process. I have observed many mentoring programs with mentors who at least act as if cloning themselves is their purpose.

Today's educators recognize the cloning model of mentoring as less than professional and out of sync with current conceptions of learning and teaching as more of a constructivist process. They know excellence in teaching and excellence in learning to teach is as much an art as it is a science. Thus, I propose that the mentors that educators need today must act more as models of continual learning than as individuals who have all the answers. This is a crucial understanding to reach and to implement in induction and mentoring processes. This conception of teaching and learning cannot be learned by new teachers if they are inducted into the profession any other way.

Simply stated, if mentors act as if they have all the answers and are not continuing to learn, new teachers will learn to look for and act as if they have all the answers, encouraging the idea that they do not need to keep learning once they have found a teaching style that works. Put such a teacher into a classroom and you get students who perceive their roles as getting the right answers, and when they have done that, it is okay to stop learning. This is exactly what educational leaders do not want to see.

What leaders *do* want to see is an aligned three-layer model of continual learning:

1. Leaders want to see mentors who model the excitement of learning every day, openly, and in front of their peers. They want to see mentors with a drive to find ever better ways to help their students *and* their colleagues succeed.
2. With this kind of mentoring, beginning teachers become models of continual learning, and do so openly, in front of their students. Leaders want to see beginning teachers whose passion is finding ever better and more effective ways of ensuring their students' success.
3. Leaders need this kind of beginning teachers, because they know it is the best way to help students become lifelong learners and collaborative workers who are open to learning from each other, always searching for better and more effective ways to achieve their own goals.

Clarifying what mentors should model is an absolutely critical step in developing induction and mentoring programs that can actually improve teaching and increase student success. Leaders who are responsible for the success of induction and mentoring programs and of beginning teachers need to establish this starting point before they make the next set of decisions.

The Evolving Picture of the Protégé

It is becoming quite surprising to review the range and diversity of prior experience found in new employees at a typical start-of-school orientation meeting. Some are twenty-one years old, recently graduated from college, and ready to assume their first paid position in a new career. Some of these individuals have never held a paid position before, not even a part-time job for a few weeks during school breaks. Others may be in their late thirties or older, have raised several children, and are now returning to a career they started fifteen years earlier. Some have been actively teaching for a number of years and are merely changing districts or schools, or even just grade levels. Still others have been working for a number of years in a corporate position or the military, have recently attained a teaching degree and certification, and are changing careers to become teachers. A more recent phenomenon is the new employee who has worked in another career, has no preparation as a teacher, is filling a teaching position in a subject area where candidates are scarce, and is entering this role under an alternative certification program.

Creators of induction and mentoring programs must carefully seek ways to adjust the support provided to such a diverse range of new employees so that the assistance they receive remains appropriate to the varying levels and types of experience new employees bring to their work. It is critical that the program address the individual needs that determine the ability of the person to develop professionally. It is also essential to explicitly model how important it is for all educators to work for the success of individual learners.

Induction and mentoring are frequently tailored to the different levels of new employee experience. Following are three terms induction and mentoring programs often use to distinguish these levels of need and the way the program delivers its services. Those who lead an induction program need to select, define for others, and consistently use a similar set of terms in their work. (See also Figure 1.1)

1. **Protégé:** The labels programs give new participants in mentoring vary considerably, from mentee to partner teacher to colleague. I use the term *protégé* and reserve it exclusively for those new or beginning educators who are assigned to and actively work with a mentor. This is to distinguish the protégé from all other new employees, regardless of their level of experience, who are not working with mentors.

2. **Beginning educator:** This term includes both teachers and others such as school social workers, school psychologists, school nurses, or learning center directors. *Beginning educator* usually describes someone with little or no previous professional educational experience, such as those with a year or less of teaching experience. The label *beginner* also assumes no previous experience. In other words, someone who taught for four years, then raised a family, and is now returning to teaching should *not* be called a beginning educator, even if the lack of recent experience suggests a need for intensive mentoring.

A mentor assigned to a beginning educator needs to be cautious, for the protégé frequently has other kinds of experience that greatly impact his or her professional development needs. For example, mentors should not treat a twenty-one-year-old college graduate the same way they would a thirty-five-year-old individual who has entered the profession through an alternative route to teaching after working in a related content field, or the same way as a forty-two-year-old beginning educator who has just raised two children, and has recently completed requirements for a teaching certificate. Both the individuals mentioned in the last two circumstances represent people who have life experiences that have prepared them well for many aspects of the role of educator, even though they may have little or no paid educational experience. Nevertheless, in all three cases the term *beginning educator* applies.

How does mentoring of a beginner get started? Beginning educators may not know all the questions they need to ask, and so they may feel well prepared and ready to go to work when, in fact, they are not well prepared. Mentors should expect that beginning educators may not always be ready to accept help immediately, but that they may become ready and more open to help a little later in their teaching experience. During that time mentors must remain visibly and continually available and accepting of the level of readiness their protégé expresses. The experience of organizing and running one's own classroom and the sense of responsibility for student success is a huge reality check for many beginning teachers. This is why they may have an intense and sudden need for mentoring once the first days or weeks of the school year are past.

Mentors need to stay on top of their own responsibilities, trying to accomplish their own work well in advance of when things usually have to be done. This is important because when the beginning teacher grasps the reality of teaching and becomes aware of his or her need for help, the mentor must have time to provide the necessary support. For example, if a mentor waits to complete her own grading until just before report cards are due, she will not be available to help her protégé with that task when the need arises. In this case, the opportunity to explain issues of student assessment and fairness, discuss district assessment expectations and processes, and demonstrate important decision-making processes are lost. Or, the mentor may make time to help the protégé, but may end up with insufficient time to do justice to his or her own grading.

3. **New educator:** This term refers to educators who are newly hired to the district, but have at least two years of paid professional teaching experience. They may have been recently employed as educators in another district or may be returning to education after an extended leave, but they have nearly similar needs for orientation to the school, district, community, curriculum, key people, procedures, and the traditions and culture of the school. However, they do not always need the same amount of time and the same intensity of mentoring to become well oriented to these things. That is why it is critical to distinguish between beginning and new educators.

Structures for Induction and Mentoring Programs

Experienced but new educators know most of the questions that should be asked and are usually not timid about asking those questions or seeking the assistance they know they need. As a result, they can anticipate many of their needs and can learn the ropes much faster. Mentors assigned to an experienced educator may find their protégé provides as much leadership in the relationship and in accomplishing tasks as they do. Mentors who know this pattern may occur will view it as a good sign. They will be comfortable when this occurs, knowing that the new educator's needs are being met one way or the other and that their protégé is developing appropriately.

Mentors who are not well prepared to do mentoring may feel disappointed that they cannot help this kind of protégé more, and may be defensive and insistent about who should be leading in the mentoring relationship. Such a reaction is unfortunate and should be avoided. A strong mentor training program, a focus on meeting the varying needs of the protégés, and a mentoring process that predicts the phases through which new employees will move all help mentors to anticipate what they need to do to remain appropriate in their mentoring and to facilitate their protégés' professional growth.

Administrators and educational leaders who want their induction and mentoring programs to have a major positive impact on the success of their new employees need to ensure that their program components are structured to take into account the diversity of protégés' experience. Orientation seminars, for example, can begin with whole group activities, but should be customized to grade or course level for introductions to curriculum and strategies that are specific to particular levels of instruction. The support should also be individualized, although it does not necessarily have to be delivered individually. Mentoring is provided precisely to ensure that the critical knowledge gained in group settings is individualized to the needs of the educator, successfully mastered, and applied in every teacher's classroom.

Individual or Team Mentoring?

Even though most programs adopt the traditional one-to-one mentoring relationship for their program's approach, some may question whether that is the best structure. Other possibilities exist, which is why the mentor was defined earlier as the person who assumes the primary responsibility to provide mentoring. Individual, one-on-one mentoring is the prevalent structure because it is the easiest way to resolve a number of issues. Reducing mentoring to a pair context makes it easier to create the safe, confidential, and trusting relationship that must be present if mentoring is to successfully prompt the risk-taking and professional growth needed. Also, one-to-one mentoring simplifies assigning the responsibilities necessary in a mentoring relationship, simplifies the training and support needed by mentors, and is the most practical structure for mentoring in many schools, especially those with only a few teachers in any given grade or department. However, other approaches can be successfully used.

The use of a team approach to mentoring is increasing, especially as program leaders decide they want to develop beginning teachers who see teaching as a team function, not just as an isolated, individual role. Schools that are consciously trying to help all students succeed often structure the staff in teams so that the diverse strengths of team members can be better used to address the diverse needs of students. This conception of teaching suggests that mentoring should also be a model of team collaboration so that it reinforces other efforts to develop beginning teachers for the team environment. In such a context, group or team mentoring makes a great deal of sense, even though there are several challenges to implementing the strategy effectively and efficiently. Leaders can help make the process go smoothly by providing the time and facilitating the conversation needed to coordinate a team's responsibilities for mentoring. Providing training for a team of people is more difficult to coordinate and may be more costly. However, the effort is worth it as it increases the number of experienced teachers involved in mentoring. This helps a school to create an experienced faculty with the very skills excellent teachers need. After all, mentoring strategies and skills are also critical for good teaching.

Even in a team mentoring situation, however, one person should be identified as responsible for making sure the protégé is effectively supported. This is necessary regardless of whether the mentor or other team members are actually the individuals who provide the specific assistance that is needed. In this way, the person who is assigned the oversight responsibility often acts more as a linking agent between the protégé and the team, helping the protégé assess his or her own needs and access the people and resources available from the team.

There is another reason to consider the use of team mentoring. Almost all induction and mentoring programs are based on the idea that separation of mentoring from summative evaluation is required to ensure that the environment in the mentoring relationship is conducive to candid self-assessment, risk-taking, learning, and professional growth. In some novice teacher support programs, however, tricky roles and tasks must be assigned. For example, some state-mandated programs require evaluation of the beginning teacher for purposes of earning a professional certificate. In these types of situations, team mentoring can be used to separate the assigned responsibilities so that a principal on the support team does the observation and conferences for purposes of evaluation, contract extension, and certification, and mentors observe and confer with the protégé for purposes of supporting improvement in performance. Such a delineation of roles recognizes that principals do play critical mentoring roles, but also acknowledges that novice teachers are not likely to seek help from an evaluator, and thus mentoring should be kept separate from evaluation.

Full-Time or Part-Time Mentoring?

The most common mentoring structure is a teacher with a full-time teaching responsibility assigned to also serve as a mentor for a beginning teacher. In this case, the mentoring pair must find the time to plan, problem solve, observe, discuss teaching, set goals, and so forth (Moller 1999). This approach to mentoring is frequently accompanied by a stipend for the mentor in recognition of the tremendous amount of extra time it takes to be an effective mentor. For example, it is often necessary for mentors to use their own planning periods to assist their protégés. Providing a stipend is recognition that a mentor teacher's own work of calling parents, developing materials, or conducting planning must be done outside of the school day on his or her own time. In some situations, leaders of induction programs may not have the resources or may not wish to provide a mentoring stipend, but they also know there is a need for time for mentoring, particularly if instructional improvement is a program purpose. In that case, the mentoring pair is often provided with a budget of substitute time on which to draw throughout the year whenever planning time, staff development, observations, or coaching conferences are needed in the mentoring process.

In smaller schools and school districts, providing substitute teachers is often the most practical way to create the time needed for effective mentoring. However, finding substitutes at certain times of the year is difficult and results in the best teachers being sometimes absent from their own classrooms. While it is fairly logical to justify the sacrifice made today on behalf of the students who will benefit throughout the protégé's entire career, the arrangement does cause breaks in instructional consistency and other problems. The fact is, at least using this approach, the time for mentoring must be taken from time in the mentor's own classroom (Moller 1999), or the additional time must be purchased, either through a stipend or extended contract and school year.

A different approach makes finding time for professional development a greater priority. This approach is generally described as restructuring, and it often requires a complete analysis of how time is currently spent compared to the needs for professional development and school improvement on a daily basis during the school day. This step is frequently taken when district or school administrators realize they must align the use of time to their expectations that teachers improve their professional practice. Simply put, they decide they must provide the tools for people to do the work that is expected. Barkley (1999) reflects this approach and provides some powerful means for resolving the issue of making time available for initiatives such as mentoring and coaching. I have found the following strategies to be helpful in resolving time issues:

- Release mentors from hallway and/or study hall supervision or other non-instructional duties.
- Allow for team teaching between two mentors, or a mentor and a protégé.
- Use technology, mathematics/science, or literacy staff development funds to provide a year or two release for a teacher to serve as a mentor to beginning teachers and to experienced teachers in the target staff development program.

The Benefits of Full-Time Mentoring

Some larger mentoring programs have concluded they have a sufficient number of novice teachers to assign a full-time mentor to a number of protégés for a period of two to three years. Such a configuration is much more common today, and is used in cities such as Milwaukee, Minneapolis, and Baltimore, and in some suburban systems such as Cherry Creek Schools in Colorado (Romer 1999). In these situations, mentors are released from all teaching responsibilities, replaced by another teacher, and assigned to work intensely with as few as five or as many as twelve to fifteen protégés at a time. This range results from the different kinds of expectations placed on the mentor for improving instruction and other goals. Generally, the more complex the assignment, the more time needed with each protégé to attain the desired results within the formal mentoring period.

Despite the cost of additional salaries, these districts find a sufficient return on their investment to warrant the use of this approach. Consider what Terri Romer, a full-time mentor in Colorado's Cherry Creek Schools S.T.A.R. (Staff Training Assistance and Review) Mentor Program has to say about full-time mentoring:

I think that one tremendous plus in being a full-time mentor is not having the responsibilities of a classroom full of children and being able to concentrate solely on the needs and growth of our mentees.

We were told recently by a secondary administrator that the first year teachers in his school who have had a S.T.A.R. mentor have grown at a pace that equals three or more years of a new teacher without a mentor. This fantastic growth is due to three facts:

1. Full-time mentors can exclusively devote their time to assisting, advising, and coaching the mentees to cause that growth!

2. Full-time mentors can spend in-depth, extended time with their mentees as needed. No other commitments get in the way. As a result, we get to know our mentees so quickly and "intimately" that individual needs, worries, plans, idiosyncrasies, strengths, etc., can really be discovered and acted on. I truly know each mentee so well as an individual that I am able to be a better mentor.

3. The third reason we are so successful is what we call our data curtain. What we mean is that, in our program, there is an imaginary wall around the mentoring relationship. Nothing discussed within the mentoring pair can ever be shared outside that relationship. We have found that this data curtain protects the confidentiality of the mentoring dialogue and ensures that the mentee will feel free to discuss their real problems and concerns with me. Then we go to work on whatever it is. Of course, this is something part-time mentors should do too.

With this kind of closeness and time, great strides can quickly be made in developing trust and achieving candid and open communication with every mentee. That is why full-time mentoring increases the opportunity for growth and mentee improvement accelerates so much. Other mentoring programs should consider the use of full-time mentors too.

(Romer 1999)

Structures for Induction and Mentoring Programs

Every educator knows the terrible tensions created by the scarcity of time in schools. The Cherry Creek S.T.A.R. Mentor Program and others like it around the country have learned how to avoid that problem while better supporting their beginning teachers. These programs are achieving outstanding results. The return on investment they have found also comes from cost and other savings, including the following:

- Eliminated costs of mentoring stipends
- Decreased problems with finding and frequency for using substitute teachers
- Decreased costs for substitute teachers
- Eliminated disruptions to instruction in the mentor's classroom
- Accelerated professional growth for both the mentor and protégé
- Decreased costs for recruitment, orientation, and training of new teachers because of increased retention of teachers
- Decreased waste of administrative time because of increased teacher retention
- Decrease in the administrative time required to supervise and evaluate new teachers since their performance is better because of their work with their mentor

Full-time assignment of a mentor is effective, because it restructures the use of time and aligns it with the priority of improving instruction in the protégé's classroom. Such dedicated time clarifies for all staff the district's commitment to the innovative practices that time supports (Hayes et al. 1999). Furthermore, full-time mentoring eliminates the inherent conflict between the need of the students in the protégé's classroom for a quality teacher and the need of the students in the mentor's own classroom for a quality teacher. When that conflict is left unresolved or is even increased by placing excessive expectations on part-time mentors, the students in the mentor's classroom will win, and the mentoring process and the students in the protégé's classroom will lose. This conflict is really a lose-lose situation, because it is always unfair to someone (Moller 1999).

While the full-time assignment of mentors is not a configuration that is appropriate for every mentoring program, it is a
win-win situation many programs should consider. It is a solution to a number of the problems that occur when the mentoring role is added on top of everything else a mentor is already
doing as a full-time teacher.

Critical Distinctions That Make All the Difference

One concern of educational leaders involves the interaction of
mentors with nonparticipant colleagues within the traditional
egalitarian culture of schools. In this culture, all teachers are
perceived as the same except for differences in teaching style.
Leaders often want to avoid the "sibling rivalry" and resulting
ostracism that can occur when teachers are singled out as
unique (Magee 1999). However, leaders also want to establish
a culture of shared leadership in which teachers can offer
themselves as resources for professional responsibilities that
go beyond teaching, such as mentoring (Gusky and Peterson
1996). Of course, leaders know there are often enormous differences in the effectiveness of some teachers, in teachers'
people skills, in their willingness to help others, and so forth.
These are the very things leaders consider when selecting and
matching mentors to novice teachers. Effective leaders match
the needs of a beginner to the strengths of a mentor and
expect that considerable transfer of experience and professional learning will occur. For example, a principal may hire a
beginning teacher with excellent credentials, but no previous
experience and few technology skills. To increase the opportunity for this teacher's success, the mentor should have considerable experience—especially in using technology in the
curriculum. Leaders know the difference between the partners
will challenge assumptions, lead to discoveries, and prompt
the professional growth all beginning teachers need. Without
the difference between mentor and protégé, beginning teachers' assumptions about the ability of all students to learn, the

Structures for Induction and Mentoring Programs

role of the teacher, and even the career of teaching may remain those that they formed during their previous years as students. These assumptions are often inadequate when applied to today's schools and students.

The mentor is able to function as a mentor precisely because of greater experience and knowledge, deeper insights into student learning, and greater skills at facilitating that learning. The differences between the mentor and the protégé make the mentoring worthwhile for the beginning educator. Protégés stand to gain more from working with someone who is different from them than from someone whose experiences and perspectives are similar to their own. By design, therefore, effective mentoring cannot be a peer relationship.

Nevertheless, the traditional school culture reinforces peer relationships, and this can make mentors uncomfortable if they feel singled out for different status and use of time than their colleagues (Moller 1999). This dilemma must be explicitly addressed in program design and during mentor training so that mentors are prepared to deal with it positively (Bird 1986). People who are not participating in a mentoring program may be uncomfortable with teacher leadership, and these colleagues may make comments that reflect that discomfort. Teaching mentors to respond positively to the discomfort can ultimately save a mentoring program from becoming a very limited orientation program in which the mentor's role in facilitating professional growth is too frightening for some to undertake.

Dealing with Distinctions

Clarity about vocabulary can be a helpful starting point for dealing with these tricky distinctions. For example, when coaching occurs within a mentoring relationship, I suggest that it not be called peer coaching. Such a label seems imprecise in that while the job description (teacher) may be the same, there are a number of significant differences between the beginning and the experienced teachers in the mentoring pair. I suggest that the term *peer coaching* be reserved to describe the coaching that occurs between two or more veteran educators who may have differing strengths but whose years of experience are more similar.

Those who choose to label mentoring as peer mentoring or a mentor's coaching as peer coaching are usually trying to distinguish it from the mentoring and coaching done by a supervisor or administrator who is also an evaluator of the beginning teacher. I suggest that leaders find other, more helpful ways to make these vital distinctions, such as differentiating between the process and purposes of coaching and evaluation. Figure 1.3 offers guidance regarding how leaders can do this.

Use of the term *peer* in the mentoring context is also a reaction to the discomfort described earlier. Traditionally, teachers have tried not to call attention to the ways in which they are different from each other. Such an approach is understandable but often unfortunate, for it limits the opportunities for learning from each other. The use of mentoring raises issues of teacher leadership because leadership is what the role of the mentor requires. In fact, establishing teacher leadership as a norm is one of the biggest benefits of mentoring. As important as this is for school improvement, it is still a big change for many teachers, and leaders need to know how to successfully facilitate that transition.

Clarifying the Critical Differences in Roles

Features	Mentor Coaching	Peer Coaching	Supervisory Evaluation
The Focus of the Observation	Set by the interests and needs of the teacher to be observed, often after observation of an effective teacher that prompts discovery of a need to improve	A mutual inquiry into increased use of the best instructional practices in both parties' teaching	Comparison of the teacher's skills with a model of excellent teaching or a set of teaching standards to determine minimal competency
The Direction of the Focus	Protégé ⇄ Mentor	Best Practices ↗↖ Teacher A Teacher B	Teacher ← Evaluator
The Goals of the Activity	• To develop a more trusting and collegial professional relationship • To develop reflective, analytical and self-assessment skills in protégés and mentors • To develop more effective teaching strategies • To improve student learning	• To develop a more trusting and collegial professional relationship • To develop reflective, analytical, and self-assessment skills of both • To develop more effective teaching strategies for both • To improve student learning in both classrooms	• To judge teacher competence for decisions about certification and continued employment • To apply pressure to increase teacher performance and accountability • To improve student learning
Observation Initiated By	Mentor, first by invitation to the protégé to observe the mentor at work. Then, after comfort is established, mentor observation in the protégé's classroom	Either teacher in the peer coaching pair	The supervising administrator in response to legal and contractual requirements
The Paper Trail and Use of the Observational Data	• Copies kept by both • Both look for data patterns • Mentor asks protégé reflective questions to teach him or her how to self-assess and reflect	• Given to the teacher who was observed to analyze • Coach asks reflective questions to prompt teacher's analysis	• Evaluator analyzes the data and prescribes needed improvement • Papers go into personnel file as documentation of evaluation

Figure 1.3

GUIDEBOOK

REFERENCES

Barkley, S. G. 1999. Time: It's made, not found. *Journal of Staff Development.* 20(4): 37–39.

Bird, T. 1986. *The mentor's dilemma.* San Francisco: Far West Regional Educational Laboratory.

Gusky, T., and K. D. Peterson. 1996. The road to classroom change. *Educational Leadership.* 53(4): 10–14.

Hayes, C., P. Grippe, and G. Hall. 1999. Firmly planted. *Journal of Staff Development.* 20(4): 17–21.

Magee, M. 1999. The curse of the trophy. *Journal of Staff Development.* 10(4): 23–26.

Moller, G. 1999. At issue: Teacher leadership. *Journal of Staff Development.* 20(4): 11–15.

Romer, T. 1999, November. An e-mail message to Barry Sweeney regarding the benefits and results of full-time mentoring.

Sweeny, B. W. 1994. *Promoting the growth of new teachers: A mentor training manual.* Wheaton, IL: Resources for Staff and Organization Development.

———. 1998. *A survey of state-mandated mentoring and new teacher induction programs in the 50 United States.* Wheaton, IL: Best Practice Resources. Online at <www.teachermentors.com/MCenter%20Site/StateList.html>.

Two Blackline masters are provided on the pages that follow:
- Suggested Mentor Activities Before Starting School
- Suggested Mentor Activities During First and Second Weeks

Both offer ideas for mentors in the beginning of the induction and mentoring process. Once mentors understand the terms and basic structure of the mentoring process, as described in this selection, they may use these lists to jump start the induction and mentoring program.

Suggested Mentor Activities Before Starting School

Not every task on this list makes sense for every teacher when they first begin teaching. Identify appropriate activities given the experience of your protégé, and then check off tasks as you complete them.

BUILDING TOUR:

School layout and location of:

- ❏ Washrooms
- ❏ Lounge
- ❏ Office
- ❏ Supply room
- ❏ Custodian
- ❏ Media center and audiovisual equipment
- ❏ Bus entrance and teacher parking
- ❏ Rooms for specialists, nurse, social worker, psychologist, music/art/physical education

TOUR OF OTHER IMPORTANT PLACES:

- ❏ The school service center (administration building)
- ❏ Location and time of first day institute activities (map?)
- ❏ The teacher center (and their hours and services)
- ❏ Local "teacher store"
- ❏ Good lunch spots

BUILDING PROCEDURES:

- ❏ Hours for teachers, building use at other times
- ❏ Extra duties, bus, clubs, activities, chaperoning
- ❏ Attendance policies
- ❏ Movement of children, entry/exit from building, washrooms, lunch
- ❏ Student and teacher dress code
- ❏ Fire/disaster drills
- ❏ Lunch supervision, eating arrangements
- ❏ Homework, testing policies
- ❏ Student accidents, emergencies
- ❏ Pullout programs and the need for flexibility

(continued on next page)

ACCESS TO RESOURCES:
- ❏ Classroom and teaching supply requisitions, budget process
- ❏ Audiovisual equipment requests
- ❏ Computer access for teacher use and for student use
- ❏ Discretionary funds (saving receipts)
- ❏ Shared equipment and materials
- ❏ Textbooks, supplemental materials

STUDENT DISCIPLINE:
- ❏ Behavior expectations for hallway, lunch, washroom, playground
- ❏ Establishing and enforcing classroom behavior expectations and routines
- ❏ What works for me with our children
- ❏ Consequences for extreme behavior problems (contact parent, referral)
- ❏ Expected staff supervision outside of classroom
- ❏ Referral process for students with special needs (gifted, special education)

CURRICULUM:
- ❏ Guides/manuals
- ❏ District curriculum development process and resulting expectations for teachers
- ❏ Central office staff in curriculum and staff development (Department of Instruction)
- ❏ Management of the curriculum demands and pacing of learning
- ❏ Introduction to texts and available supplemental materials
- ❏ Lesson plan procedures and expectations
- ❏ Classroom assessment system, rubrics, and tests as feedback for instruction
- ❏ Subject matter experts on the building staff
- ❏ Teaching teams or shared responsibilities
- ❏ Grading procedures for day-to-day records (report cards later)
- ❏ Opening day schedule, appropriate plans, administrative details
- ❏ A plan for the first week's lessons (allow for organizing and behavioral teaching)
- ❏ Curriculum mapping (scope and sequence)

(continued on next page)

Blackline 1.1 (continued)

ACCOUNTABILITY FOR STUDENT LEARNING:

- ❏ District strategic planning process and objectives, and implications for teaching
- ❏ School improvement planning process, implications of the plan for grade/department level decisions, and individual teaching practices
- ❏ Student learning standards and district curriculum goals and expectations for teaching
- ❏ State assessment schedules and process and preparation approach (overview only)
- ❏ District assessment system, rubrics, standardized test schedules

ORGANIZING THE CLASSROOM:

- ❏ Options for room arrangement and its effect on teaching and learning
- ❏ Traffic patterns
- ❏ Student work collection and distribution system
- ❏ Storage and access to materials
- ❏ Student access to texts, equipment, and teaching centers

PERSONAL AND PROFESSIONAL DECISIONS AND PROCEDURES:

- ❏ Calling in sick and personal or professional days
- ❏ Expectations for sharing with colleagues; what others can do for you
- ❏ Adjustment to a new job
- ❏ Performance review (evaluation)
- ❏ Professional portfolios

Blackline 1.1 (continued)

Suggested Mentor Activities During First and Second Weeks

Not every task on this list makes sense for every teacher, but many will be important to do soon after your protégé arrives at your school. Identify which of these activities are appropriate for your school and for your protégé, then check off those tasks as you complete them.

HOW IS IT GOING?
- ❑ Don't wait—ask about concerns, new ideas, or proud moments.
- ❑ Share your experiences too. (We all work at these same issues.)
- ❑ How can I help? *I'm available at . . . ,* or *Let's work together on . . . .*
- ❑ Provide encouragement, show enthusiasm for successes, and look for ways to celebrate.
- ❑ Only provide feedback or other options when requested or when the answer is clearly one "right way."
- ❑ Give protégés the okay to blow the whistle when they are about to overload on too much information or extra time.

BUILDING AND DISTRICT REQUIREMENTS:
- ❑ Sub folder, lesson plans, requests for specific substitutes
- ❑ Faculty members, timing, and schedule for team meetings, etc.
- ❑ School calendar for the year including end of quarter, holidays, and assemblies
- ❑ Progress report procedures
- ❑ Report card processes and deadlines
- ❑ Professional staff evaluation process
- ❑ Contractual requirements for non-tenured staff such as workshops or visits

HELPING CHILDREN WITH SPECIAL NEEDS:
- ❑ Staffing or placement procedures
- ❑ Cumulative records and the issue of confidentiality
- ❑ Avoid compromising situations when trying to help, such as offering rides, etc.
- ❑ Introductions to support staff, gifted, reading, LAP, LD/BD, speech, social worker, psychologist, nurse, guidance, etc.

PERSONAL AND PROFESSIONAL TOPICS:
- ❑ Opportunities for attendance at professional meetings/workshops
- ❑ Importance of attending meetings that explain expectations and changes
- ❑ Get the new teacher and a few colleagues away from the building for a social gathering to begin friendships.
- ❑ Explain mentor's class schedule and availability. Are calls at mentor's home okay?

Blackline 1.2

In order to share meaningful conversations that lead to improved teaching and improved learning for students, mentors and mentees must develop a trusting relationship built upon open communication. Pitton describes how mentors can communicate effectively with new teachers.

The Heart of Mentoring:
Trust and Open Communication

by **Debra Pitton**

Open Communication

Open communication is necessary to build trust, but trust is necessary for open communication to occur. This endless loop makes it difficult for mentors to know where to begin their focus when they are working with a mentee. It is important that mentors remember that this process is not linear, but circular, and as such a starting point is needed. Mentors can establish trust more easily while working to communicate openly if some ground rules are established for interactions. While the term *ground rules* may sound negative and perhaps unnecessary, communication conflicts can be avoided with a plan for approaching conversations. Mentors can use the guidelines in Figure 2.1 for their ground rules or create their own to fit the needs of their mentoring relationship. These ground rules can be a starting point for developing trust and open communication.

Ground rules state publicly what both partners will do for each other. The commitment to these rules provides a solid base from which trust can be developed and open communication can occur.

Adapted from *Mentoring Novice Teachers: Fostering a Dialogue Process* by Debra Pitton, pp. 20–35. © 2000 by Corwin Press. Used with permission.

The Heart of Mentoring: Trust and Open Communication

Ground Rules for Mentor and Mentee

Mentor_____   Mentee_____

Ground rules apply to both parties.

1. Honesty is key. We need to say what we are feeling and thinking when we talk to each other.

2. Ask questions. If you are not sure about what has been said, ask "What do you mean?" Avoid filling in the blanks with your own interpretation—ask for clarification.

3. Create and stick to a schedule. Regular, planned times for conversation, observation, and informal get-togethers are vital to developing the relationship.

4. Respect the other's needs. It is okay to let the other person know that the timing of an unplanned conversation is not the best. But always set up a time in the near future for a phone call or conference to discuss the issue, and follow up on all concerns in a timely fashion.

Signed by: _____ and _____   Date: _____
                 (mentor)   (mentee)

Figure 2.1

Open communication is based on honesty and takes into consideration the use of verbal, nonverbal, and paralinguistic interactions. Mentees sense that their mentors are truthful from the words that they use (verbal), the physical expressions and body language they exhibit (nonverbal), and the tone and inflection of their voice (paralinguistic). Messages are sent when individuals communicate, but the meaning of those messages is only perceived in the mind of the individual who hears the message (Hamilton with Parker 1990). While no mentor intentionally sends his or her mentee mixed signals, often not enough attention is paid to the use of verbal, nonverbal, and paralinguistic messages, and miscommunication results, obscuring the effectiveness of the mentor/mentee relationship.

Verbal Messages

Verbal messages are often considered to be the most accurate part of a dialogue between two people. How can spoken words be misinterpreted? Yet individuals cannot be sure that the verbal messages they send are actually what is heard by the listener. One married couple, for example, often checks signals on the amount of gas left in the car before the other uses it. If the woman hears from her husband, "There is enough gas to get you there," she interprets that to mean that she has at least a quarter of a tank. However, many times after hearing this from her husband she has found the needle on the gas gauge to be near empty. The woman may feel that her husband is not giving her a straight answer, but according to his view he is telling her the truth. He believes that even if the gas indicator is near empty, there is enough gas to get her to most places she wants to go. This is his interpretation of enough gas. The woman, however, does not have the same understanding of enough gas. Over time, this couple has come to understand that they mean very different things when they say or hear the words, "There is enough gas." Their awareness of the other's understanding of the words has enabled them to prevent conflict. This example demonstrates that individuals in any relationship need to carefully check signals to be sure that what is said is what is heard by the other party.

Mentors can read the following conversation to analyze the impact of verbal signals in communication.

Scenario: Focus on a Verbal Message

Ask two people to read the exchange between a novice teacher and a mentor while you listen. After you have "heard" the exchange, list the ways that the verbal message (words only) could be interpreted by the mentee.

Mentor:	Hi, Sam. I found it really interesting observing you in class today. I'm glad we can take some time to discuss what went on.
Mentee:	Yeah, things didn't go exactly as I had planned.
Mentor:	Let's talk about that. What did you plan and how did the actual lesson vary from that plan?
Mentee:	My goal was to have the kids explore the various properties of paper by having them feel the paper, write on it, tear it, and soak it in water—and I had a whole bunch of different types of paper for them to use. I had waxed paper, construction paper, cardboard, typing paper, notebook paper, toilet paper, and paper towels.

Mentor:	There was a lot for them to explore.
Mentee:	Yeah—maybe too much. They were so busy doing the tearing and soaking that they didn't write down any of their discoveries.
Mentor:	I didn't hear any of the directions you gave the students.
Mentee:	Well, it was a discovery lesson.
Mentor:	Discovery? Hmmmm.
Mentee:	We learned about teaching by discovery in my methods class at the university.
Mentor:	Do you think that a discovery lesson fit what you were trying to do?

Dialogue: Misinterpretation

Debrief with a colleague or write out your answers. What are the various ways that the words used by the mentor could be misinterpreted? What about the word choices of the mentee? Try rewriting this dialogue using different word choices to see if you can find some language that is clearer to the listener. Ask two people to read the dialogue again, so you can practice listening to your word choices and their possible implications.

Some mentors who analyzed this conversation came up with these suggestions for clarifying the verbal message:

- Using the word *interesting* to describe the lesson might be interpreted negatively by the mentee. A simple "Thanks for letting me hang out in your class today" might be a better beginning, as it does not allow for misinterpretation.
- The question "What did you plan . . . ?" is supportive because it suggests that the mentee actually did have a plan.
- The words *Discovery? Hmmmm,* might be interpreted as a negative comment through which the mentor indicates this is not something he or she cares for, or it might be interpreted as an inquisitive comment. In

either case, the word choice is open to misinterpretation by the mentee.

- The statement "Well, it was a discovery lesson," made by the mentee might seem to be justifying his or her decision.

This role-play demonstrates that mentors need to think about their word choices to make sure they are not being misconstrued. For example, to clarify meaning after using the word *interesting* in the dialogue, the mentor might have said, "I am always amazed by all the various methods that can be used in the classroom." This kind of explanation can help avoid misinterpretation.

There is no way for individuals to be absolutely sure that what they say is interpreted by the listener in the way they intended it. Therefore, it is important that mentors check signals by asking questions when they are not sure about what they have heard, and it is equally important that mentors are sure their mentees heard their words the way they intended. If mentors think they might have heard something incorrectly, they need to ask, "So you are saying that . . . ?" or "Do you mean . . . ?" to check the accuracy of their interpretation. Without checking signals, mentors may have a false impression of what occurred in the classroom or an inaccurate view of what mentees think. If mentors have a trusting relationship with their mentees, it is easier for them to ask their mentees if they are comfortable with the communication that took place, and be sure they have gotten an honest answer.

Another way mentors can avoid misinterpretation is to give the lead to their mentees. For example, when first talking to mentees about a classroom observation, mentors should not qualify what they have seen by giving it any descriptors. Mentors can make a statement such as "Thanks for giving me the opportunity to see students in action" or "I appreciate you letting me spend time in your class." Mentees are usually eager to know if mentors liked the lesson or not; thus, a mentor's initial comments may be interpreted as a statement of "like" or "dislike" toward what happened in the classroom. A mentor's lead-in statement should not give a mentee any indicator of his or her feelings. Lead-in statements should be emotionally neutral, so mentors do not inadvertently send a signal to their mentees that interferes with the discussion. If mentees think their mentor did not like their lesson, they may become defensive and unable to hear the mentor's comments and suggestions. On the other hand, if mentees think their mentor liked the lesson, they may discount the mentor's suggestions. The use of statements such as "That was interesting," "That was nice," or "Wow, I'd be worn out after that class," are vague and can be misinterpreted by an anxious beginner. It is easy to imagine a novice teacher thinking, "An interesting class? What does that mean? Was it too rowdy? Is she saying *interesting* because she doesn't want to be critical? Was it interesting because there was so much going on that needs to be fixed?" A neutral lead-in serves as a transition from the actual lesson to the conversation that concerns the lesson.

As mentors and mentees work at open communication, having ground rules is useful as mentors can refer to them and ask their mentees if they are clear about what was said. If ground rules are established that say that both mentors and mentees will work to be open and honest with each other, and that both parties need to clarify if something is not clear, a reference point for checking signals is established. Mentors can work toward open communication by saying something such as, "In our ground rules we agreed to be open with each other. So, I would really like it if you would let me know if there is anything I said that is confusing to you or that doesn't seem to connect with what you are thinking."

Mentors can further investigate the importance of checking signals through the following exercise.

Dialogue: Exact Language

Ask another mentor or mentee (or even a family member or friend) to list what they mean when they say the following statements, and then answer the questions yourself. Next, share your interpretations with each other. What did you learn about yourself and the person you exchanged lists with regarding your individual understanding of the words? How can you use this knowledge in your work with your mentee?

What do you mean when you say these sentences? (Be as specific as possible.)
- I'll be there in a few minutes.
- Can I borrow a couple of bucks?
- Can I borrow some money?
- Come here a second.
- I'll be right there.
- It needs some work.
- It's okay.
- I've done that a lot of times.

When you use these words, what do they mean to you?
- Sometimes
- Always
- Never
- Usually
- Maybe

This exercise demonstrates how important it is to use exact language to help avoid misinterpretation. If, for example, a mentor states that his or her mentee never gets the students refocused after a disruption, the imprecise language may create a barrier as the mentee might think, "It's not true that I never get the students refocused." The mentor might have used the word *never* for impact or just failed to consider how the word might be interpreted. "That was good," "I liked that," and "That needs some work" are all statements that do not use exact language. Mentors can prevent misinterpretation by telling the mentee specifically what was good, exactly what occurred in the classroom that they liked and why, and identifying what needs some work. By being specific, communication can be much more accurate and effective.

The Heart of Mentoring:
Trust and Open Communication

Nonverbal Messages

Many people have probably heard the statement, "It's not what you said, it's how you said it." This statement exemplifies how the nonverbal components of communication must be considered as well as the verbal. Nonverbal signals include facial expressions, vocal tone, inflection, and body stance. It is important that nonverbal messages match verbal messages, as people often tend to pay more attention to these signals than to words.

People's faces and bodies often reveal what they are feeling, even if their words do not. If someone frowns as she tells her guest that she is glad he dropped by to visit, the guest gets the message that she is really not very pleased to see him. If a person lowers his eyes and looks away as he tells a colleague that he likes her idea, she may get the message that he is not sincere. Listeners add meaning to the messages they hear as they make sense of the words and interpret nonverbal signals. Sending contradicting verbal and nonverbal signals is a common cause of miscommunication. Mentors can communicate more accurately by being aware of nonverbal messages.

Vocal tone is a component of nonverbal language called *paralanguage,* and it is what is remembered more than the actual words used when a person speaks. According to research by George Trager (1958), vocal tone is what occurs in conversations beyond or in addition to the words we speak. The match or mismatch between what is said and the tone used is very important in conversations. If the tone matches the words, the message is believable; if the tone is not congruent with the words, it is the tone that delivers the message.

It is important that mentors match their tone to their verbal message. If a mentor tells her mentee that she wants to support him, but uses a contradictory or inconsistent tone when uttering the words, the words will not be heard by the mentee. For example, if a mentor tells a mentee that he likes the way she called on her students in class, but he says it hesitantly while looking away, the mentor sends a nonverbal cue that he does not necessarily mean what his words convey. Mentors can try the following exercises to heighten their awareness of nonverbal communication and the use of paralanguage.

Dialogue: Nonverbal Practice 1

Say the following phrases to another mentor or videotape yourself. Try to convey the positive emotion listed in the parentheses. If you are using a videotape, watch your physical stances, gestures, and facial expressions and listen to your verbal tone when you play back the video. If you are having another mentor watch you, have your partner reflect back to you what they see in your face and body and what tone and voice they hear. Answer the questions at the end of the exercise. The goal is to get a sense of how you convey these emotions.

- I think you're doing a great job! (enthusiasm)
- When you said that to the student, what was their response? (thoughtfulness)
- The class was on task, even if they were a bit loud. (confidence)
- I know it's hard to find time to create your lesson plans. (support)
- Do you want me to give you some suggestions? (questioning)
- I really enjoyed watching the students interact in their small groups yesterday. (pleased)
- It's tough when a parent gets angry with you. (empathy)
- I saw what you did with the fourth grade math lesson on fractions yesterday. (awe)

Follow-up questions:
- From your observations or the feedback you received, how would you describe how your nonverbal signals matched your messages?
- What might you need to do to change your tone, facial expressions, or body language to more accurately reflect the words you are speaking?

Mentors who discussed the questions following the dialogue exercise above identified that it was not always easy to match their vocal tone and nonverbal signals. They noted that having an awareness of their use of tone and the ways in which they created the tone they wanted was important. By listening to themselves and working with peers, these mentors felt they were able to monitor their own use of tone and nonverbal signals to create accurate messages when they communicated. Mentors agree that it is important to convey confidence to mentees, even if there is some doubt in the mentor's mind about the novice teacher's capabilities, and the vocal tone is very important when conveying confidence. If mentees hear mentors tell them they are improving, but hear uncertainty in the mentor's voice, they probably will not believe the mentor. This leads mentees to have a lack of confidence in themselves, and to begin to distrust their mentor. Mentees expect honesty, and if they get a sense that their mentor does not mean what they say, the relationship is negatively impacted.

Mentors can engage in the following dialogue exercise to identify nonverbal and paralinguistic signals that go with negative emotions. By becoming aware of the signals of these emotions, mentors can work to avoid them.

Dialogue: Nonverbal Practice 2

Practice saying the phrases listed below using the identified negative emotion and accompanying nonverbal signals. Videotape yourself or have another mentor provide feedback. This exercise strengthens your awareness of the tone, stance, gestures, and facial expressions that accompany negative emotions, so you can monitor your own interactions to avoid inadvertently sending a message that you do not intend.

- I think you're doing a great job. (hesitancy)
- When you said that to the student, what was their response? (anger)
- The class was on task, even if they were a bit loud. (sarcastic)
- I know it's hard to find time to create your lesson plans. (unbelieving)
- Do you want me to give you some suggestions? (demanding)
- I really enjoyed watching the students interact in their small groups yesterday. (sarcastic)
- It's tough when a parent gets angry with you. (unconcerned)
- I saw what you did with the fourth grade math lesson on fractions yesterday. (disbelief)

Follow-up questions:
- What did you pay more attention to, the words or the emotion (nonverbal message) of each phrase?
- How would you feel if you heard these messages (and tone)?
- What could you do to create a more positive tone/emotion to match these verbal and nonverbal messages?

The reflection questions following the phrases identify the contradiction that occurs when a person says words that by themselves might seem positive, but are reflected using a negative tone and body language. When this happens, the listener often focuses on the emotion conveyed in such a contradictory message.

It is important that mentors practice matching their tone to the words they speak, especially when conversing with a mentee. Awareness of tone, facial expression, and body language helps the mentor match verbal and nonverbal messages. Mentors can use a mirror or practice with a friend to increase their ability to monitor their tone and nonverbal messages.

Nonverbal communication also includes factors such as the distance people stand from one another as they speak, eye contact, the way people take turns talking, how people listen, and when people choose to communicate. Some of these aspects of communication are cultural and some are gender based (Samovar, Porter, and Jain 1981). If a mentee and mentor do not share the same cultural background, it is important that the mentor think carefully about these differences. During the getting-acquainted process at the beginning of the mentoring relationship, it is critical that both parties talk about how they communicate, and perhaps also include diverse communication perspectives in the ground rules. For example, during an initial conversation with a mentee, mentors should identify their personal preferences for communication and ask the mentee to share what their preferences are. A mentor might say, "I really find that I like to think about an issue for a while before I am ready to decide what to do about the problem. I know that some of my colleagues like to jump right in with solutions, but I like to mull things over. So, I may be very quiet about things while I am thinking. This doesn't mean that I am not happy about what I have observed or what we are discussing, it just means I am thinking. I wanted you to know that so you can get a sense of my communication style. What about you? How do you like to approach issues?"

Mentors who often react with intense emotions, speak loudly and with authority, or are aware that they really do not like to spend a lot of time hashing over an issue should communicate these things to their mentee. Mentees may use or prefer other communication styles, and mentors need to be aware of these differences to set up ground rules that identify and validate these differences in communication styles.

In addition, mentors should keep in mind that various patterns of communication have been described as gender related. For example, Deborah Tannehill (1989) states that male communication responses to a problem often include specific ideas for solving the issue, while female communication responses lean more toward nurturing and empathic statements. These patterns need to be explored to determine if they reflect the individuals involved, and mentors should definitely consider these patterns if they have a different problem-solving style than their mentees.

The following aspects of nonverbal communication identify a European-American cultural perspective and the impact these components may have on a conversation. These components should be given attention in all mentoring relationships. Mentors who are mentoring someone with different cultural communication standards should explore these aspects of intercultural communication. Mentors can start by asking their mentees about their comfort level with the following aspects of communication.

Proximity

As everyone has a certain comfort level with the personal space that surrounds them, standing too close to another during conversation can create discomfort for a person. In a situation where a mentee may perceive the mentor as having more power (e.g., in a student teaching situation), standing too close while talking may heighten the sense of dominance. This is not productive when trying to develop trust.

Turn-Taking

A speaker who does not allow someone to complete what he or she is saying, but rather jumps in with comments or suggestions, can give the impression of not caring if he or she hears what the other person is saying. Interrupting someone minimizes his or her contributions to the conversation. In open communication, each member of the conversation has an equal right to speak, and taking turns is important. Mentoring is not about one person telling the other what to do—it is about sharing information to reach conclusions about educational practice.

Eye Contact

Most Americans expect people to look them in the eye when they talk to them, and if the listener looks away, the speaker may perceive a lack of interest. On the other hand, when someone stares at another person with an intense gaze, it can be disarming as well. Mentors should strive to use the appropriate level of eye contact to reflect their interest and support when speaking with their mentees.

Listening

There is a listening stance that communicates that someone is paying attention to what is being said in a conversation. A person who is leaning forward and concentrating on what the speaker is saying signals that he or she is listening. Another aspect of listening is balance in the conversation. Mentors need to keep this in mind, giving their mentees plenty of opportunities to talk about what is happening in their classrooms.

Use of Time

Allowing significant time for a conversation to occur is another signal that the message is important. If mentors set up a time to talk with their mentees and then frequently change the meeting time or look at their watches and seem eager to get going,

The Heart of Mentoring:
Trust and Open Communication

mentees may feel that what they have to say is not valued. This undermines trust and prohibits open communication.

By paying attention to the process of communication, mentors can develop trust and provide for open dialogue with their mentees. Without trust and open communication little is accomplished because the mentee will not share important issues or concerns. In order to have important discussions that can lead to improved teaching and higher levels of learning for students, mentors must pay attention to these components of their relationship with their mentees.

REFERENCES

Hamilton, C., with C. Parker. 1990. *Communicating for results.* Belmont, CA: Wadsworth.

Samovar, L., R. Porter, and N. Jain. 1981. *Understanding intercultural communication.* Belmont, CA: Wadsworth.

Tannehill, D. 1989. Student teaching: A view from the other side. *Journal of Teaching in Physical Education.* 8: 243–253.

Trager, G. 1958. Paralanguage: A first approximation. *Studies in Linguistics.* 13: 1–12.

Mentors can use Figure 2.1 to initiate an open discussion with protégés on trust in the mentoring relationship. Mentors may also want to practice communicating openly and honestly with their protégés.

Level 1

MENTORING GUIDEBOOK

SECTION II

Observing the Novice Teacher

New teachers who engage in the developmental cycle of planning, teaching, reflecting, and applying what they have learned are on the road to becoming competent practitioners.

—Lucas 1999

ne of the key components of most mentoring relationships is the observation of the new teacher while he or she is teaching students. Part of the process involves holding a pre-conference to talk with the new teacher about the lesson to be observed and what the mentor should look for during the observation. The new teacher may want feedback on a particular aspect of the classroom such as questioning techniques, behavior patterns, transitions between activities, or specific teaching strategies. Correia and McHenry (2002) believe that the pre-conference should address the "objectives or purpose of the lesson, the area(s) which the new teacher identifies as a concern, the link to standards, the student assessment procedures, and the role of teacher self-reflection and evaluation" (7).

In Selection 3, **Observation,** Sausen discusses the clinical supervision and cognitive coaching models of observation. She also describes the importance of the pre-conference in targeting specific elements of a lesson the protégé would like the mentor to focus on during the observation. The post-observation conference provides opportunities for the mentor to give feedback and help the protégé reflect on ways to improve his or her teaching skills.

In Selection 4, **Data-Gathering,** Sausen describes the various data tools mentors can use to gather objective information during the observations that can be used during the post-conference. Mentors may not be familiar with some of the options for data-gathering because data tools may not have been used during their teaching careers. Data, however, provides objective information about what is happening in the classroom and allows the mentor and protégé to analyze and interpret the information in order to modify or change practice based on their thoughtful analysis of the problems.

Villani (2002) believes that "prompting self-reflection through the collection and sharing of data from classroom

The effective mentor serves as a mirror that reflects what is happening in the classroom.

observations, as well as asking thoughtful questions that promote reflection, are the key strategies of successful cognitive coaching" (12).

REFERENCES

Correia, M. P., and J. M. McHenry. 2002. *The mentor's handbook: Practical suggestions for collaborative reflection and analysis.* Norwood, MA: Christopher-Gordon Publishers.

Lucas, C. 1999. How a veteran teacher can help a beginner. *Educational Leadership* 56(8): 27–29.

Villani, S. 2002. *Mentoring programs for new teachers: Models of induction and support.* Thousand Oaks, CA: Corwin Press.

> Sausen discusses the importance of pre-conferences, observations, and post-conferences in the mentoring process. She emphasizes the nonjudgmental nature of objective observations.

Observation

by Julie Sausen

Compassion with a critical eye is a motto I have used when I mentor new teachers in my school. Compassion because we are working with human beings who are fledglings in a new profession . . . a critical eye because we have the knowledge and expertise to point out issues and to ask the right questions to guide new teachers through the first difficult years.
> —Delgado 1999

Before mentors and their protégés begin the observation process, they need to be clear about the expectations of their roles. People in charge of mentoring programs also need to clarify what to expect. Pitton (2000) provides issues that could be discussed and prioritized by mentors and their protégés before starting observations. (See Figures 3.1 and 3.2.)

An important role of a mentor is observing protégés with a friendly and critical eye or in a nonjudgmental manner. There is a distinctive difference in the purpose of why *mentors* observe beginning teachers (protégés) and why *evaluators* observe beginning teachers. Administrators, department chairs, lead teachers, or other educational staff who observe beginning teachers for evaluations can be intimidating because evaluations are part of the teacher retention and/or tenure process.

Expectations for the Protégé

The following list identifies expectations for the protégé in the mentoring relationship. Review the list and select five key expectations that you feel are critical for a successful mentoring relationship that meets the needs of the protégé.

The protégé will

1. come to the first year of teaching exhibiting enthusiasm, a love for learning, and a genuine liking for young people.

2. be open to developing a relationship with the mentor.

3. be willing to try new ideas and suggestions offered by the mentor.

4. bring to the experience a solid knowledge base.

5. bring to the experience a willingness to work hard.

6. be willing to create an interactive classroom via discussion groups, cooperative learning lessons, and by engaging students in higher-order questions, projects, and activities.

7. develop lesson plans that reflect varying formats.

8. develop and articulate a classroom management plan.

9. develop flexible lesson plans that can change when schedules and student needs dictate.

10. implement a variety of assessment strategies.

11. commit to teach a unit that they develop, without relying on a text.

12. observe teachers from a variety of subject areas and varying grade levels.

13. plan lessons that engage students of varying degrees of ability.

14. get involved in the total school experience, via extracurricular activities and all teacher duties, meetings, etc.

(continued on next page)

Adapted from *Mentoring Novice Teachers: Fostering a Dialogue Process*, by Debra Pitton, pp. 17–18. © 2000 Corwin Press.

Figure 3.1

15. communicate with the mentor teacher daily.

16. exhibit a strong presence—the ability to stand up in front of the room and capture and hold student interest.

17. address the various multiple intelligences and multicultural identities of his or her students.

Other Expectations

_____

_____

_____

_____

_____

_____

_____

_____

_____

_____

_____

_____

Top Five Critical Expectations — Key Words

☐ _____

☐ _____

☐ _____

☐ _____

☐ _____

Adapted from *Mentoring Novice Teachers: Fostering a Dialogue Process*, by Debra Pitton, pp. 17–18. © 2000 Corwin Press.

Figure 3.1 (continued)

Expectations for the Mentor Teacher

The following list identifies expectations for the mentor teacher in the mentoring relationship. Review the list and select five key expectations that you feel are critical for a successful mentoring relationship that addresses the needs of the protégé.

The mentor teacher will

1. communicate his or her expectations and objectives for the student teacher/first-year teacher at the start of the mentoring relationship.

2. allow the protégé to develop his or her own teaching style.

3. review the protégé's management plan and inform the protégé of school and district discipline policies.

4. arrange for introductions to other staff members, administrators, and school personnel.

5. maintain confidentiality.

6. arrange/encourage observations in other classes to see different ability levels and grade levels.

7. provide an opportunity for the protégé to videotape his or her teaching both early and late in the year.

8. encourage the protégé to implement a variety of curricular, teaching, and assessment strategies.

9. model infusion of multiculturalism on a daily basis (beyond the curriculum, as a part of life in the school).

10. model instruction that is differentiated for students with varying needs.

11. model effective interpersonal communication skills (in parent conferences, with administration and other faculty, and with students).

12. discuss the legal issues of education with the protégé.

13. provide protégé with information on state requirements and mandates and describe processes in place for meeting these expectations in the classroom.

14. be aware of what is going on in the protégé's classroom by observing on a regular basis.

15. provide evidence of the protégé's classroom interactions and teaching strategies to the protégé following observations.

16. review lesson plans (check written plan and/or have protégé rehearse, discuss, or visualize).

(continued on next page)

Adapted from *Mentoring Novice Teachers: Fostering a Dialogue Process*, by Debra Pitton, pp. 18–19. © 2000 Corwin Press.

Figure 3.2

17. provide the protégé with the opportunity to develop and teach his or her own curricular materials.

18. review the observational tool that will be used.

19. offer suggestions in areas requested by the protégé.

20. share curricular materials.

Other Expectations

_____
_____
_____
_____
_____
_____
_____
_____
_____
_____
_____
_____

Top Five Critical Expectations—Number and Key Words

\# [ ] _____

\# [ ] _____

\# [ ] _____

\# [ ] _____

\# [ ] _____

Adapted from *Mentoring Novice Teachers: Fostering a Dialogue Process,* by Debra Pitton, pp. 18–19. © 2000 Corwin Press.

Figure 3.2 (continued)

Many boards of education require beginning staff to be evaluated for a specific period of time. Most often these evaluations are in written format and are used to make decisions on letting teachers go or granting teachers tenure. Besides state and district evaluation requirements, there are also state licensing laws and professional standards beginning teachers need to meet for certification renewal. While it is the mentor's responsibility to guide the beginning teacher in meeting these requirements, it is the evaluator's responsibility to make sure the beginning teacher is upholding the district requirements and state licensing and professional standards. A few examples of what beginning teachers need to demonstrate in order to meet requirements and standards are positive classroom management techniques, professional conduct, efforts toward earning continuing education credits, and professional growth portfolios. Most states post requirements on a Web site or mail requirements to administrators. Mentors can better guide protégés if they are aware of these requirements.

Observation versus Evaluation in the Mentoring Relationship

Evaluations can be threatening for teachers. The evaluator is charged with bringing about change and may be seen as an adversary. Placing mentors in the role of evaluator does not work for the mentoring process or for the evaluation process. To develop an effective and trusting mentor-protégé relationship, the observation process needs to be a nonthreatening, nonevaluative, and nonjudgmental. Most school district administrators do not have mentors formally evaluate their protégés because doing so violates the terms of a successful mentoring relationship.

Trust and Confidentiality

Trust and confidentiality in the mentor-protégé relationship is key to its success. Trust is important to a mentoring relationship because it allows the mentor to guide the beginning teacher in the improvement of problematic areas. "New teachers and many experienced teachers must be guided in understanding the knowledge of the curriculum they are teaching and in developing educational goals and purposes so they are viable for them" (Gold and Roth 1999, 105). Protégés who do not trust their mentors will not share problems or issues with their mentors nor will they be willing to listen to their mentors' ideas on curriculum, teaching strategies, or classroom management techniques. Professional growth can diminish if the beginning teacher does not trust his or her mentor.

If the information the protégé shares with his or her mentor is evaluated, the protégé will be reluctant to discuss important elements for professional growth. Confidentiality prevents mentors from sharing the protégé's classroom difficulties with an administrator or supervisor unless the problems negatively impact the students or their learning. When Lee Shulman (as cited in Tell 2001) was asked whether a mentor should ever have an evaluative role, he pointed to the mentor's access through observations and conversations to views and perspectives of the protégé. Through the mentor-protégé relationship, the mentor may discover, for example, that the beginning teacher did not know content and was hurting students academically. The mentor might also discover that the protégé was hurting students physically or psychologically. Shulman says it would be unethical for the mentor to withhold such information. The mentor would need to report the problem to an administrator or supervisor. The mentor's role is to guide the protégé in best practices and professional growth; any evaluative role or any breach of confidentiality only applies in cases of harm to students' learning or well being.

Learning from Mistakes

For the mentor-protégé relationship to have a real effect on a protégé's teaching, the protégé needs to believe he or she can take chances and make mistakes. The goal of mentoring is to let the novice teacher become independent and make decisions. However, beginning teachers may make mistakes repeatedly or may make serious errors that put students at risk.

With a mentor's guidance, protégés can learn from mistakes, and can improve over time. An effective mentoring relationship built on trust and communication gives beginning teachers a sense of security to take risks and make mistakes without feeling penalized or judged. If mentors take on an evaluative role, beginning teachers lose that safety net.

The mentor's role, therefore, is complicated. Mentors need to know when to step in and when to give protégés their independence to learn on their own. Sweeny (2001) warns mentors not to develop a trial and error philosophy for protégés to find their way—the mistakes could be detrimental to the academic and social welfare of the students. Shulman feels new teachers should be allowed to make mistakes, "but on the other hand, we want to protect the society, the community, and the students from the insufficient preparation or limited motivation of some practitioners" (cited in Tell 2001, 8). Mentors can familiarize themselves with policies, regulations, and procedures to help them determine what is appropriate in the classroom.

The mentor as evaluator can hinder the mentoring process. If the trust and confidentiality of a mentor-protégé relationship is compromised, beginning teachers will not be able to grow professionally. However, observation is a useful tool in the mentoring process as long as the observation is conducted without an evaluative component. The following section offers models of observation that can be adapted to the needs of mentoring.

Models of Observation

Mentors can guide a protégé in professional growth through observation. During observation, a mentor can get a firsthand view of how his or her protégé is emerging in the areas of classroom management, instructional strategies, curriculum alignment with state learning standards, and professional growth. There are two main types of observation: the clinical supervision model and the cognitive coaching model.

GUIDEBOOK

Clinical Supervision Model

Pitton (2000) describes observation as a three-step process:

1. pre-conferencing to set guidelines for the observation;
2. observing the beginning teacher in the classroom; and
3. post-conferencing for discussing and reflecting on the observation.

These steps link observation data to professional growth goals and standards. This format is derived from the clinical supervision model that is the best known and most widely used structure for working with classroom teachers. Glickman, Gordon, and Ross-Gordon (2001) review the format in five sequential steps (see Figure 3.3).

Although the clinical supervision model is associated with a formal evaluation of the teacher being observed, the process of observation for the supervisor-teacher can also be applied to a mentor-protégé relationship.

Cognitive Coaching Model

Cognitive coaching is another model of observation. Costa and Garmston (2002) use the term *cognitive coaching* to define a nonjudgmental process built around a planning conference, observation, and a reflecting conference. The cognitive coaching model emphasizes collaboration and a sense that "we are all learners." The ultimate goal of coaching is for both the teacher and the mentor (or coach) to learn so that all involved—the mentor, beginning teacher, and the students—will benefit. See Figure 3.4 for a description of the coaching process.

Supervision Model

Step 1: Pre-conference with teacher
Determine the
- reason for and purpose of the observation,
- focus of the observation,
- method and form of observation to be used,
- time of the observation, and
- time of the post-conference.

Step 2: Observation of classroom instruction
The observer records descriptions of the actual events and the interpretations are the meanings inferred from those events.

Step 3: Analysis and interpretation of the observation and determination of conference approach
The observer can take one of the following two approaches:

1. Direct Control: Present observation and interpretations.
   - Ask for teacher input.
   - Set a goal.
   - Tell the teacher which actions to take (direct control) or provide teacher with alternative actions from which to choose.
   - Share observations (collaborative).
   - Allow teacher to present his or her own interpretations.
   - Negotiate mutual contract for future improvement.

2. Nondirective Control: Explain observations.
   - Encourage teacher to analyze and interpret data.
   - Encourage teacher to make his or her own plan.

Step 4: Post-conference with teacher
Discuss analysis of observation and, if needed, produce a plan for instructional improvement.

Step 5: Critique of previous four steps
Review whether the format and procedures were satisfactory and whether revisions might be needed before repeating the sequence.

Adapted from *Leadership for Learning: How to Help Teachers Succeed* by C. D. Glickman. Alexandria, VA: Association for Supervision and Curriculum Development. © 2002 ASCD. Reprinted with permission. All rights reserved.

Figure 3.3

The Cognitive Coaching Process

Phase 1: Planning Conference
The teacher to be observed
- clarifies lesson, goals, and objectives,
- shares anticipated teaching strategies,
- identifies data on student achievement to be collected, and
- identifies data the coach is to collect during the lesson.

Phase 2: Observing the Lesson
The coach gathers the data identified in Phase 1.

Phase 3: Reflecting
The teacher shares impressions of the lesson and critiques the lesson, identifying data used for conclusions.

Phase 4: Applying
The coach enocurages the teacher to
- identify what was learned,
- draw implications for future lessons, and
- share his or her impression of the coaching process.

Adapted from Harp, B. ed. 1994. *Assessment and Evaluation for Student-Centered Learning,* 2nd ed. Norwood, MA: Christopher-Gordon Publishing. Used with permission.

Figure 3.4

As shown in Figure 3.4, the mentor (cognitive coach) facilitates the learning process, but the person being observed (protégé) engages in self-assessment. This facilitation and self-assessment can be applied to the mentoring process as well. This selection includes numerous questioning strategies and reflection activities that mentors can use to engage beginning teachers in self-assessment. Self-assessment is important to the professional growth of beginning teachers. "When teachers are aware of their needs and are working on meeting them, they are less likely to look to others for solutions. These teachers will be healthier, more confident, and more successful in their work" (Gold and Roth 1999, 115).

This selection focuses on the main steps in the observation process—pre-conferencing, observing, and post-conferencing.

Observation

Careful preparation makes the observation process successful. Throughout the process, it is important for mentors to schedule specific dates and times for each step. Mentors should be careful not to skip any steps. Taking time to complete each step—especially discussing, reflecting, and linking to professional growth—is worth the effort for both mentor and protégé.

Step One: Pre-Observation Conference

One of the early steps [in planning and collaboration] is working with the teacher to assist in her or his diagnosis of needs, interests, and concerns. Part of this may be focused on determining the teacher's general philosophical orientation to learning, and the teaching process"

—Gold and Roth 1999

The goal of the pre-observation conference is to determine what a mentor will look for during an observation. "The major purpose of the planning conference is to provide an opportunity for the teacher to think carefully and explicitly about instruction, including its relation to content. This prologue to the lesson helps to reduce pitfalls, randomness, and reliance on intuition" (Pajak 1993, 56). The pre-conference is considered the planning and collaboration phase by Gold and Roth (1999); the mentor and protégé schedule a time to pre-plan and discuss what elements will be the focus of the observation.

Glickman (2002) believes that the process for determining what to look for in the observation is as important as the structures and formats for communicating feedback and making plans for further implements. The implementations or new strategies can be recorded later during the post-conference to help the novice teacher link the observation data to professional growth. Discussing the professional needs and objectives of the protégé can help determine what elements to look for during the observation. "Usually, issues concerning short- and long-term objectives are addressed during the planning stages as well as the appropriateness of the content to be taught" (Pajak 1993, 56). The determination factor might be a new classroom management or teaching strategy, a particular phrase, word, or motion a protégé is concerned about using during a lesson, or essentials related to a specific professional growth goal.

If the protégé is having a difficult time determining what the mentor should look for during the observation, the mentor should ask guiding questions during the pre-observation conference. Beginning teachers may not be aware of any weaknesses in their teaching or they may not be willing to admit they need to work on a specific area. "Ineffective teachers usually know they are having difficulty, but may begin a conference by denying any concern" (Pajak 1993, 45). This is when the mentor becomes a powerful model in helping beginning teachers to recognize strengths and weaknesses in their teaching practice. "Modeling flexibility and intuitiveness and above all, exhibiting humane sensitivity are very important when working with teachers who are having difficulty" (Pajak 1993, 45). Strategies such as active or guiding questioning help the protégé draw from prior knowledge, experiences, and specific situations. According to Pitton (2000), guiding questions can help a mentor lead the protégé to recognize where he or she might want assistance. "Guiding questions are always appropriate and helpful, as they allow mentors to gently redirect and focus a mentee's thinking while encouraging the development of the mentees' decisions" (Pitton 2000, 40).

After a broad discussion about the needs and goals of the protégé, mentors begin to refine and narrow the observation elements. According to Costa and Garmston (2002), the mentor and protégé are not ready for an observation until they have "clarified instructional goals and how [they] will collect evidence of their achievement and have "determined . . . exactly what data should be collected for teacher growth and how it should be recorded" (49). Figure 3.5 is a sample completed pre-observation conference planning form. (See Blackline 3.2 at the end of this selection for a blank template.) Mentors can use the pre-conference planning form as a guide to determine what elements he or she will give attention to during the observation. Mentors who do not use some form of observation

Observation

Sample Pre-Observation Conference

Mentor or Coach: Chris Jackson   **Protégé:** Lisa Chu

Title of Lesson: French Vocabulary: Around the City

Objectives of Lesson:
- Introduce students to beginning French words for city objects.
- Students will be able to incorporate new words into vocabulary.

What will be the format of the lesson? (Circle one.)

(Direct Instruction (Lecture)) Facilitation (Cooperative, Inquiry Learning)

What element of the lesson would you like to be observed?
Instructions to students

What student element would you like to be observed?
Are students A, B, and C on task?

What teacher element would you like to be observed?
Am I calling on a number of students or always the same ones?

What difficulties might arise during the lesson?
Some students will catch on to the vocabulary quickly, while others will take longer. I may lose some students along the way.

Based on the above elements, what observation tool will be used?
Use a classroom seating chart for tallying the above elements. It will be more effective to place tallies by the students that are called on and an X by the students who are off task or lost.

Where will the observer sit?
On the side of the room, until group work, then walk around the room to observe groups

Figure 3.5

tool can have trouble staying on target during the actual observation. Something that happens during the observation period could easily become the focus of the observation rather than the defined element if the mentor veers off target. However, the mentor must remember that if the new element does not endanger the safety or learning of the students, the new element should be noted, and may be focused on in a later observation.

Step Two: The Observation

The focus of the observation is usually derived from preceding events. These events may be prior experience with the teacher, a teacher's indication of what he or she is seeking assistance with, a pre-observation conference, or combination of any of these.   —Gold and Roth 1999

The mentor who builds a trusting relationship can directly observe the protégé's classroom and can guide the protégé to build his or her repertoire of teaching skills by trying new strategies in his or her classroom. "When conducting observation-assessment activities, the relationship between the [mentor or coach] and teacher is not likely to be contaminated, particularly if trust and rapport have been established" (Gold and Roth 1999, 10). One ingredient to build a trusting relationship is remaining nonjudgmental and focused during the observation. The friendly and critical eye helps mentors to stay focused on the objectives or elements decided in the pre-conference and to remain nonjudgmental during an observation. Cogan (as cited in Pajak 1993) defines observation as "those operations by which individuals make careful, systematic scrutiny of the events and interaction occurring during classroom instruction" (84). Cogan endorses classroom observation "as a tool for improving instruction, rather than a way of evaluating or identifying weakness in a teacher" (84).

An observation is a two-part process: (1) describing what has been seen, and (2) interpreting what it means (Glickman,

Observation

Gordon, and Ross-Gordon 2001). Using a friendly and critical eye during observations helps the mentor to describe what is happening in the classroom—these are the facts. During the second part of the observation process—interpreting what these facts mean (why they occurred)—the mentor determines whether or not the observed facts had a positive or negative impact on student learning. For example, if a mentor walked by the classroom and observed that the students were talking to each other, he or she may describe what was observed (the facts) as a classroom management problem. If the mentor had stopped to observe the class and taken the time to interpret what was observed, he or she may notice that the students were talking with peers in a cooperative learning activity and remained on task during the activity, a positive impact on student learning.

General Observation

According to Gold and Roth (1999) there are several types of observation. One approach to observation is *general observation.* General observation does not require a pre-conference—identifying elements for the mentor to look for during the observation is not done. The mentor simply records what he or she observes in the classroom. The general observation might be used in a peer-coaching situation between two experienced teachers. Although this is a valid form of observation, it is suggested that this type of obervation should not be used every time the mentor or coach observes the protégé. Though the mentor can certainly provide feedback using general observation, this feedback is given only through the mentor's perspective. By not including the protégé in the observation process through pre-conferencing, the protégé loses an opportunity for professional growth. In general observation, the protégé is not given the opportunity to state what he or she would like to be observed by the mentor. Therefore, the protégé does not have the opportunity to share what he or she feels is problematic in his or her teaching practice, missing the opportunity to set goals for professional development.

Specific Focus Observation

The preferred type of observation is called *specific focus*—it requires identification of the observed elements during a pre-conference. The specific focus observation is critical to helping novice teachers reach professional growth goals. The ultimate goal of observation is to provide information on *what* to improve and suggestions for *how* to improve. If protégés identify areas they are concerned about (the *what*), they become more invested in the observation process and more inclined to receive feedback (the *how*). The protégé will then be able to take the *what* and the *how* of the observation and create goals for improving his or her instruction, practice, and classroom management techniques.

A few minutes before the specific focus observation takes place, the mentor can review the observation elements with the protégé to make sure what was stated in the pre-conference is accurate to avoid any misunderstandings. After the review, the mentor can sit in the classroom where he or she can easily see and hear. A recording tool can assist mentors in remaining focused on collecting the observation data.

Recording Observation Data

"During the classroom observation, the [mentor] simply monitors for and collects data regarding the teaching behaviors and student learning as discussed in the planning conference" (Costa and Garmston 2002, 49). Mentors can use several methods to record observation elements. "There is a wide range of options for ways of actually collecting information and providing a description of the classroom. These include event sampling, time sampling, checklists, general scripting, and focused scripting" (Gold and Roth 1999, 225). Mentors should "record specific examples, incidences, or exchanges pertaining to what the teacher has asked them to observe" (Barbknecht and Kieffer 2001, 53). Mentors need to decide how they will be collecting information ahead of time, preferably with the protégé at the pre-conference. See Figures 3.6 and 3.8 for data collection tools; see Figures 3.7 and 3.9 for samples. (See the end of this selection for blackline masters.)

Mirroring the Classroom Observation Tool

Observation Elements		
The mentor or coach writes the elements discussed in the pre-conference to observe in this area.		
I Saw	**I Heard**	**I Think**
*In this column, the mentor or coach records what he or she **sees** happening in the classroom. Information recorded in this column is factual and relates to the elements discussed in the pre-observation conference.*	*In this column, the mentor or coach records what he or she **hears** happening in the classroom. Information recorded in this column is factual and relates to the elements discussed in the pre-observation conference.*	*In this column, the mentor or coach records what they **think** about the lesson, the classroom environment, and the actions taking place. The information in this column is opinion and should not be shared with the protégé.*

Adapted from p. 105 of *Mentoring Novice Teachers: Fostering a Dialogue Process* by D. Pitton. © 2000 Corwin Press. Reprinted by permission.

Figure 3.6

Sample Mirroring the Classroom Observation Tool

Observation Elements		
1. *Student transitions from individual to group work* 2. *Wait time when asking student questions*		
I Saw	**I Heard**	**I Think**
Student A and B chatting with each other during instructions	*Teacher assigning students' roles for group work*	*If roles were written on the board, the students might have a clearer understanding of what they need to do*
Teacher allowing students to move desks to get into groups	*Students' voices raising during transitional move to group work*	*If room is arranged for group work before students come in, that could reduce transition time and noise level*

Adapted from p. 105 of *Mentoring Novice Teachers: Fostering a Dialogue Process* by D. Pitton. © 2000 Corwin Press. Reprinted by permission.

Figure 3.7

Guided Reading Question Observation Tool

Observation Elements
The mentor or coach writes the elements discussed in the pre-conference to observe in this area.

I Saw	I Heard
In this column, the mentor or coach records what he or she sees happening in the classroom. The information recorded in this column is factual and relates to the elements discussed in the pre-observation conference.	In this column, the mentor or records what he or she hears happening in the classroom. The information recorded in this column is factual and relates to the elements discussed in the pre-observation conference.

Five Guided Questions
In this area, the mentor or coach writes five questions to ask in the post-conference. The answers to these questions will help the protégé reflect and connect the results of the observation to professional growth and improving his or her teaching practice.

Adapted from p. 105 of *Mentoring Novice Teachers: Fostering a Dialogue Process* by D. Pitton. © 2000 Corwin Press. Reprinted by permission.

Figure 3.8

Sample Guided Reading Question Observation Tool

Observation Elements
1. Are students remaining on task during the lesson?
2. Am I calling on the same students all the time?

I Saw	I Heard
Teacher direct instruction; students on task	Students quiet during instruction
Students talking with neighbors during material pass out	Students chatting about weekend activities with neighbors during material pass out
Student groups 1, 3, 4, 5 on task	Student group 1 talking about task
Student group 2 off task	Student group 2 talking about what friends are doing after school
Teacher walking around room helping groups	Teacher redirecting group 2 back on task

Five Guided Questions
1. How do you think the lesson went?
2. What did you notice about student groups?
3. What are some other ways to distribute materials?
4. How did you feel about the redirection of student group 2?
5. What do you think you would change about this lesson for the future?

Adapted from p. 105 of *Mentoring Novice Teachers: Fostering a Dialogue Process* by D. Pitton. © 2000 Corwin Press. Reprinted by permission.

Figure 3.9

Observation

Cogan (as sited in Pajak 1993) strongly suggests when a person—in this case a mentor—is finished observing a lesson, he or she should not make any type of comment on the lesson, teacher behaviors, or students immediately. A wait time of no more than two hours is necessary before any comments are given to the teacher who was observed. If too much time passes between the observation and some form of feedback, however, the significance of the observation loses its meaning. This wait time is important because it allows the person who observed the lesson to reflect on what happened, to review notes or observation tools, and to refine comments into helpful feedback for the teacher. Such feedback is best suited for the post-observation conference.

Step Three: Post-Observation Conference

After the mentor has observed the protégé, it is time to discuss and reflect on the happening that took place in the classroom. This conference gives the teacher who was observed an opportunity to reflect on the entire process and share feeling in a one-on-one situation. —Barbknecht and Kieffer 2001

The post-observation conference gives the mentor an opportunity to provide the protégé with feedback on what he or she observed in the classroom in a safe, nonthreatening environment. The protégé can use what the mentor says in the post-conference to reflect on what happened in the classroom and to brainstorm methods of improvement. (The mentor may need to lead the protégé to reflect using guided questions.) The post-conference schedule should be discussed in the pre-conference along with the other elements of the observation process. The post-conference should take place soon after the observation. Although Cogan suggests giving the protégé comments on the observation no more than two hours after the observation, Barbknecht and Kieffer (2001) recommend that the post-observation conference take place within a week of the observation, ideally in a face-to face meeting.

Regardless of which timeframe mentors adhere to, delaying the post-observation conference results in the disconnection of the link to professional growth. Without timely feedback from the observation, protégés do not have the opportunity to correct or improve the elements that were observed. Those elements observed lose meaning long after the observation because the protégé may move on to other areas of concern. Novice teachers are constantly looking for ways to improve their practice—timely feedback offers them a step toward that improvement.

Recapping the specific focus observation elements or objectives that were decided during the pre-conference is a good way for a mentor to begin the post-observation conference. The mentor can then begin asking the protégé guided questions to help him or her to reflect on the lesson that was observed. "As the reflecting conference begins, the coach encourages the teacher to share his impressions of the lesson and to recall specific events that support those impressions" (Costa and Garmston 2002, 49). Through reflective questioning, the mentor can assist the protégé to recall the classroom events that occurred during the observation. "Reflection is a higher-order skill capable of producing large effects on classroom instruction and student learning" (Blasé and Blasé 1998, 99). It is through reflective questioning that the protégé links observation elements to professional growth and improvement of teaching strategies. "If mentees do not identify issues to address from the classroom reflection, mentors can ask guiding questions to help them consider the classroom interaction more thoughtfully" (Pitton 2000, 46). The mentor may use guided questions specifically connected to what he or she noted during the observation, or mentors can use the following sample guided questions in Figure 3.10.

Sample Guided Questions

- What do you think was a positive outcome of the lesson?
- What do you think were the strengths of the lesson?
- How do you feel about the students' behaviors?
- How do you feel about the transition of groups?
- How can you use this lesson to improve your teaching practice?
- How has this teaching lesson demonstrated your growth as a professional?

Figure 3.10

If the protégé is having a difficult time recalling the events of the observation through reflective questioning, the mentor can then use more direct questioning (Pitton 2000). "If questions do not help to prompt a novice teacher's awareness of areas for growth, mentors must be more directive" (Pitton 2000, 46). See Figure 3.11 for examples of direct questioning. Notice the use of "I" messages in the first question. Use of "I" questions in a feedback conversation takes the focus off of the protégé's weaknesses and directs attention to ways the mentor can help strengthen the protégé's teaching.

Sample Direct Questions

1. I wonder what would happen if you tried _____?
2. What do you think would happen if you did _____?
3. Do your actions have any relation to the students' behavior?
4. How do you think the students' behavior relates to your actions?
5. How might your actions affect the students' behavior?

Adapted from p. 105 of *Mentoring Novice Teachers: Fostering a Dialogue Process* by D. Pitton. © 2000 Corwin Press. Reprinted by permission.

Figure 3.11

GUIDEBOOK

A tool such as Mrs. Potter's Questions (Bellanca and Fogarty 2002) can also be used to help a protégé reflect on the observation elements. Teachers often use questioning such as Mrs. Potter's Questions to help students reflect on a specific lesson. Mentors can adapt the questions to fit the reflection needs of their protégés. Protégés may transition the tools used in the mentoring relationship to the classroom. See Figure 3.12 for the original Mrs. Potter's Questions. See Figure 3.13 for sample adapted questions.

Mrs. Potter's Questions

1. What were you supposed to do?
2. In this assignment, what did you do well?
3. If you had to do this task over, what would you do differently?
4. What help do you need from me?

From *Blueprints for Achievement in the Cooperative Classroom.* © 2002 by SkyLight Professional Development, Arlington Heights, IL.

Figure 3.12

Sample Adapted Questions

1. What were the expectations for the observation?
2. What do you think went well in the lesson?
3. If you could teach the lesson over again, what would you do differently?
4. What help can I give you?

Figure 3.13

After the protégé has recalled information and reflected on the observation, it is important for the mentor to help the protégé link the recalled information to the professional growth process. "As the reflecting conference continues, the [mentor] will encourage the teacher to project how future lessons might be rearranged based on new learnings, discoveries, and insights" (Costa and Garmston 2002, 50). A mentor needs to guide the protégé in this part of the post-conference. "[Protégés] need assistance in drawing from their prior knowledge and reflecting on and critically analyzing their previous experiences they have encountered. [Mentors] can be an essential part of their learning as they offer interpretations of situations the [protégés] are sharing" (Gold and Roth 1999, 105). Mentors can offer insights, resources, and new strategies to beginning educators when a problem arises. The protégé who is in a trusting relationship relies on the mentor to guide them in improving instructional practice. The mentor can link new issues to a second observation and repeat until problems are resolved. The record of observations becomes the protégé's professional growth plan.

Beginning teachers are continually defining and outlining their professional strengths and weaknesses. A mentor or coach can be the ideal assistant throughout this process. Mentors can model teaching practices, share resources, and direct beginning teachers to view peer teachers' classrooms. These types of mentor behaviors lead beginning teachers into a deeper level of reflection. "Another element, developing teacher reflection, included behaviors such as modeling, classroom observation, dialogue, suggestion, and praise. The essence of reflection, as we found, was associated with collegial inquiry, critical thinking, and expanding teacher repertoires" (Blasé and Blasé 1998, 156). See Figure 3.14 for a sample post-observation conference record; see the end of this selection for a blackline master.

Sample Post-Observation Conference Guide

Mentor or coach: Sally Marks   **Protégé:** Joe Coral

Title of Lesson: Narrative Essays

Outcomes of the Lesson:
- Students outlined differences between expository and narrative essays
- Student chose an event that happened to them for their essays
- Students reviewed writing rules for grammar, punctuation, and paragraph style

What element(s) of the lesson went well?
Students were very interested in choosing their own topics for the narrative essay.

How do you think the students responded to the lesson?
Students did not respond well to the lesson when they heard it was a writing assignment, but once the instructions were given there was an increase in interest.

How did you feel about your instructions of the lesson?
The instructions began well, but then I felt as if I were talking and the students were not participating like I wanted.

What difficulties do you think arose during the lesson?
Students began to lose focus during the review of grammar, punctuation, and paragraph structures.

Based on the above what will you change, if anything, for next time?
I would have students work in a jigsaw structure when it was time to review grammar, punctuation, and paragraph structures.

How can this lesson or teaching strategy show signs of professional growth?
Realizing what the strengths and weaknesses of the lesson were, and thinking about adding a jigsaw component to the lesson, encourages me to try a new teaching strategy and research how this strategy will best fit the lesson.

Figure 3.14

Conclusion

The coach [mentor] 'leads' a person to locate and amplify his or her own internal resources—states of mind or knowledge—necessary to deal effectively with a problem situation.
—Costa and Garmston 2002

The process of observation is not to be taken lightly by a mentor or protégé. The observation process is the key that opens conversations to building trust and exploring new opportunities within the mentor-protégé relationship. Beginning teachers are more likely to explore new ideas and expand teaching practices if the process of observation is taken seriously. The planning, observing, and reflecting conversations are powerful ways to foster professional growth. The steps of the observation process outlined throughout this selection should not be skipped.

The observation process is extremely important to the mentor and protégé, because both can learn from the outcomes of the observation and guide each other to improve teaching practices. The steps of the mentor observation and supervisor evaluation are the same, but the advantages of the mentor observation can lead to open and honest exploration of teaching practices.

BIBLIOGRAPHY

Barbknecht, A., and C. W. Kieffer. 2001. *Peer coaching: The learning team approach.* Arlington Heights, IL: SkyLight Training and Publishing.

Bellanca, J. and R. Fogarty. 2002. *Blueprints for achievement in the cooperative classroom.* Thousand Oaks, CA: Corwin Press.

Blase, J., and J. Blase. 1998. *Handbook of instructional leadership: How really good principals promote teaching and learning.* Thousand Oaks, CA: Corwin Press.

Costa, A., and R. Garmston. 2002. *Cognitive coaching: A foundation for renaissance schools,* 2nd ed. Norwood, MA: Christopher-Gordon Publishers.

Delgado, M. 1999. Developing competent practitioners. *Educational Leadership* 56(8): 45–48.

Garmston, R. J., and B. M. Wellman. 1999. *The adaptive school: A sourcebook for developing collaborative groups.* Norwood, MA: Christopher-Gordon Publishers.

Glanz, J., and R. F. Neville. 1997. *Educational supervision: Perspectives, issues, and controversies.* Norwood, MA: Christopher-Gordon Publishers.

Glickman, C. D. 2002. *Leadership for learning: How to help teachers succeed.* Alexandria, VA: Association of Supervision and Curriculum Development.

Glickman, C. D., S. P. Gordon, and J. M. Ross-Gordon. 2001. *Supervision of instruction and developmental approach,* 4th ed. Needham Heights, MA: Allyn and Bacon.

Gold, Y., and R. A. Roth. 1999. *The transformational helping professional: A new vision: Mentoring and supervising reconsidered.* Needham Heights, MA: Allyn and Bacon.

Harp, B, ed. 1994. *Assessment and evaluation for student learning,* 2nd ed. Norwood, MA: Christopher-Gordon Publishers.

Herman, J. L., L. Morris Lyons, and C. T. Gibbon-Fitz. 1987. *Evaluator's handbook.* Newbury Park, CA: Sage Publications.

Millman, J., and L. Darling-Hammond, eds. 1990. *The new handbook of teacher evaluation: Assessing elementary and secondary school teachers.* Thousand Oaks, CA: Corwin Press.

Pajak, E. 1993. *Approaches to clinical supervision: Alternatives for improving instruction.* Norwood, MA: Christopher-Gordon Publishers.

Pitton, D. 2000. *Mentoring novice teachers: Fostering a dialogue process.* Thousand Oaks, CA: Corwin Press.

Stronge, J. H. 1997. *Evaluating teaching: A guide to current thinking and best practices.* Thousand Oaks, CA: Corwin Press.

Tell, C. 2001. Appreciating teaching: A conversation with Lee Shulman. *Educational Leadership* 58(5): 6–11.

Vella, J., P. Berardinelli, and J. Burrow. 1998. *How do they know they know: Evaluating adult learning.* San Francisco: Jossey-Bass.

Villani, S. 2002. *Mentoring programs for new teachers: Models of induction and support.* Thousand Oaks, CA: Corwin Press.

Mentors and protégés can use the following blacklines to plan observations.

- Blackline 3.1 can be used to schedule when they will conduct the phases of observation.
- Blackline 3.2 can be used to decide what elements mentors will look for in the observation.
- Either Blacklines 3.3 or 3.4 can be used to take notes during the observation.
- Blackline 3.5 can be used to lead the discussion during the post-observation conference.

MENTORING

Phases of Observation Schedule

Pre-conference

Date: _____

Room: _____

Time: _____

Observation

Date: _____

Room: _____

Time: _____

Post-Conference

Date: _____

Room: _____

Time: _____

Blackline 3.1

GUIDEBOOK

Pre-Observation Conference

Mentor or Coach: **Protégé:**

Title of Lesson:

Objectives of Lesson:

What will be the format of the lesson? (Circle one.)

Direct Instruction (Lecture)   Facilitation (Cooperative, Inquiry Learning)

What element of the lesson would you like to be observed?

What student element would you like to be observed?

What teacher element would you like to be observed?

What difficulties might arise during the lesson?

Based on the above elements, what observation tool will be used?

Where will the observer sit?

Circle items needed or fill in here:

Seating Chart	Copy of Lesson Plans	Copy of Discipline Procedures
Class Name List	Tape Recorder	Video Camera

Blackline 3.2

Mirroring the Classroom Observation Tool

Observation Elements		
I Saw	**I Heard**	**I Think**

Adapted from p. 105 of *Mentoring Novice Teachers: Fostering a Dialogue Process* by D. Pitton. © 2000 Corwin Press. Reprinted by permission.

Guided Question Observation Tool

Observation Elements:

I Saw	I Heard

Five Guided Questions

1.

2.

3.

4.

5.

Adapted from p. 105 of *Mentoring Novice Teachers: Fostering a Dialogue Process* by D. Pitton. © 2000 Corwin Press. Reprinted by permission.

Observation

Post-Observation Conference Guide

Mentor or coach: Protégé:

Title of Lesson:

Outcomes of the Lesson:

What element(s) of the lesson went well?

How do you think the students responded to the lesson?

How did you feel about your instructions of the lesson?

What difficulties do you think arose during the lesson?

Based on the above what will you change, if anything, for next time?

How can this lesson or teaching strategy show signs of professional growth?

Data is like a mirror that reflects feedback. Sausen describes various data tools mentors can use to provide objective feedback that new teachers can use to improve their skills.

Data Gathering

by **Julie Sausen**

Observation is an essential component for the protégé's professional growth. After a well-planned observation, the mentor or coach can guide the protégé to improved teaching through analyzing the data observed and through careful reflection of that analysis. It is the collection of data gathered during the observation and the analysis of that data that is key to a successful observation that can lead to professional growth. The instruments used to collect information in the observation will determine how the data is analyzed—instruments can focus on specific content areas, classroom management issues, instruction and interaction, and student engagement in classroom activities (Gold and Roth 1999). Several data-gathering instruments that can be used during observations are provided in this selection. Completed samples are also included.

The first part of this selection gathers resources from three experts on data-collecting methods that mentors can use while observing protégés. Collecting appropriate data that matches the observation elements set in the pre-conference is important to protégés, because this data will be analyzed in the post-conference and reflected on for setting professional growth goals. Pitton (2000) and Stronge (1997) both cite Airasian and Gullickson's (1996) methods for gathering data for reflection, which provide specific data-gathering methods as well as examples of tools that can be used by mentors during the observation. Glickman's (2002) research provides strong evidence that data is an important part of the mentoring or coaching process.

Data Gathering

The second part of this selection examines the process of data analysis and how a mentor can use the data collected to prompt discussion with his or her protégé. Analysis of the data is extremely important to the professional growth of the beginning teacher. Data gathered during an observation, however, is meaningless if it is not reflected upon and put into a human perspective. "Data has no meaning on its own. Meaning is a result of human interaction with data" (Garmston and Wellman 1999, 22). It is the mentor's responsibility to collect the data and analyze the data before the post-conference. The analysis of the data paints a factual and human picture of the teaching accomplished during an observed lesson. For the beginning teacher, the analyzed data is the evidence needed to show strengths in teaching practices. The analyzed data is also non-judgmental, nonthreatening evidence needed to determine areas for improvement; the professional growth journey begins with identifying areas of weakness. The analysis of the data also provides the foundation that the beginning teacher needs to develop new goals related to one's practices.

While the analysis of the data provides the groundwork for setting new goals, the reflection is the foundation upon which professional growth goals are built. The last part of the selection provides evidence and research on the importance of reflecting on data and how this reflection leads to establishing new and meaningful professional growth goals. "Teachers can improve teaching if they better understand the reality of what goes on in the classroom. Classroom data can be used to identify behavior patterns unique to the individual teacher" (Goldhammer as cited in Glanz and Neville 1997, 246). It is through observation, gathering and analysis of data, and reflection that mentors can guide beginning teachers into becoming superior educators.

Data Gathering Methods

Data is not just used for the purpose of fixing what is wrong. It is also used to continuously monitor and improve performance. Without a plan or tool to guide data collection, mentors may record unnecessary or incorrect data. The data collected must have an impact on the professional growth of the teacher. As Herman, Morris, and Fitz-Gibbon (1987) suggest, mentors should "plan to measure or observe only those things which you can feasibly measure or observe with some degree of reliability and validity" (35). Mentors need to keep this in mind when pre-conferencing and when deciding on how to gather data. Glickman, Gordon, and Ross-Gordon (2001) state that "Data-gathering methods are ways to collect data from sources. Examples include testing, observations, content analysis, case studies, review of records, administration of rating scales and surveys, and interviewing" (276). This selection focuses on observation and data collection. Pitton (2000) describes ten different data gathering methods for mentor observations and supplies tools that can be used for each method (see Figure 4.1).

Data as Reflection

Conzemius and O'Neill (2001) believe that data is like a mirror—it gives educators feedback about our systems, our students, and ourselves. That is why the use of data for improvement can be referred to as reflection. The data mentors collect through scripting, note taking, anecdotal records, free writing, focused scripting, and visual and auditory evidence proximity analysis all provide information to the new teacher. The information may be in the form of numbers, descriptors, or perceptions. Whatever the form, the information is valuable because it offers a chance to understand what happened and, even more important, it offers the chance to understand why something happened and how to correct or improve a situation. The more sources of information sought out, the more well rounded the understanding of any situation will be (Conzemius and O'Neill 2001).

Data Gathering

Ten Data Gathering Techniques

Scripting
"Mentors need to be unbiased recorders of the events that occur in a classroom. Scripting involves taking notes that represent a script of classroom interactions. Mentors sit in a location in the classroom that provides them with a good view of the students and the teacher and write down what they see and hear" (Pitton 2000, 96).

Proximity Analysis
"The goal is to capture the teacher's movement in the classroom, indicated by an arrow and/or line. The mentor can include an indicator of where the teacher stops during the lesson by numbering the stops, or perhaps by noting the time for each pause in teacher movement" (Pitton 2000, 107).

Anecdotal Record
"The anecdotal record is a form of scripting that allows the observer to note events that occur at particular times during the lesson and includes a place for comments so that interpretations might be captured and set aside for later discussion with the mentee" (Pitton 2000, 98).

Verbal Flow
"Looking at the verbal flow in the classroom allows mentors to gather evidence of the way teachers and students engage in conversation during the lesson. This is an especially useful tool to use during class discussions, when mentees are working to involve all students in the conversation" (Pitton 2000, 109).

Free Writing
"This concept does not attempt to capture specific statements and observations, but rather describes in a paragraph format the overall sequence of events" (Pitton 2000, 100).

Numeric Data
This data can be used when mentees use a word or phrase that could distract student learning. The mentor would count the number of times the word or phrase is spoken in a particular lesson. This method can also be used to track teacher or student behavior. (Pitton 2000, 113)

Focused Scripting
"In focused scripting, the observer (mentor) looks for evidence in classroom interactions that support the language and expectations defined in the lens [pre-conference outline]" (Pitton 2000, 100).

Videotaping and Audiotaping
Videotaping and audiotaping mirror exactly what is being said or done in the classroom. This type of data recording should be looked at by both the mentor and mentee because it may overwhelm some beginning teachers. (Pitton 2000, 114)

Visual/Auditory Evidence
"The mentors write down what they saw, what they heard and, if they wish, what they thought" (Pitton 2000, 42).

Portfolio
"The use of a portfolio to document lesson plans, creative units, and classroom management plans can be a very helpful way for beginning teachers to organize this evidence" (Pitton 2000, 115).

Adapted from *Mentoring Novice Teachers: Fostering a Dialogue Process* by D. Pitton. © 2000 Corwin Press. Reprinted by permission.

Figure 4.1

The mentor must choose the type of data-collecting tool to use when he or she meets with the protégé at the pre-observation conference. Once the mentor and protégé identify the elements of the observation, they can choose the appropriate tool. During the pre-conference, the mentor can discuss how the data gathered will be used after the observation. This will help the protégé link the collected data to professional growth. By selecting the tool together, the mentor creates more trust and the protégé will feel more comfortable with the observation process.

Whatever data collection method is used, data gathering can be focused and meaningful if the mentor and protégé discuss during the pre-conference what elements to focus on during the observation. Glickman (2002) offers ideas to help focus scripting:

> Perhaps the observer will write a narrative during the lesson of what teacher and students say to each other, or observe a predetermined five or six students, or interview a few students about how they analyze integrate, and assess the ideas just discussed in class. The idea is to focus observations through agreed upon, open-ended questions with a way of recording (for example, verbatim, segments, computer-entered, etc.) that will be helpful to later discuss with the teacher. (29)

After the observation is completed, the mentor should take time to analyze the data and create questions to help guide the protégé into reflection; discussion takes place with the protégé at the post-conference.

Mentors can choose from several methods for observation and data collection; beginning teachers can choose from several methods for reflection. Varying the tools, methods, and reflections can offer both mentors and protégés a wide variety of data for analysis of teaching strategies. Figure 4.2 shows eight ways to gather data for reflection. Mentors can use this chart in the pre-conference to help determine what type of data should be collected during the observation. When the mentor and protégé determine what type of data collection tool will be used during the observation they can also discuss the kind of reflection that will follow.

Eight Ways to Gather Data for Reflection

Teacher Self-Reflection	Teacher Shared Reflection	Student Input for Teacher Reflection
Tools Checklists, rating scales, and questionnaires can be passed out to students, parents, or other teachers to provide data necessary for self-reflection.	**Portfolios** Collect and analyze data to provide evidence of professional growth. Working with a colleague or sharing information with a colleague can help provide deeper insight.	**Feedback** Questionnaires, surveys, and journals can be given to students to provide data for teachers to improve upon weaknesses and look at strengths.
Media Audiotaping and videotaping can be used to record happenings of the classroom and be reviewed to look for strengths and weaknesses in teaching.	**Peer Observation** Mentor or coach can observe colleague to record and discuss evidence for reflection on teaching practice.	**Performance Data** Classroom or standardized test results, essays, and projects can be used to help a teacher gather evidence of student growth and link evidence to professional growth.
Journaling Records of events and happenings in the classroom can be recorded and retained in a folder or notebook to use for evidence of professional growth.	**Collegial Dialogue** Sharing information and talking with others can give new insights to teaching strategies, as well as provide continual reflection practices for professional growth.	

From Stronge, James. *Evaluating Teaching: A Guide to Current Thinking and Best Practices.* pp. 226–227, © 1997 by Corwin Press. Reprinted by permission.

Figure 4.2

Data Gathering Tools

Tools used for data collection can be informal, such as a class seating chart, or more formal, such as a prepared chart with specific categories listed. Figure 4.4 is an example of a seating chart that can be used to record information about students.

For example, the mentor can note students who are on task, students who are off task, or students who are displaying certain behavior problems. A seating chart can also be used to mark where a beginning teacher stands in the room (proximity to students) and the pattern of movement during a lesson. See the end of this selection for a blackline master of a seating chart.

Another tool is shown in Figure 4.3. This figure shows two samples of verbal/behavioral charts that mentors can use to record words, phrases, or behaviors in the classroom that were identified by the protégé in the pre-conference. On the left side of the chart, mentors can record the predetermined phrases. Mentors can tally the number of occurrences by checking the boxes on the right side of the chart.

Sample Verbal/Behavioral Checklist—Teacher Behaviors

Phrases, Words, or Behaviors	Make a checkmark in the boxes below for each occurrence.																		
Umm . . .	-	-	-	-															
like . . .	-	-																	
ah	-	-	-																

Phrases, Words, or Behaviors	Make a checkmark in the boxes below for each occurrence.																		
Teacher is allowing students to talk without listening to others	-	-	-	-															
Using shhh . . .	-	-	-	-	-	-													
Calling on students who shout out answer	-	-	-	-	-														

Figure 4.3

Classroom Seating Chart

Classroom Arrangement

X Bobby	X Carrie	X Judy	// Mia	X Alem	X Marco
X Tsu	X Marlen	X Pei-Kans	/ X Graham	/ Thiago	X Sean
X Debbie	X Raimi	X Sara	/ Fisnik	/ Uriel	X / Mike
// Vlad	X X Andre	X Remy	/ Akiko	// Jenny	X Rich
/ Teshi	X Susan	X X Phil	X Ken	/ Steve	X Marla

Observation Elements

1. Look for students who are off task. Put a tally mark inside the box.
2. Look for students on task. Put an X inside the box.

Figure 4.4

88 | Mentoring Guidebook Level 1: Starting the Journey

GUIDEBOOK

A third tool shown in Figure 4.5 can be used for focused
scripting. The mentor can write the observation elements
determined at the pre-conference in the magnifying glass.
The mentor then brings the form to the observation and uses
the box below the magnifying glass to record elements as
they occur and what the mentor sees and hears during the
observation.

There are also more formal methods of data collection,
including videotaping or audiotaping a lesson for the mentor
and protégé to view or listen to and note observation elements
identified in the pre-conference. The methods and tools mentioned in this selection can help mentors remain focused on
specific elements during observations of beginning teachers.
Mentors can, of course, use any method they want to record
data during an observation. However, if the data is not focused
and is not recorded carefully or in an organized method, analyzing that data may pose a challenge. If the observation is
focused and data can be organized during an observation, the
analysis of the data becomes targeted and can lead to a deeper
reflection. Whatever method a mentor chooses to observe a
beginning teacher, experts agree that one method is not
enough for collecting data. Several methods of data collection
should be used throughout the mentoring relationship to provide an accurate picture of professional growth.

"Data collected should always be detailed enough to allow a
systematic analysis which can point to specific behaviors,
events and instances rather than generalities. Teacher behavior, the context in which it appears, and its outcome for students are especially useful information. Such details facilitate
later analysis, interpretations, and understanding of the classroom environment as a whole" (Pajak 1993, 84).

MENTORING

Sample Pre-Conference Focused Elements

1. Calling on both boys and girls

2. Moving away from podium

3. Using visuals during explanations

Element Number	I Saw	I Heard
1	Group of boys and girls raising hands	*Called on Sue*
1	Group of boys and girls raising hands	*Called on Trevor*
3	Use of geometric shapes	
2	Walked to the window	

Figure 4.5

GUIDEBOOK

Analyzing Data

Protégés need to have an accurate, nonjudgmental reflection of the observation in order to set and meet professional growth goals. According to Pitton (2000), without evidence, the conversations become centered on what mentors thought they observed, rather than what actually occurred. Mentors must remember that their observation is nonevaluative—the more factual, nonthreatening data presented to a protégé, the greater the chances he or she will link data to improving professional teaching practices. "Presenting the data collected during the observation assists teachers in acquiring a clear picture of what happened in the classroom. It also provides a means for them to hone their skills in observing and diagnosing their own instructional practice" (Gold and Roth 1999, 249).

Glickman, Gordon, and Ross-Gordon (2001) recommend that after the observation, the mentor review and study the recorded pages from the observation. Mentors may look for recurring patterns, incidents that happened in the classroom during the observation, and performance indicators that were or were not present. Mentors must make sense out of the information gathered and be able to communicate the data to their protégés. Making sense out of the data helps the mentor lead the protégé into a deeper reflection. Taking time after the observation gives mentors a chance to examine the recorded data and organize it into a fashion that will be useful to their protégés during the post-conference discussion. Too much time should not pass after the observation or the data loses meaning.

Mentors can use a graph to organize collected observation data for a one-time period or for several different observations. Graphs are an easy tool to use for locating areas of weaknesses or strengths. The graph should be completed before the post-conference. The completed graph then may be discussed at the post-conference after each observation and kept in the protégé's portfolio. Figure 4.6 is a sample graph of data from an observation where the identified elements involved specific words and phrases.

Sample Graph of Gathered Data

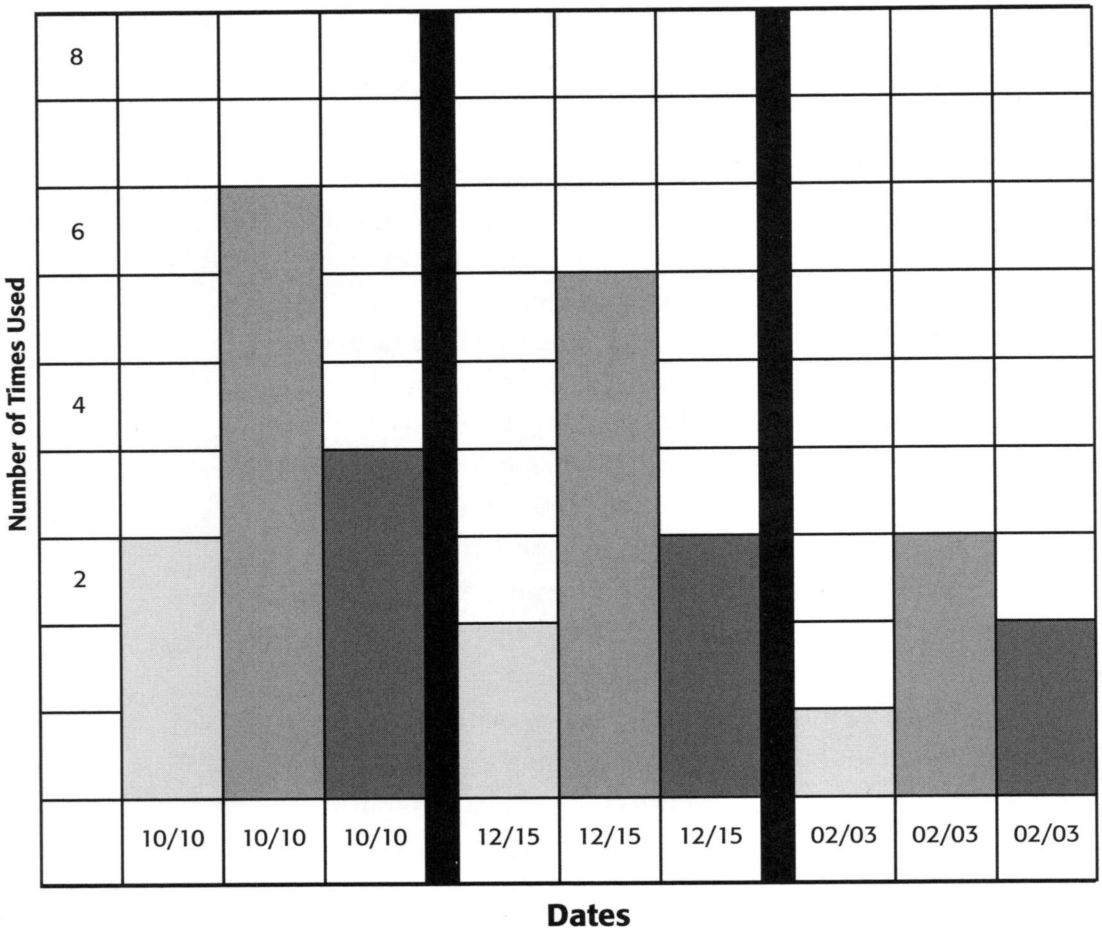
8
6
4
2
Number of Times Used
10/10
10/10
10/10
12/15
12/15
12/15
02/03
02/03
02/03
Dates

Observation Elements: Using inappropriate expressions

Like	
Umm	
Ah	

Figure 4.6

Linking Reflection to Professional Growth

Many beginning teachers need strong guidance from mentors in linking reflection to professional growth. The process of reflection can be challenging for many new teachers, because they have not had much experience with reflection. The process of reflection often asks a person to recognize not only strengths but also weaknesses. It can be difficult for new teachers to recognize weaknesses, because they may feel pressured to try to do everything exactly right so they can earn tenure or keep their job. No matter how difficult the process may be, reflection is necessary if the beginning teacher wants to improve his or her teaching practices.

After the mentor analyzes and organizes the data, he or she can create a list of questions to ask during the post-conference. These questions should help guide the beginning teacher to deeper reflection and lead her or him to set new professional growth goals. See Figure 4.7 for sample questions.

Sample Post-Conference Data Reflection Questions

After analyzing and organizing the observation data, write out five reflection questions to help guide your protégé in reflection.

DATA REFLECTION QUESTIONS

1. What does the data represent about your teaching?

2. What about the data surprised you?

3. What does the data confirm to you about your teaching?

4. How can you use this data to show improved teaching practices?

5. As a result of viewing the data, what area(s) do you want to focus on in your next observation?

Figure 4.7

The Post-Conference

When the mentor believes he or she is ready to discuss the data with the protégé, the post-conference can begin. It is not good practice to delay the post-conference and reflection too long after the observation. The observation will lose meaning and reflection will not occur.

At the post-conference, the mentor guides the protégé through an examination of the data. "Mentors can facilitate a mentee's reflective thinking by providing evidence or data from the mentee's classroom and asking him or her to respond to it" (Pitton 2000, 97). This response can be directed by the reflective questions. Pitton (2000) continues, "The evidence gathered should reflect both areas of concern and strengths of the teaching interaction" (97). Showing a protégé the hard data provides the evidence that he or she needs to determine strengths and weaknesses. Since the data is factual, the mentor remains in a nonjudgmental role.

Not only should mentors share information about the data at the post-conference, but mentors must also provide resources that will help the protégés relate data to professional development and give them an understanding of why professional growth is a continuous process. "The effects of sharing professional and research literature with teachers were usually very positive and included increases in teacher motivation, reflection on teaching and learning, and reflectively informed instructional behavior" (Blasé and Blasé 1998, 57). Figure 4.8 is a list of resources a mentor teacher can share with his or her protégé.

Resources allow beginning teachers the opportunity to explore solutions to their weaknesses and evidence to support their strengths in teaching. Mentors should provide resources that are related to the protégés and their needs. If the resources are related to the protégés' needs, they are more likely to be interested in exploring other research through a variety of resources. Research is a vital part of professional growth—it provides the background and means in which to improve teaching practices.

Educational Resources for Beginning Teachers

- Educational journals
- Web sites
- Educational videos
- Community resources
- Educational magazines and newspaper articles
- Books
- Conferences, workshops, and symposiums
- College or university courses

Figure 4.8

Conclusion

The data-gathering tools and techniques discussed in this selection are designed to help mentors guide protégés in the development of continual professional growth practices. The use of data is powerful when new teachers begin to set professional growth goals for themselves. Mentors gather, analyze, and organize data to guide the protégé to analyze the data, reflect on data, and to set professional growth goals.

The data a mentor gathers should not be used to evaluate the beginning teacher. If data collected by mentors are used to evaluate protégés, the data becomes threatening and the mentor then becomes an evaluator rather than a guide. The data should be used in a non-judgmental manner to help the beginning teacher improve practices and set goals for professional growth.

There is a variety of tools for gathering and collecting data. The observation elements that a mentor looks for during the observation period is determined in the pre-conference. The mentor discusses with the protégé what type of data should be gathered and what tool should be used to gather the observation data. Next, the mentor or coach analyzes and organizes the data to use during the post-conference discussion. Many experts agree that the mentor should analyze and organize the data alone before the post-conference. At the post-conference, the mentor and protégé can further analyze the data and reflect on the findings the data presents. This helps the protégé to continue to reflect on and research strengths and weakness. The protégé then sets new professional growth goals. This process is a continuous cycle. Even if teachers have years of experience, the observation and data-gathering process can help to determine professional growth goals.

BIBLIOGRAPHY

Airasian, P. W., and Gullickson, A. R. 1996. *Teacher self-evaluation tool kit.* Thousand Oaks, CA: Corwin Press. A Sage Publications Company.

Barbknecht, A., and C. W. Kieffer. 2001. *Peer coaching: The learning team approach.* Arlington Heights, IL: SkyLight Training and Publishing.

Blase, J., and J. Blase. 1998. *Handbook of instructional leadership: How really good principals promote teaching and learning.* Thousand Oaks, CA: Corwin Press.

Conzemius, A., and J. O'Neill. 2001. *Building shared responsibility for student learning.* Alexandria, VA: Association for Supervision and Curriculum Development.

Costa, A., and R. Garmston. 2002. *Cognitve coaching: A foundation for renaissance schools,* 2nd ed. Norwood, MA: Christopher-Gordon Publishers.

Garmston, R. J., and B. M. Wellman. 1999. *The adaptive school: A sourcebook for developing collaborative groups.* Norwood, MA: Christopher-Gordon Publishers.

Glanz, J., and R. F. Neville. 1997. *Educational supervision: Perspectives, issues, and controversies.* Norwood, MA: Christopher-Gordon Publishers.

Glickman, C. D. 2002. *Leadership for learning: How to help teachers succeed.* Alexandria, VA: Association of Supervision and Curriculum Development.

Glickman, C. D., S. P. Gordon, and J. M. Ross-Gordon. (2001). *Supervision of instruction and developmental approach* 4th ed. Needham Heights, MA: Allyn and Bacon.

Gold, Y., and R. A. Roth. 1999. *The transformational helping professional: A new vision: Mentoring and supervising reconsidered.* Needham Heights, MA: Allyn and Bacon.

Harp, B., ed. 1994. *Assessment and evaluation for student learning,* 2nd ed. Norwood, MA: Christopher-Gordon Publishers.

Herman, J. A., L. Morris, and C. T. Fitz-Gibbon. 1987. *Evaluator's handbook.* Newbury Park, CA: Sage Publications.

Millman, J., and L. Darling-Hammond, eds. 1990. *The new handbook of teacher evaluation: Assessing elementary and secondary school teachers.* Thousand Oaks, CA: Corwin Press.

Pajak, E. 1993. *Approaches to clinical supervision: Alternatives for improving instruction.* Norwood, MA: Christopher-Gordon Publishers.

Pitton, D. 2000. *Mentoring novice teachers: Fostering a dialogue process.* Thousand Oaks, CA: Corwin Press.

Stronge, J. H. 1997. *Evaluating teaching: A guide to current thinking and best practices.* Thousand Oaks, CA: Corwin Press. A Sage Publications Company.

Vella, J., P. Berardinelli, and J. Burrow. 1998. *How do they know they know: Evaluating adult learning.* San Francisco: Jossey-Bass.

Villani, S. 2002. *Mentoring programs for new teachers: Models of induction and support.* Thousand Oaks, CA: Corwin Press.

Six Blackline masters follow.

- Mentors can use Blacklines 4.1–4.3 to gather data during observation.
- Mentors can use Blackline 4.4 to graph data collected during one or more observations.
- Before meeting with the protégé during the post-observation conference, mentors can use Blackline 4.5 to develop five questions that will help the protégé reflect on the data gathered in the observation.
- Mentors can use Blackline 4.6 to recommend resources that will help the protégé improve his or her teaching.

GUIDEBOOK

Classroom Seating Chart/Diagram for Gathering Data

Classroom Arrangement

Observation Elements

1.

2.

Complete the Classroom Arrangement Chart and use symbols such as an X or a slash to note observed elements. The symbols can be recorded inside the boxes.

Blackline 4.1

GUIDEBOOK

Classroom Seating Chart/Diagram for Gathering Data

Classroom Arrangement

Observation Elements

1.

2.

Complete the Classroom Arrangement Chart and use symbols such as an X or a slash to note observed elements. The symbols can be recorded inside the boxes.

Blackline 4.1

Verbal/Behavioral Checklist

Name: _____   Date: _____

Phrases, Words, or Behaviors	Make a checkmark in the boxes below for each occurrence.																

Blackline 4.2

Pre-Conference Focused Elements

Element Number	I Saw	I Heard

Adapted from p. 105 of *Mentoring Novice Teachers: Fostering a Dialogue Process* by D. Pitton. © 2000 Corwin Press. Reprinted by permission.

Blackline 4.3

Gathering Data

Shade areas in the graph below to represent number of occurrences of an observation element. (Use a different color for each element.)

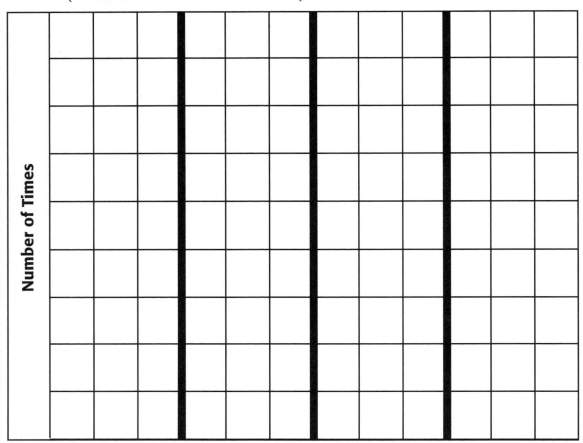

Number of Times

Dates

Observation Elements:

	color _____
	color _____
	color _____

Post-Conference Data Reflection Questions

After analyzing and organizing the observation data, write out five data reflection questions to help guide your protégé to reflect.

Data Reflection Questions

1.

2.

3.

4.

5.

Blackline 4.5

Data Gathering

Educational Resources for: _____

Observation Elements:

Recommended Resources:

Level 1

MENTORING GUIDEBOOK

SECTION III

Designing Lesson and Unit Plans

If mentoring is to serve as a viable process in the midst of change, we must focus on how a person can become a mentor and be a mentor, as opposed to simply doing mentoring
—Sullivan 1992

entoring is more than showing a new teacher around a school or giving him old lesson plans and tests. A mentor serves as a formal guide who plans the educational itinerary with the protégé. The new teacher, of course, makes the final decision, but the mentor guides the protégé by giving advice on how to meet objectives, standards, and academic goals. Trust in a mentoring relationship may form the foundation of a strong partnership, but the new teacher also needs to know how to plan lessons, design engaging units, and create learning experiences that meet the diverse needs of all learners. Allowing the new teacher to learn by trial and error is not always appropriate for effective teaching and optimal student learning. Since the first weeks of school establish a pattern, presenting effective lessons and units become critical components that need to be discussed and planned *prior* to the start of school.

In Selection 5, **Basic Instructional Design,** Jan Skowron provides templates to help protégés plan a lesson design that correlates to standards and provides a description of what students must demonstrate in order to show they have met or exceeded the standards. New teachers often need help in developing the components of an effective lesson plan, even though their preservice training may have included some information. Often, undergraduates spend weeks in a college course preparing one lesson plan. The reality of planning four or five lessons each day in most schools overwhelms many new teachers; moreover, ineffective lesson planning can result in a disastrous beginning for students and teachers. Protégés may need help to create motivating lesson hooks, select appropriate teaching strategies, group students, and assess student work. One of the most critical decisions teachers make every day is determining what type of learning activities will help students achieve deep understanding of the content. The decision to use graphic organizers, role-play scenarios, or create projects is important because various strategies meet the needs of diverse students.

A mentor serves as a formal guide who plans the educational itinerary with the protégé.

In Selection 6, **The Artistry of Teaching For, With, and About Multiple Intelligences,** David Lazear introduces Howard Gardner's theory of multiple intelligences and the implications for meeting the needs of learners in the classroom. He describes the variety of instructional strategies, projects, and performances teachers can use while teaching and assessing. He provides lesson planning ideas and assessments for Howard Gardner's eight intelligences. It is important to meet standards and curriculum goals, but it is also important to motivate students to learn in a variety of ways.

In Selection 7, **Creating a Unit Plan Using the Multiple Intelligences,** I describe a user-friendly process where teachers can work in teams to brainstorm appropriate activities classified by the multiple intelligences. The multiple intelligences grid serves as a template for planning two- to three-week units designed to motivate students as well as address multiple curriculum goals. Protégés can cluster standards and design an integrated unit that shows connections to various subject areas as well as provides a multimodal method of delivery.

In Selection 8, **Performance Tasks and Rubrics,** I share examples of performance tasks and sample rubrics that measure the same criteria listed in the standards and reflect real-life problem scenarios. Checklists and rubrics can help students evaluate their own work. With the proper time and attention given to assessment, students can internalize the criteria for quality work and become more independent learners, not totally dependent upon teachers for feedback and evaluation. Section III is really focused on creative curriculum planning. Mentors can work with protégés to help implement lesson plans and unit plans that align with curriculum goals and standards as well as motivate students to learn.

REFERENCES

Sullivan, C. G. 1992. *How to mentor in the midst of change.* Alexandria, VA: Association for Supervision and Curriculum Development.

Trust in a mentoring relationship may form the foundation of a strong partnership, but the new teacher also needs to know how to plan lessons, design units, and manage a classroom.

Good teaching begins with a thoughtful lesson plan designed to integrate appropriate activities, resources, and assessments to achieve the desired results for students. Often, mentors must introduce new teachers to lesson planning. Mentors can use the basic design plan to help new teachers begin with the end in mind.

Basic Instructional Design

by Janice Skowron

The Basic Instructional Design Planning Guide is a thinking process approach to guide decision making for basic instructional planning. It is comprised of three sections: (1) Desired Results, (2) Lesson Design, and (3) Evidence of Learning. Each of the three sections includes three columns: Planning Questions and Decisions, Information and Data Sources, and Notes and Comments. The Planning Questions and Decisions column poses a series of key questions to guide and stimulate thinking during the planning process. The Information and Data Sources column lists the types of resources and data sources that will facilitate answering the questions in column one. The Notes and Comments column provides information that will further clarify and assist in answering questions in column one. A detailed explanation of each section follows.

PLANNING GUIDE–BASIC INSTRUCTION
SECTION 1: DESIRED RESULTS

Use these questions to plan a basic instructional design.

PLANNING QUESTIONS AND DECISIONS	INFORMATION AND DATA SOURCES	NOTES AND COMMENTS
1. What learning standards/ benchmarks will be taught?	District curriculum guides, district and state standards documents, student needs based on test data (formal and informal), school improvement goals, district goals, state initiatives	A decision regarding what is to be taught is made before completing the rest of the planning process.
2. What is the specific learning standard?	_____	A clear statement of what students are to do provides clarity and focus in planning.
3. What assessment activities will enable students to demonstrate they have met the learning standard?	Recommended and required assessments, textbook materials	Planning for assessment is a recursive process. Assessment strategies and tools are tentatively outlined in the initial stages of instructional design, reconsidered and modified as the design emerges, and then finalized as the design is completed.
4. What performance expectations are there for students to show the extent of learning that has occurred?	District, state expectations for performance and/or teacher developed expectations	
5. How will students' difficulties be recognized along the way?	Formative assessments, observational techniques	
6. What assessment materials are available and what materials need to be developed?	Rubrics and assessments in district curriculum guides, teacher manuals, other sources	
7. How will assessment results be communicated to students and parents?	Report cards, grading scale, narrative report, conference, portfolio	Select the assessment strategy that is most appropriate. If the assessment results are to be incorporated into a grade, appropriate documentation should be made.

Figure 5.1

(continued on next page)

Section 1: Desired Results

Learning Standards

The process of instructional design begins with the learning standards—what students are expected to know and do (see Figure 5.1). It is this desired end result that drives the planning process and provides the focus and direction for the lesson. Wiggins and McTighe (1998) tell us to begin with the end in mind—think first about the desired results.

GUIDEBOOK

SECTION 1: DESIRED RESULTS
Planning Questions and Decisions

Science Class Grade 7

1. What learning standards/benchmarks will be taught?
The standard is part of the district curriculum in physical science and part of the sequence in understanding solutions. It aligns to state and NSTA standards.

2. What is the specific learning standard?
Students will distinguish between mixtures that are solutions and those that are not.

3. What assessment activities will enable students to demonstrate they have met the learning standard?
Students will enter findings and conclusions in their science log. A forced choice assessment will show what factual knowledge students have acquired. (I may modify the assessment to include additional information.) Students will develop an outline for their presentation. (The presentation rubric will be used.)

4. What performance expectations are there for students to show the extent of learning that has occurred?
Science logs will have appropriate detail and diagrams. (Corrections are expected if necessary.) Students will answer 80% of the questions on the forced choice test correctly. (Corrections are expected if necessary.) Students will develop an outline for their presentation. (The presentation rubric will be used.)

5. How will students' difficulties be recognized along the way?
Student responses during class discussion will be noted to determine understanding. (I need to ask several questions during class discussion to ascertain students' understanding. I will use my class list to note which students appear to need further assistance. They will be paired with a "stronger partner" for a study buddies activity.)

6. What assessment materials are available and what materials need to be developed?
Instructions for the experiments and a rubric describing levels of performance for the science log entries will be developed and discussed prior to the lesson.

7. How will assessment results be communicated to students and parents?
Students will receive a copy of the rubric showing the assessment of their science log with teacher comments. Students will understand that the science log assessment and the forced choice test will be included in their quarterly report card grade.

Figure 5.1 (continued)

Objective Objection

Educators may state learning benchmarks (objectives) in such precise terms that they become confused with activities. A clear distinction and an obvious connection exists between a benchmark and an activity. The benchmark is what the student will know and be able to do as a result of engaging in the activity.

Start with the standard or benchmark, determine what evidence to acquire to assess whether the standard or benchmark is met, and plan the activities to get to this end.

Section 2: Lesson Design

A lesson plan is what the teacher does to teach the learning standard (see Figure 5.4). The components of a lesson plan are described below (see also Figure 5.2).

Opening

The opening of the lesson sets the stage for what is to follow. The "anticipation" that is created motivates students and piques their interest (Hunter 1984). It activates students' schemata by tapping into their prior knowledge and making connections to new learning. Calling to mind what is already known is critical for learning. Jensen (2000) says that the more associations and connections one makes, the more firmly new information is "woven in neurologically." There is greater depth of meaning when new information is connected to existing knowledge. The lesson opening, therefore, should be structured to help students recall what they already know, understand the relevance of what they will learn, and be aware of what they will know and be able to do as a result of the learning activity. In other words, students should consciously connect new learning to previous learning. The teacher facilitates this process through appropriate opening activities.

Components of an Effective Lesson Plan

- Opening
- Teaching strategies/activities (input)
- Student activities
- Materials/resources
- Grouping pattern
- Monitoring student progress
- Ending/summary/reflection
- Practice activities/assignments

Figure 5.2

Teaching Strategies/Activities (Input)

Teaching strategies are selected based on the type of content to be taught and the needs and abilities of the students. They include demonstrating, modeling, explaining, questioning, and coaching. Teaching strategies are what the teacher does to develop background and set the stage for the learning activities students will engage in. The input provided at this point gives students enough information to proceed confidently with the learning tasks (see Figure 5.3). It does not preclude exploration and discovery on their part.

Content-Specific Examples of Teaching Input

- Demonstrating pulley operation
- Modeling a think-aloud during a poetry reading
- Explaining the life cycle of a frog
- Questioning and discussing to elicit higher-order thinking related to legislative decisions
- Coaching for sound articulation

Figure 5.3

Student Activities

In selecting or developing an instructional activity, it is important to consider its "fit" with the learning standard and student needs and abilities. An instructional activity is always related to the learning standard—it is not an end in itself. To learn, a student engages in an activity. A learning activity may be as simple as reading a selection, or it may be a more complex activity such as gathering data from multiple sources for problem solving. Today, a plethora of instructional activities are offered in teaching manuals, professional journals, books, newsletters, software, and the Internet. Far more activities are available than can possibly be used. The teacher must be selective.

Engaged Learning How students learn is just as important as what they learn. Student engagement is a high-priority in instructional design. Danielson (1996, 95) states: "Engaging students in learning is the *raison d'etre* of education. All other components are in the service of student engagement . . .". But engaged learning activities are not selected merely for their hands-on quality and potential for enjoyment. The purpose of engagement is to involve students in developing important concepts, skills, and processes. Engagement provides the condition in which concepts are made meaningful.

Basic Instructional Design

PLANNING GUIDE—BASIC INSTRUCTION
SECTION 2: DESIGN
Use these questions to plan a basic instructional design.

PLANNING QUESTIONS AND DECISIONS	INFORMATION AND DATA SOURCES	NOTES AND COMMENTS
1. What are the learning standards/ benchmarks to be achieved?	See Section 1: Desired Results.	
2. What is a motivating opening for the lesson?		
3. What strategies or activities will be used to teach the standard?	Curriculum guides, teaching manuals, professional literature, best practices information, etc. are sources of information for lesson development.	
4. What materials are needed to support and enhance learning?		
5. What is the appropriate use of technology?		
6. How will students be grouped for this activity?		
7. What opportunities will students have to reflect on their learning?		
8. How will student progress be monitored?		
9. What forms of additional practice may be necessary?		
10. How long will the lesson take?		
11. Are there any foreseeable pitfalls in this lesson?		
12. What alternatives are there if the lesson doesn't work out?		

Figure 5.4

(continued on next page)

Types of Learning Activities Learning activities are designed to enable students to reach specified standards. This is not as simple as it may sound. Other considerations affect the design of learning activities. Student interest impacts motivation, which affects attention and retention (Cummings 1980).

SECTION 2: LESSON DESIGN
Planning Questions and Decisions
Science Class Grade 7

1. What are the learning standards/benchmarks to be achieved?
Students will distinguish between mixtures that are solutions and those that are not.

2. What is a motivating opening for the lesson?
Set up as a problem-solving activity related to a real-life application: forensic scientist working with a detective to solve a criminal case. Show two containers of liquid and how they would identify the one that has water and the one that contains another substance. Ask students why such identification is necessary or important. Record responses for later review.

3. What strategies or activities will be used to teach the standard?
Possibilities include: Review and develop background information through discussion, reading, research, and questioning the teacher. Use KWL strategy. Invite a chemist from a local industry to talk with students about real-life applications. Conduct demonstration or experiment. Use lab record/report activity.

4. What materials are needed to support and enhance learning?
Safety goggles, lab aprons, graduated cylinders, clear plastic glasses or beakers, stirring rods, six prepared mixtures (water/milk, water/sugar, water/oil, water/rubbing alcohol, water/drink mix, sand/salt); for Tyndall effect: flashlight, cardboard, metric ruler, pencil

5. What is the appropriate use of technology?
Students may keep notes on word processing program. The computer probe equipment is also a possibility, perhaps as a demonstration.

6. How will students be grouped for this activity?
Students will work in groups of three for the lab experiment. The class as a whole will discuss findings and outcomes.

7. What opportunities will students have to reflect on their learning?
At the conclusion of the lesson, students will write about three new things they learned as a result of the lesson and how these three things have application to their everyday lives. (This could be part of the assessment.)

8. How will student progress be monitored?
During lab work, the teacher will observe students and check for proper use of equipment and following directions. Spot checks of lab book entries will be made.

9. What forms of additional practice may be necessary?
Students who miss this session or need further input may review textbook diagrams and explanations of the Tyndall effect and solutions. A video disk segment on solutions may be viewed. Or, they could partner with another student to review science log entries.

10. How long will the lesson take?
Two class periods will be scheduled for this lesson. I may have to provide additional time to get all presentations in—or I could have just a few groups present. Other groups could present for other lessons.

11. Are there any foreseeable pitfalls in this lesson?
Students must perform the experiment carefully to obtain the desired results. Students will need teacher supervision and direction in carrying out the experiment to ensure safety and proper use of lab equipment. Extra mixtures will be available in case of spills.

12. What alternatives are there if the lesson doesn't work out?
A demonstration will be used if the student activity doesn't work out as planned. Students will observe and record their findings in their science logs.

Figure 5.4 (continued)

Basic Instructional Design

Designing Learning Activities

Literal Learning. Literal learning defines a relatively simple activity for acquiring basic information and facts. The following are examples of literal learning activities:
- Name the steps in the scientific method.
- Identify the President of the United States during the Great Depression.
- Match the Generals to their Civil War battles.
- Identify given rocks and minerals.

Relational Learning. In relational learning students relate or connect information from one or more sources including their own background knowledge. Some examples of relational learning activities follow:
- Locate the ancient civilization of Mesopotamia on a modern-day map.
- Compare the population of Illinois and Chicago over time.
- Predict the next action in a story.

Transformational Learning. Transformational learning requires the student to transcribe or apply learning in a different way. Some examples of transformational learning activities are as follows:
- Rewrite the ending to a story.
- Demonstrate the operation of a simple machine.
- Dramatize a historical event.

Extensional Learning. Extensional learning activities ask students to take their learning and extend it using literal, relational, and transformational strategies to create, produce, originate, evaluate, and in other ways exhibit their learning in a unique way. Some examples follow:
- Critique a novel.
- Design a rubric for a learning task and use it to assess the task.
- Justify the actions of the main character in a story.

Figure 5.5

Therefore learning activities should be appealing and interesting to students. An appropriate level of challenge is necessary to maintain interest; therefore learning activities should be designed to meet a wide range of student needs.

It is apparent that some learning standards relate to simple information and fact acquisition. Other standards require the learner to relate, transform, or extend concepts. The wording of the learning standard is a guide in developing learning activities. The wording of the learning activity guides the students in the learning task.

The categorization of learning into literal, relational, transformational, and extensional domains allows teachers to use the wording of state learning standards. The categories do overlap. Strictly defined, separate categories of learning activities may not be possible, but understanding general categories of learning helps to focus planning of activities in relation to the learning standards (see Figure 5.5). All students should participate in all types of learning. It would be a drastic mistake to treat these categories as a hierarchy in which students begin with literal learning, staying there until the teacher decides mastery is obtained, and then move on to the next category. Linear use of learning categories is neither indicated nor effective. It is contrary to theory and research, which suggests an overlap and integration of the various types of thinking (Good and Brophy 1997). It is not possible to totally isolate levels of thinking into separate compartments—they are interrelated and iterative (Ellis and Fouts 1997).

Describing Learning Activities A critical part of instructional planning is the description, explanation, or directions for a learning activity. The wording of the description is carefully chosen to convey precisely what students are to accomplish. Selecting appropriate terminology for the learning activity is necessary to design coherent and organized instruction. If the students are asked only to list events in chronological order, it is not fair to expect that they will analyze those events. If analysis behavior is expected, the terminology that conveys this expectation must be used. The key word in the description of an instructional activity is the linchpin and, therefore, must be carefully chosen. A list of suggested terms for learning activities is contained in Figure 5.6. Teachers may find it helpful to refer to this list in describing instructional activities.

Designing Learning Activities: Terms to Use

Use the following terms to help recognize the type of learning required in a standard and to design instructional activities that correspond to the learning standard.

Literal Learning

count	label	outline
define	list	quote
find	match	recall
identify	name	tell

Relational Learning

compare	differentiate	locate	restate
conclude	discuss	measure	review
contrast	explain	paraphrase	sequence
demonstrate	generalize	predict	show
describe	interpret	report	summarize

Transformational Learning

analyze	collect	diagram	rewrite
apply	compute	distinguish	select
change	debate	dramatize	separate
characterize	deduce	examine	use
choose	demonstrate	research	

Extensional Learning

appraise	criticize	judge	prioritize
assess	decide	justify	produce
choose	design	make up	propose
compose	develop	originate	prove
conclude	evaluate	perform	rank
construct	integrate	plan	rate
create	invent	pretend	

Figure 5.6

Learning Activities

1. Graphic Organizers

Use graphic organizers to create mind maps for students, thereby strengthening learning and subsequent recall of material. When the graphic organizers are personalized to match the needs and backgrounds of the students, they become even more powerful. A slightly different twist is to use pictures or drawings instead of words to create a mind map.

2. Creative Retelling

Weave content information into a story using known genres such as fables, tall tales, songs, and myths. In this manner, the information is transformed into a different setting.

3. Peer Presenting

Use an "each one, teach one" model, or in some manner allow students to teach one another. Explaining strengthens understanding.

4. Model Making

Create models (two- or three-dimensional) to produce a concrete representation of an abstract concept.

5. Performance

Transform information or a concept into a performance using drama, music, or dance. Write about the solution to a math problem or create a poem about a science concept.

6. Role Playing

Provide opportunities for some students to assume the role of historical or fictional characters while other students take on the role of reporter in an interview activity that contributes to whole learning through a simulated experience.

Figure 5.7

(continued on next page)

Brain-Frame Activities Recent research into how the brain learns provides a rich source of information for teachers as they plan instruction. Teachers frame instruction around brain-compatible learning to maximize learning. Robin Fogarty (1997) tells us that brain-compatible classrooms differ from others in three major ways. First, brain-compatible learning is integrated, not isolated. Second, threat and anxiety are diminished, allowing students to function at high levels. And third, learning involves real or simulated "whole" experiences that tap into many ways of thinking, expressing, and doing. Teachers may use many effective brain-based strategies to deepen students' understanding. Figure 5.7 is adapted from the work of Eric Jensen (2000). Figure 5.8 connects some brain-framed activities to the thinking functions they support.

Materials/Resources

The variety of instructional materials available is extensive and at times overwhelming. Learning resources and materials must be appropriate to the needs and interests of the students. Sometimes the only materials needed are a pencil and paper (or word processor). Other times, more extensive resources are needed for exploration and research. Generally the teacher selects learning resources for young learners. But as students take more responsibility for their learning, they begin to search out information and learning resources on their own. Guidance and support at this stage helps students become independent learners and users of the vast number of resources at their disposal.

Some schools use a commercial textbook program as the required curriculum. When this is the case, state or district learning standards are used as a filter in selecting what is important to teach from the textbook. A comparison of learning standards and textbook objectives points out instructional priorities and enables the teacher to eliminate some textbook material. This standards-driven approach makes the curriculum more manageable.

Technology-related materials can support and enhance student learning. However, those that are technology based should be carefully chosen. Technology to support teaching the learning standards is the foremost consideration. Some technology-based applications can include the following:

- Explore a concept using video discs, computer software programs, or the Internet.
- Present a concept or idea using video discs, computer software, or presentational tools (PowerPoint, HyperStudio).
- Analyze and sort data and information using database programs.
- Create artistic products using graphic and sound design.

Other resources for learning extend beyond the classroom into the community. Partnerships with governmental agencies, local businesses, and professional organizations can be a source of extended learning opportunities for students. Joining resources helps build greater understanding of the relationship between schooling and real-world applications.

7. Debate, Discuss, Debrief
Provide opportunities for students to explain their thinking in a nonthreatening environment. Communication is the key for deepening understanding.

8. Game Making
Use a known game genre into which the new concepts and material are incorporated.

9. Presentations
Provide opportunities for students to use technology or visual aids, or to process information and transform it for others.

Activities such as those described in this figure allow students to do something—to use concepts, ideas, strategies, and processes. This use and manipulation of material is the vehicle to deepen understanding by weaving it into existing knowledge.

Figure 5.7 (continued)

Basic Instructional Design

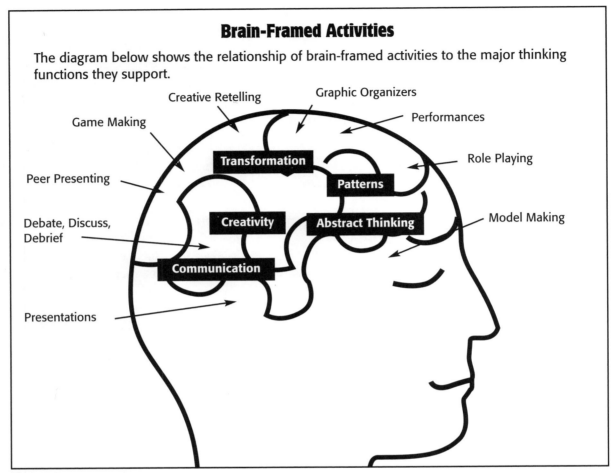

Brain-Framed Activities

The diagram below shows the relationship of brain-framed activities to the major thinking functions they support.

Figure 5.8

Grouping Pattern

The benefits of cooperative learning groups have been known for many years. Students in cooperative learning settings tend to perform better academically than students taught in individualistic or competitive settings (Johnson and Johnson 1984). Bellanca and Fogarty (2002) state: "Research on cooperative learning is overwhelmingly positive and the cooperative approaches are appropriate for all curriculum areas. The more complex the outcomes (high-order processing of information, problem solving, social skills and attitudes), the greater are the effects." There are times, however, when individual or whole group activities are appropriate. The key is to balance whole group, teacher-directed activities with cooperative learning groups (Zemelmann, Daniels, and Hyde 1993; Skowron 1990). Types of grouping arrangements in relation to instructional purposes are described in Figure 5.9.

Grouping Students for Instruction

GROUPING ARRANGEMENT	DESCRIPTION	PURPOSE
WHOLE CLASS	Students participate as a whole class with the teacher in a directed instructional activity.	• presentation of information • demonstration/modeling of a process • outlining directions • sharing/reporting/communicating/presenting the work of cooperative groups
COOPERATIVE GROUPS	Students work with others in a cooperative group arrangement in which students are responsible for the group's activities. The teacher is a facilitator to the groups. Not all groups necessarily work on the same topic. A jigsaw approach specifies separate topics for each group with a whole class sharing at the conclusion of the project.	• solving a problem • exploring a topic • conducting an experiment • creating a model • developing a presentation • discussing concepts and ideas
INDEPENDENT WORK	The student focuses on a task to practice, reinforce, or extend specific learning or reflect on what he or she has learned. Independent work may be used when a student has missed some instruction or has not achieved the level of proficiency necessary. Independent work may also be appropriate when a student's capabilities show he or she would benefit from in-depth exploration of a topic.	• practicing skills (math, spelling) • reading (literature selection or content information) • summarizing/reflecting on personal learning • independent research
PAIR AND SHARE	Students find it beneficial to work with one other student when they need tutoring or reinforcement of a learning concept or skill. Pair and share also provides an opportunity for students to discuss a topic of study or class event in terms of feelings and attitudes.	• reading each other's essays • listening to one another's stories • discussing what has been learned • discussing feelings and attitudes toward a given topic
SMALL GROUPS	Small group instruction is beneficial for teaching students who have common skill needs. The instruction is tailored to specifically meet the needs of the group. The groups are convened for a specific purpose and disbanded when the purpose is met.	• practicing letter/sound relationships • practicing correct use of the apostrophe in plural possessives • practicing fluency at the independent reading level • practicing the steps in using the calculator to perform specific operations • transposing music from key of C to key of F

Figure 5.9

Basic Instructional Design

Monitoring Student Progress

Monitoring students as they engage in a learning task is a crucial part of teaching. It is important for students to receive feedback on their progress throughout the learning activity. At times, encouragement or positive affirmation is all that is needed. At other times, clarification or instructional guidance is necessary to prevent misunderstandings. When confused, some students willingly ask for help. Other students do not. And still others do not even know they are confused. Monitoring all students is important to obtain diagnostic feedback and determine when intervention through reteaching or additional practice is necessary.

There are several ways to monitor students, ranging from observation in the classroom setting to performance tests and quizzes. Some general questions the teacher may use during monitoring are as follows:

Does the student exhibit confusion?

Is the student off task?

Has the student finished too soon or not soon enough?

Does the student understand the directions?

Is there some prior knowledge or prerequisite information the student needs?

Does the student's response indicate understanding?

A checklist may be used to monitor student progress during a learning activity. The checklist contains key criteria against which the students are observed (Burke 1999). A sample checklist for informational reading at the elementary level appears in Figure 5.10. The checklist will help determine which students have common difficulties. These students may then be grouped for reteaching, reinforcement, or practice activities.

Another form of student monitoring is through direct questioning on what is being learned. Questioning may be through a verbal exchange between teacher and student or in written form, through quizzes, summaries, or reflections. The type of monitoring a teacher chooses to do depends on the

GUIDEBOOK

Observation Checklist: Reading for Information																		
Name																		
Uses prediction																		
Visualization apparent through descriptive illustration																		
Understands descriptive text																		
Recalls sequence and order																		
Compares and contrasts ideas presented in text																		
Explains cause/effect relationships																		
States opinion and gives reasons																		
Connects sources of information																		
Links reading to prior knowledge																		
Uses inferential thinking																		
Self-corrects																		
Exhibits independence																		

3 = Needs further instruction
2 = Shows developing understanding
1 = Demonstrates understanding

Figure 5.10

demands of the learning situation and the level of complexity and difficulty of the learning standards. Generally, more complex learning is better monitored through observation and questioning. Literal learning is more easily monitored through written quizzes and tests.

Ending/Summary/Reflection

When one links new learning to prior knowledge, one's mental map of information, concepts, skills, processes, attitudes, values, and beliefs related to a topic is expanded. This mental map is the schema or linked collection of related thoughts and ideas and is the operating base within which new information is integrated. Schema is expanded and understanding deepened through metacognitive processing and reflection. Seifert (1999) states that reflection is the partner of experience. Reflection and experience lead us to construct meaning. It is therefore important that students have opportunities for metacognitive processing throughout and especially at the conclusion of a learning experience. Notebook journals, audio journals, and sketchpads are some means for students to reflect and record the impact of their learning and thinking.

Practice Activities/Assignments

Not all students progress at the same pace. Monitoring and observation will indicate which students need more instruction or practice. For these students, it is appropriate to provide additional activities to reinforce learning. Practice activities should be interesting, well designed, and assigned only as necessary.

Section 3: Evidence of Learning

The purpose of assessment is to determine what the student has learned in relation to the learning standard. Since assessment is aligned to a learning standard, classroom instruction likewise must be aligned to that standard. Alignment of learning standards, instructional activities, and the assessment ensures that students are assessed on what was taught. If the standard is to identify rocks and minerals by their appearance, then students are assessed as they look at rocks and minerals and tell what they are. The teaching/learning activities that occur prior to the assessment provide input and practice on the physical appearance of rocks and minerals and how to identify them. When this is the case, there is no need for additional "test prep." The learning activities themselves are the preparation—and in some cases, may even be the assessment.

Assessment Strategies

The learning standard is the basis for assessment. Assessment strategies are formulated in the initial stage of planning and reconsidered and finalized with the completed instructional plan (see Figure 5.11). The type of assessment selected will vary according to the type of learning that is expected.

In the broadest sense, assessments may be classified as selected response or performance based. Selected-response assessments include the pencil-paper "traditional" forms of testing (i.e., true-false, multiple choice, short answer). These assessments are useful in determining the student's content knowledge related to facts, information, and processes. Performance-based assessments are those that allow students to demonstrate what they can do with the learning they have acquired. Performance-based assessments include writing an essay, conducting research, preparing a report, presenting a demonstration, singing, playing a musical instrument, and performing a physical activity.

Students want to know how they will be assessed and evaluated. Parents also want to know what their student is learning and how he or she is progressing. Assessment tools such as rubrics and checklists help students understand what is to be learned by pointing out criteria and performance levels. They also clearly convey information about expectations and progress to parents (Burke 1999). When students and parents know the criteria and expectations, student performance often improves.

PLANNING GUIDE–BASIC INSTRUCTION
SECTION 3: EVIDENCE OF LEARNING
Use these questions to plan a basic instructional design.

PLANNING QUESTIONS AND DECISIONS	INFORMATION AND DATA SOURCES	NOTES AND COMMENTS
1. How will students demonstrate their learning?	See curriculum resource information and best practices information related to types of assessment: criterion-referenced assessment, performance assessment, observation, standardized.	
2. How will the assessment be scored?	Consider use of a rubric, template, or Scantron scoring.	
3. How will learning be reported?	Consider appropriate types of feedback to students, use of a grading scale, parent reports, report cards, portfolios, etc. If feasible, electronic data may also be useful.	Refer to your planning notes in section one as you finalize decisions regarding assessment.
4. How will the assessment results be used?		Use assessment results to determine student strengths and weaknesses and plan the next lessons.

Figure 5.11

(continued on next page)

GUIDEBOOK

SECTION 3: EVIDENCE OF LEARNING
Planning Questions and Decisions

1. How will students demonstrate their learning?
Science log entry of experiment—steps and conclusions
Forced choice test (20 items)
Present report to class

2. How will the assessment be scored?
Rubric
Answer key: (20 items, 5 points each). Sign up to use Scantron for scoring.

3. How will learning be reported?
Copy of rubric showing performance level will be returned to students. Teacher comments will be included as appropriate.
Go over test items with students. Grades will be determined according to the school-wide grading scale.
Copy of rubric showing performance level will be returned to students. Teacher comments will be included as appropriate.

4. How will the assessment results be used?
Determine which students need additional practice. Include results in quarterly report card grade. Students make revisions as necessary.
Determine which students need reinforcement of factual information. Students make corrections as necessary. Include results in quarterly report card grade.
The rubric will provide feedback to the student. A total of 5 points will be included in the quarterly report card grade.

Figure 5.11 (continued)

Using the Basic Instructional Design Planning Guide

The Basic Instructional Design Planning Guide is a thinking process approach to instructional planning. Preservice and novice teachers will find it helpful to follow all the steps in the guide. Understanding the thinking process underlying instructional design makes subsequent planning easier and provides a foundation for planning more complex instruction. Below are suggestions for using the planning guide.

1. Read the planning guide in its entirety.

It is good practice to become thoroughly familiar with the planning guide before using it. Doing so saves time in the long run. Get the "big picture" in mind before filling in the details.

2. Think it through.

Begin with Section 1: Desired Results. Think about the questions in column one and write down your thoughts and reactions. Consult the data and information sources suggested in column two and note the reminders and supplemental information in column three. Add notes and comments for later reference. Continue through Section 2: Lesson Design and Section 3: Evidence of Learning.

3. Synthesize the information.

The thinking process in step two provides a great deal of information which now must be synthesized into a coherent plan for instruction. The Basic Lesson Plan Form (see Blackline 5.4) is a synthesis and summary of the decisions made in working through the Basic Instructional Design Planning Guide. It is an action plan and a presentational overview for classroom instruction. An example of how this guide has been used by a seventh-grade science teacher appears in Figure 5.12.

When a novice teacher uses the planning guide over and over, he or she becomes familiar and comfortable with the planning process. With experience, the teacher is able to take shortcuts in planning by using the lesson plan form without filling out the planning guide. This shortcut is possible when the planning questions are practiced and well known.

LESSON PLAN – GRADE 7 SCIENCE

LEARNING STANDARDS/BENCHMARKS (concepts, skills, processes)
Students will differentiate mixtures that are solutions and
those that are not.

LESSON DESIGN	MATERIALS/RESOURCES	STUDENT GROUPING ARRANGEMENT
Opening (outcomes/purpose/expectations) Describe problem scenario: A forensic scientist is working with a detective to solve a criminal case. Show two beakers. Ask: How can the scientist tell which beaker contains water and which contains a mixture of salt and water? Discuss responses. Record responses for later review. Ask: Why is it important to be able to identify substances?	Beakers/mixtures Chart paper, markers	Whole class
Teaching Strategies/Activities (demonstration, modeling, explanation, directions, etc.) Describe lab set up and activity. (Refer to Lab Activity manual.) Review lab safety. Distribute/review experiment procedure.		
Student Activities Complete lab activity. Record findings in lab manual.	Safety glasses, lab aprons, graduated cylinders, clear beakers, stirring rods, six prepared mixtures, testing substances as listed in activity manual.	Three students per group (pre-arranged by teacher) Lab manual entries—individual
Closing (connections/summary/reflection) Groups 1, 2, 3 to report findings. Compare results. Verbalize conclusions. Review opening activity discussion. Discuss what was learned in the lab activity. Record two or more important concepts from this experiment in lab manual.		Whole class Lab manual entry—individual
PRACTICE ACTIVITIES/ASSIGNMENTS View video disc segment on this experiment and record results in lab manual.		Individual or small group depending on who is absent. Arrange with resource center for viewing and completion of work.
MONITORING STUDENT PROGRESS (ongoing) Informal observation and coaching during group work.		
ASSESSMENT OF STUDENT LEARNING 1. In small groups, students will use the rubric to evaluate their lab manual entries. 2. Twenty item completion test on content		**EXPECTATIONS** Students will meet or exceed all categories on rubric. Students will achieve 80% correct to meet expectations, 90% to exceed expectations.

Figure 5.12

REFERENCES

Bellanca, J., and R. Fogarty. 2002. *Blueprints for achievement in the classroom,* 3rd ed. Thousand Oaks, CA: Corwin Press.

Burke, K. 1999. *How to assess authentic learning,* 3rd ed. Thousand Oaks, CA: Corwin Press.

Cummings, C. 1980. *Teaching makes a difference.* Edmonds, WA: Teaching, Inc.

Danielson, C. 1996. *Enhancing professional practice: A framework for teaching.* Alexandria, VA: Association for Supervision and Curriculum Development.

Ellis, A. K., and J. T. Fouts. 1997. *Research on educational innovations.* Larchmont, NY: Eye on Education.

Fogarty, R. 1997. *Brain-compatible classrooms.* Thousand Oaks, CA: Corwin Press.

Good, T., and J. Brophy. 1997. *Looking in classrooms.* New York: Addison Wesley Longman.

Hunter, M. 1984. Knowing, teaching, and supervising. In *Using what we know about teaching and learning,* edited by P. Hosford, pp.169–192. Alexandria, VA: Association for Supervision and Curriculum Development.

Jensen, E. 2000. *Brain-based learning.* Thousand Oaks, CA: Corwin Press.

Johnson, D., and R. Johnson. 1984. *Circles of learning.* Alexandria, VA: Association for Supervision and Curriculum Development.

Seifert, K. L. 1999. *Reflective thinking and professional development.* Boston: Houghton Mifflin.

Skowron, J. 1990. Frameworks for reading instruction. *Illinois Reading Council Journal.* 18(1): 15–21.

Wiggins, G., and J. McTighe. 1998. *Understanding by design.* Alexandria, VA: Association for Supervision and Curriculum Development.

Zemelman, S., H. Daniels, and A. Hyde. 1993. *Best practice: New standards for teaching and learning in America's schools.* Portsmouth, NH: Heinemann.

Four Blackline masters are provided on the pages that follow:

- Planning Guide—Section 1: Desired Results
- Planning Guide—Section 2: Lesson Design
- Planning Guide—Section 3: Evidence of Learning
- Basic Lesson Plan Form

Mentors may use these guides as they coach mentees in how to plan basic lessons and choose appropriate teaching strategies, grouping plans, and assessments.

PLANNING GUIDE–BASIC INSTRUCTION
SECTION 1: DESIRED RESULTS
Use these questions to plan a basic instructional design.

PLANNING QUESTIONS AND DECISIONS	INFORMATION AND DATA SOURCES	NOTES AND COMMENTS
1. What learning standards/ benchmarks will be taught?		
2. What is the specific learning standard?		
3. What assessment activities will enable students to demonstrate they have met the learning standard?		
4. What performance expectations are there for students to show the extent of learning that has occurred?		
5. How will students' difficulties be recognized along the way?		
6. What assessment materials are available and what materials need to be developed?		
7. How will assessment results be communicated to students and parents?		

Blackline 5.1

Basic Instructional Design

SECTION 2: DESIGN

Use these questions to plan a basic instructional design.

PLANNING QUESTIONS AND DECISIONS	INFORMATION AND DATA SOURCES	NOTES AND COMMENTS
1. What are the learning standards/ benchmarks to be achieved?		
2. What is a motivating opening for the lesson?		
3. What strategies or activities will be used to teach the standard?		
4. What materials are needed to support and enhance learning?		
5. What is the appropriate use of technology?		
6. How will students be grouped for this activity?		
7. What opportunities will students have to reflect on their learning?		
8. How will student progress be monitored?		
9. What forms of additional practice may be necessary?		
10. How long will the lesson take?		
11. Are there any foreseeable pitfalls in this lesson?		
12. What alternatives are there if the lesson doesn't work out?		

Blackline 5.2

PLANNING GUIDE—BASIC INSTRUCTION
SECTION 3: EVIDENCE OF LEARNING
Use these questions to plan a basic instructional design.

PLANNING QUESTIONS AND DECISIONS	INFORMATION AND DATA SOURCES	NOTES AND COMMENTS
1. How will students demonstrate their learning?		
2. How will the assessment be scored?		
3. How will learning be reported?		
4. How will the assessment results be used?		

Blackline 5.3

Basic Instructional Design

BASIC LESSON PLAN FORM

LEARNING STANDARDS/BENCHMARKS (concepts, skills, processes)

LESSON DESIGN Opening (outcomes/purpose/expectations)	MATERIALS/RESOURCES	STUDENT GROUPING ARRANGEMENT
Teaching Strategies/Activities (demonstration, modeling, explanation, directions, etc.)		
Student Activities		
Closing (connections/summary/reflection)		
PRACTICE ACTIVITIES/ASSIGNMENTS		
MONITORING STUDENT PROGRESS (ongoing)		
ASSESSMENT OF STUDENT LEARNING		EXPECTATIONS

Blackline 5.4

> Teachers can use Gardner's theory of multiple intelligences to energize their instruction. Lazear shares ideas for planning interactive and motivating lessons.

The Artistry of Teaching For, With, and About Multiple Intelligences

by **David Lazear**

What is intelligence? How can we measure it? And once it's been measured, what should we do with it?

For many centuries humankind has been trying to understand the workings of the mind—sometimes through magic, sometimes through psychology, sometimes through sociology and anthropology, sometimes through religion, and sometimes through medicine. In the last thirty to fifty years, researchers from every walk of life, and from virtually every profession and academic discipline have begun a new set of explorations of a new frontier—the human mind and how it works. And they have been coming up with some astonishing discoveries,

Adapted from *Eight Ways of Teaching: The Artistry of Teaching with Multiple Intelligences* by David Lazear, pp. 1–14, 28, 43, 60, 75, 104, 119, 135. © 1999 by Corwin Press. Used with permission.

The Artistry of Teaching For, With, and About Multiple Intelligences

many of which have called into question all previous understandings about humanity and its potentials:

- **Right brain/left brain.** In 1981 Dr. Roger Sperry received a Nobel Peace Prize for his research into the different ways the left and right hemispheres of the brain process information. In the left hemisphere, processing is more linear and sequential, while the right brain's processing tends to be more simultaneous and creative. These two modalities are brought together in a new area of research known as *whole-brain processing*.

- **Triune brain.** Dr. Paul MacLean, Chief of the Laboratory of Brain Evolution and Behavior at the National Institute of Mental Health in Washington, D.C., has done an important research study that suggests that within our one brain there are three separate brains that come from our earlier development as a species. As humans developed, and the need for more involved levels of thinking and mental processes were required, the brain simply grew new layers, each more complex and more intricate than its predecessor. While all three brains are still present in humans, they operate as a unified whole giving us the wisdom and potentials from our evolutionary past.

- **Intelligence can be enhanced and amplified.** In the past, intelligence was viewed as a fixed, static entity. It was something you were born with and were stuck with for life. However, contemporary brain-mind researchers, such as Dr. Jean Houston, Dr. Robert Masters, Dr. Willis Harman, and Dr. Luis Machado, are suggesting that possibly the only limits to our intelligence are self-made and are related to our beliefs about what is possible. What is more, Israeli psychologist and researcher, Dr. Reuven Feuerstein, along with a number of others, suggest that at any age, and at almost any ability level, one's mental functioning can be improved. We can, apparently, all learn to be more intelligent by consciously activating perception and knowing on more levels than we usually use!

- **The brain is like a hologram.** Dr. Karl Pribram of Stanford University has proposed a fascinating theory of the brain as a hologram. In a hologram, all of the basic information of the whole is stored within each part of the hologram, so that if it is in some way shattered, each piece contains and is capable of reproducing all of the information of the former whole. Pribram suggests that memory storage may work like this in the brain. Think for a moment about times when a very small fragment of a memory is able to bring back a full-sensory experience of something that may have happened in your childhood.

- **Intelligence is a multiple reality.** Dr. Howard Gardner and his team of Harvard researchers involved in Project Zero have postulated that there are many forms of intelligence—many ways by which we know, understand, and learn about our world—not just one. And most of these ways of knowing go beyond those that dominate Western culture and education, and they definitely go beyond what current IQ tests can measure. He proposed a schema of eight intelligences and suggests that there are probably many others that we have not yet been able to test!

It is the research of Howard Gardner on which this selection is primarily based. Let me briefly summarize the eight intelligences Gardner identified:

Verbal/linguistic intelligence is responsible for the production of language and all the complex possibilities that follow, including poetry, humor, storytelling, grammar, metaphors, similes, abstract reasoning, symbolic thinking, conceptual patterning, reading, and writing. This intelligence can be seen in such people as poets, playwrights, storytellers, novelists, public speakers, and comedians.

The Artistry of Teaching For, With, and About Multiple Intelligences

Logical/mathematical intelligence is most often associated with what we call scientific thinking or inductive reasoning, although deductive thought processes are also involved. This intelligence involves the capacity to recognize patterns, work with abstract symbols (such as numbers and geometric shapes), and discern relationships and/or see connections between separate and distinct pieces of information. This intelligence can be seen in such people as scientists, computer programmers, accountants, lawyers, bankers, and of course, mathematicians.

Visual/spatial intelligence deals with the visual arts (including painting, drawing, and sculpting); navigation, map-making, and architecture (which involve the use of space and knowing how to get around in it); and games such as chess (which require the ability to visualize objects from different perspectives and angles). The key sensory base of this intelligence is the sense of sight, but also the ability to form mental images and pictures in the mind. This intelligence can be seen in architects, graphic artists, cartographers, industrial design draftspersons, and of course, visual artists.

Bodily/kinesthetic intelligence is the ability to use the body to express emotion (as in dance and body language), to play a game (as in sports), and to create a new product (as in invention). Learning by doing has long been recognized as an important part of education. Our bodies know things our minds do not and cannot know in any other way. For example, our bodies know how to ride a bike, roller-skate, type, and parallel park a car. This intelligence can been seen in such people as actors, athletes, mimes, dancers, and inventors.

Musical/rhythmic intelligence includes such capacities as the recognition and use of rhythmic and tonal patterns, and sensitivity to sounds from the environment, the human voice, and musical instruments. The consciousness altering effect of music and rhythm on the brain is probably the greatest. This intelligence can be seen in advertising professionals (those who write catchy jingles to sell a product), performance musicians, rock musicians, dance bands, composers, and music teachers.

Interpersonal intelligence involves the ability to work cooperatively with others in a group as well as the ability to communicate, verbally and nonverbally, with other people. It builds on the capacity to notice distinctions among others such as contrasts in moods, temperament, motivations, and intentions. In the more advanced forms of this intelligence, one can literally pass over into another's perspective and read his or her intentions and desires. One can have genuine empathy for another's feelings, fears, anticipations, and beliefs. This form of intelligence is usually highly developed in counselors, teachers, therapists, politicians, and religious leaders.

Intrapersonal intelligence involves knowledge of the internal aspects of the self, such as knowledge of feelings, the range of emotional responses, thinking processes, self-reflection, and a sense of or intuition about spiritual realities. Intrapersonal intelligence allows us to be conscious of our consciousness; that is, to step back from ourselves and watch ourselves as an outside observer. It involves our capacity to experience wholeness and unity, to discern patterns of connection within the larger order of things, to perceive higher states of consciousness, to experience the lure of the future, and to dream of and actualize the possible. This intelligence can be seen in such people as philosophers, psychiatrists, spiritual counselors and gurus, and cognitive pattern researchers.

Naturalist intelligence involves the ability to discern, comprehend, and appreciate the various flora and fauna of the world of nature as opposed to the world created by human beings. It involves such capacities as recognizing and classifying species, growing plants and raising or taming animals, knowing how to appropriately use the natural world (e.g., living off the land), and having a curiosity about the natural world, its creatures, weather patterns, physical history, etc. This intelligence can be seen in such people as farmers, hunters, zookeepers, gardeners, cooks, veterinarians, nature guides, and forest rangers.

The Artistry of Teaching For, With, and About Multiple Intelligences

On the following pages are a summary of the multiple intelligences (Figure 6.1) and the Multiple Intelligences Capacities Wheel (Figure 6.2). I created the wheel to show some of the specific capacities (what Gardner sometimes calls subintelligences) that are related to the eight ways of knowing.

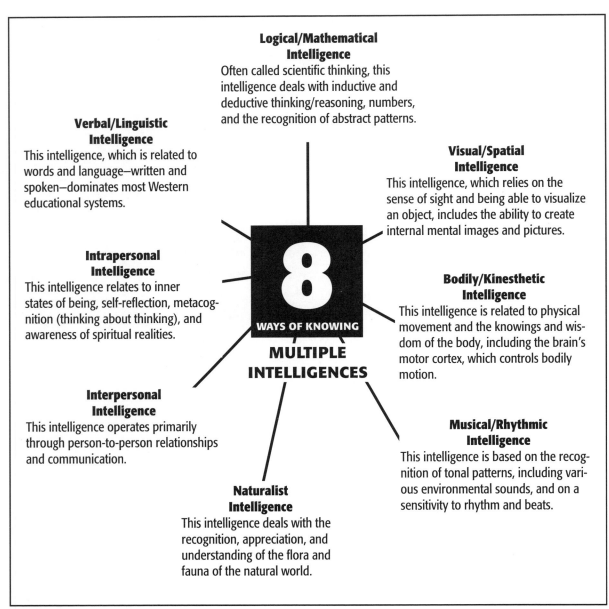

Logical/Mathematical Intelligence
Often called scientific thinking, this intelligence deals with inductive and deductive thinking/reasoning, numbers, and the recognition of abstract patterns.

Verbal/Linguistic Intelligence
This intelligence, which is related to words and language–written and spoken–dominates most Western educational systems.

Visual/Spatial Intelligence
This intelligence, which relies on the sense of sight and being able to visualize an object, includes the ability to create internal mental images and pictures.

Intrapersonal Intelligence
This intelligence relates to inner states of being, self-reflection, metacognition (thinking about thinking), and awareness of spiritual realities.

Bodily/Kinesthetic Intelligence
This intelligence is related to physical movement and the knowings and wisdom of the body, including the brain's motor cortex, which controls bodily motion.

Interpersonal Intelligence
This intelligence operates primarily through person-to-person relationships and communication.

Musical/Rhythmic Intelligence
This intelligence is based on the recognition of tonal patterns, including various environmental sounds, and on a sensitivity to rhythm and beats.

Naturalist Intelligence
This intelligence deals with the recognition, appreciation, and understanding of the flora and fauna of the natural world.

8 WAYS OF KNOWING
MULTIPLE INTELLIGENCES

Figure 6.1

Multiple Intelligences Capacities Wheel

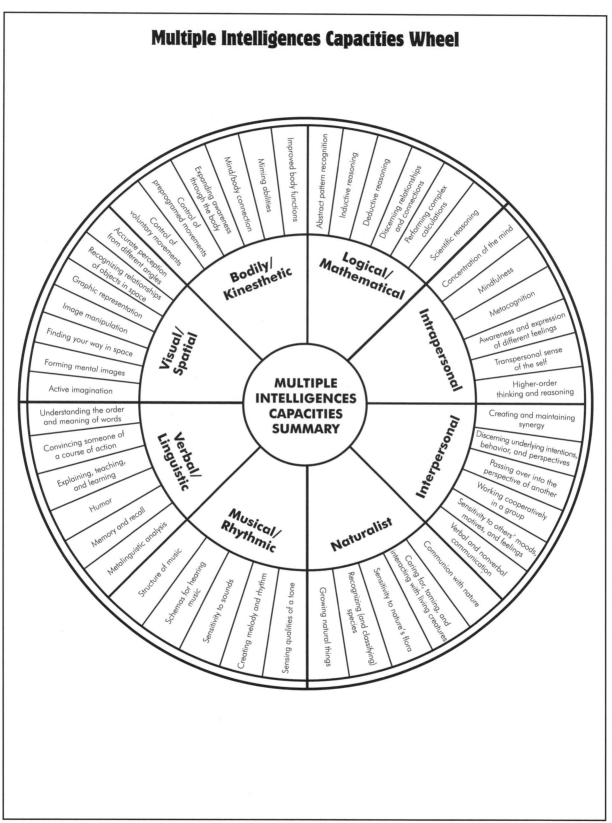

Figure 6.2

The Artistry of Teaching For, With, and About Multiple Intelligences

The good news is that each of us have all of these intelligences, but not all of them are developed equally and thus we do not know how to use them effectively. In fact, it is usually the case that one or two intelligences are stronger and more fully developed than the others. But, this need not be a permanent condition. *We have within ourselves the capacity to activate all of our intelligences!*

What are possibilities of teaching for, with, and about multiple intelligences in the classroom?

There are at least three different types of lessons that are needed:

1. **Intelligence as a subject unto itself (teaching for multiple intelligences).** Each of the intelligences can be taught as a subject in its own right: music skills, language, art as a formal discipline, mathematical calculation and reasoning, skillful body movement (physical education, dance, and drama), and various social skills necessary for effective functioning in our society. Teaching these subjects requires a grasp of the developmental stages of each intelligence as well as an understanding of the accumulated cultural wisdom on the subject, the formal knowledge base, and the practical methods, skills, and techniques of the intelligence.

2. **Intelligence as a means to acquire knowledge (teaching with multiple intelligences).** Each of the intelligences can be used as a means to gain knowledge in areas beyond itself: using body movement to learn vocabulary words, music to teach math concepts, art (drawing, painting, and sculpture) to bring to life different periods of history and different cultures, debate to explore various perspectives on current events, and the skill of comparing and contrasting to analyze characters in a Shakespearean play.

3. **Meta-intelligence—intelligence investigating itself (teaching about multiple intelligences).** Lessons that deal with meta-intelligence processes are concerned with teaching students about their own

multiple intelligences—how to access them, how to strengthen them, and how to actively use them in learning and in everyday life.

OK, I buy the eight ways of knowing! What does it take to teach in this way? What's involved in lessons that take into account the reality of multiple intelligences in the classroom?

Generally speaking, there are four stages necessary to teach *with* multiple intelligences: awaken, amplify, teach, and transfer (see Figure 6.3).

Stage I: Awaken. We must be aware that we possess multiple ways of knowing and learning and that we must learn various techniques and methodologies for triggering an intelligence within the brain-mind-body system.

Stage II: Amplify. We must learn how particular intelligences (ways of knowing) work; that is, what the various capacities and/or skills are, how to access them, and how to use and understand different intelligence modalities. This involves both practice in strengthening intelligence capacities as well as learning how to interpret and work with the different kinds of information we receive from each intelligence. We must learn to understand the unique language of each intelligence; that is, how each expresses itself. For example, the language of bodily/kinesthetic intelligence is physical movement, *not* words, sentences, writing, and speech.

Stage III: Teach. We must learn how to teach content-based lessons that apply different ways of knowing to the specific content of a given lesson. My first presupposition is that **we can teach all students to be more intelligent** in more ways, and on more levels than they (or we) ever dreamed. My second presupposition is that ***anything* can be taught and learned through all of the intelligences.** This means that we as teachers must learn how to use the intelligences in the teaching and learning process. About ninety-five percent of the

The Artistry of Teaching For, With, and About Multiple Intelligences

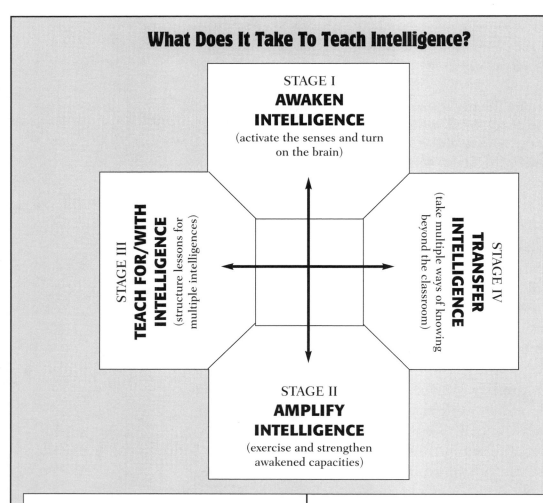

What Does It Take To Teach Intelligence?

STAGE I
AWAKEN INTELLIGENCE
(activate the senses and turn on the brain)

STAGE III
TEACH FOR/WITH INTELLIGENCE
(structure lessons for multiple intelligences)

STAGE IV
TRANSFER INTELLIGENCE
(take multiple ways of knowing beyond the classroom)

STAGE II
AMPLIFY INTELLIGENCE
(exercise and strengthen awakened capacities)

STAGE I **AWAKEN INTELLIGENCE**	STAGE II **AMPLIFY INTELLIGENCE**
Each of the intelligences is related to the five senses. In general, a particular intelligence can be activated or triggered through exercises and activities which use the sensory bases—sight, sound taste, touch, smell, speech, and communication with others—as well as inner senses—intuition, metacognition, and spiritual insight.	This involves practices for expanding, deepening, and nurturing an awakened or activated intelligence. As with any skill, intelligence skills cannot only be awakened, but can also be improved and strengthened if used on a regular basis. And, like any skill, they will also go back to sleep if not used.
STAGE III **TEACH FOR/WITH INTELLIGENCE**	STAGE IV **TRANSFER INTELLIGENCE**
This stage involves learning how to use, trust, and interpret a given intelligence through knowing, learning, and understanding tasks. In this selection, teaching *with* intelligence is approached from the perspective of classroom lessons that emphasize and use different intelligences in the teaching/learning process.	This stage includes the integration of an intelligence into daily living and its appropriate application to solving problems and meeting the challenges faced in the so-called real world. The goal of this stage is for the intelligence to become a regular part of one's cognitive, affective, and sensory life.

Figure 6.3

material we have to teach comes prepackaged in a verbal/
linguistic or logical/mathematical form. However, in planning
lessons that teach this material, we need not be bound by this
packaging. My goal is to help you learn to design and implement lessons that emphasize all intelligences.

Stage IV: Transfer. We must teach our students how to use
all of the intelligences to improve their effectiveness in dealing
with the issues, challenges, and problems we face in the task of
daily living. This is primarily a matter of approaching these
tasks on multiple levels, with a variety of problem-solving
methods that use different intelligences.

The model in Figure 6.3 is intended to demonstrate the fundamental dynamics that I believe need to be present in lessons
that are designed to emphasize the different ways of knowing
and learning when teaching content-based information.

> **Let's get practical now. Enough theory! How do I
> plan lessons that take into account multiple intelli-
> gences? What is the nitty-gritty of this?**

A model lesson (A History Lesson with Musical/Rhythmic
Intelligences) is provided at the end of this selection and
emphasizes one of the intelligences as the primary mode of
knowing and learning. As a preface to this lesson I must men-
tion that in the normal person the intelligences operate in
concert with each other, generally in well orchestrated ways,
although certain of the intelligences do tend to be stronger or
more developed than others. You will notice all of the intelligences get into the act, so to speak, even though the lesson is
designed to focus on and use one intelligence in particular.
In my own teaching I generally try to involve at least three
ways of knowing *beyond* the verbal/linguistic and
logical/mathematical. I believe this is a good rule of thumb for
classroom lessons as well. Remember, the more intelligences
you can incorporate into a lesson, the deeper and more
thorough the learning will be.

The Artistry of Teaching For, With, and About Multiple Intelligences

The Multiple Intelligences Toolbox (Figure 6.4) contains practical techniques, methods, tools, and media for accessing the eight intelligences. They must be used in conjunction with other parts of the lesson and adapted for dealing with content-based information, but these tools can help you move quickly into various ways of knowing in a lesson.

The following elements will also help you understand the model lesson and design your own lessons:

1. **Lesson Palette.** The use of the palette as a metaphor for lesson planning is a technique I have found very helpful to remind myself that, as teachers, we are artists who are creating curriculum eventfulness for students. The palette can help you select tools that are appropriate for your objectives as well as help you see how to integrate the different intelligence tools into the lesson. The palette for the lesson lists the ten tools (from the toolbox) for the intelligence being emphasized. I have checkmarked the specific tools used in the lesson as well as the other intelligences that are involved. (See Blackline 6.10 for a template to use.)

2. **The Lesson at a Glance.** This two-page model is a brief overview of the processes of awakening, amplifying, teaching, and transferring as they apply to the intelligence being emphasized in the lesson. (See Blackline 6.11 for a template to use.)

3. **Lesson Procedures.** The lesson is intended to be a model from which you can design your own lessons. This lesson is a step-by-step procedure written from the perspective of the teacher—what you do to get students involved in using their multiple intelligences in the classroom.

4. **Spiral Adaptations of the Lesson.** Each lesson focuses on one grade level (elementary, middle, or secondary). I have therefore included this section in order to provide some suggestions for other levels. This adaptation relies on the research of Jerome Brunner on spiraling the curriculum. He said that we can teach

Logical/Mathematical

- Abstract Symbols/ Formulas
- Calculation
- Deciphering Codes
- Forcing Relationships
- Graphic/Cognitive Organizers
- Logic/Pattern Games
- Number Sequences/ Patterns
- Outlining
- Problem Solving
- Syllogisms

Verbal/Linguistic

- Creative Writing
- Formal Speaking
- Humor/Jokes
- Impromptu Speaking
- Journal/Diary Keeping
- Poetry
- Reading
- Storytelling/Story Creation
- Verbal Debate
- Vocabulary

Visual/Spatial

- Active Imagination
- Color/Texture Schemes
- Drawing
- Guided Imagery/ Visualizing
- Mind Mapping
- Montage/Collage
- Painting
- Patterns/Designs
- Pretending/Fantasy
- Sculpting

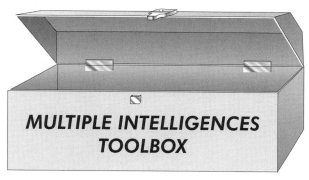

MULTIPLE INTELLIGENCES TOOLBOX

Musical/Rhythmic

- Environmental Sounds
- Instrumental Sounds
- Music Composition/Creation
- Music Performance
- Percussion Vibrations
- Rapping
- Rhythmic Patterns
- Singing/Humming
- Tonal Patterns
- Vocal Sounds/Tones

Bodily/Kinesthetic

- Body Language/Physical Gestures
- Body Sculpture/Tableaus
- Dramatic Enactment
- Folk/Creative Dance
- Gymnastic Routines
- Human Graph
- Inventing
- Physical Exercise/Martial Arts
- Role Playing/Mime
- Sports Games

Interpersonal

- Collaborative Skills Teaching
- Cooperative Learning Strategies
- Empathy Practices
- Giving Feedback
- Group Projects
- Intuiting Others' Feelings
- Jigsaw
- Person-to-Person Communication
- Receiving Feedback
- Sensing Others' Motives

Intrapersonal

- Altered States of Consciousness Practices
- Emotional Processing
- Focusing/Concentration Skills
- Higher-Order Reasoning
- Independent Studies/Projects
- Know Thyself Procedures
- Metacognition Techniques
- Mindfulness Practices
- Silent Reflection Methods
- Thinking Strategies

Naturalist

- Archetypal Pattern Recognition
- Caring for Plants/Animals
- Conservation Practices
- Environment Feedback
- Hands-On Labs
- Nature Encounters/Field Trips
- Nature Observation
- Natural World Simulations
- Species Classification (organic/inorganic)
- Sensory Stimulation Exercises

Figure 6.4

anything to anyone, at any age, if we as teachers take the time to get inside their worldview and speak the language that is meaningful to them in that world and at that age.

5. **Assessment Tips.** These assessment ideas are related to the completed lesson. These will make extensive use of student portfolios (see Figure 6.5) and journals.

6. **Look to the Past and Look to the Future.** These lesson palettes are designed to help the teacher reflect on how a past or future lesson could be restructured to incorporate the intelligence being emphasized in the lesson.

7. **Lesson Planning Ideas.** This is a chart of ideas for lessons in a given intelligence area. I have tried to address all major subject areas we teach in our schools, such as history, mathematics, language arts, social studies, science, health, geography, computer science, physical education, industrial arts, home economics, and fine arts. The ideas in the chart are lesson seedlings which you may want to plant, water, put in the sunlight, and see if they grow (see Blacklines 6.1–6.8)

I hope you have fun with this selection and that it sparks many new ideas for you and your students. I believe that the next stages of the research on multiple intelligences will happen in the laboratory of the normal school classroom. It will be based on what you discover as you conduct various experiments with eight ways of teaching, helping students activate and use their eight ways of knowing.

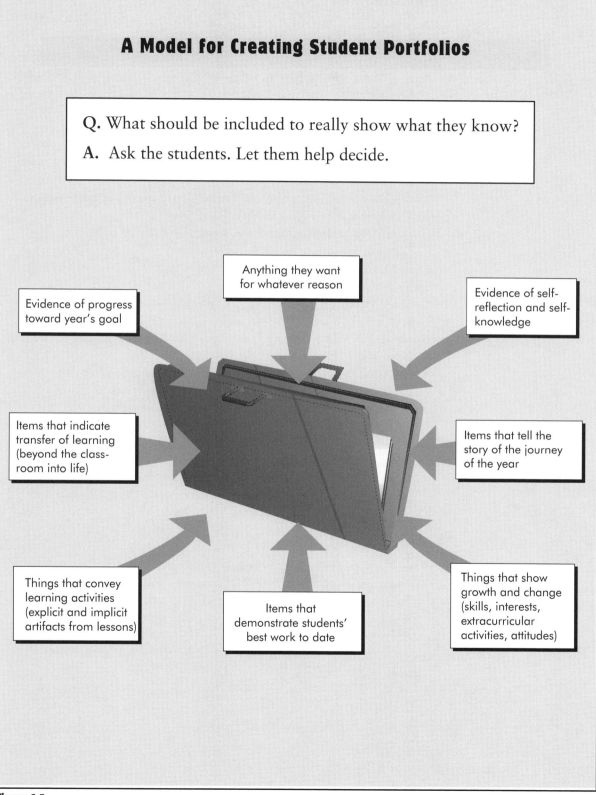

A Model for Creating Student Portfolios

Q. What should be included to really show what they know?

A. Ask the students. Let them help decide.

Anything they want for whatever reason

Evidence of progress toward year's goal

Evidence of self-reflection and self-knowledge

Items that indicate transfer of learning (beyond the classroom into life)

Items that tell the story of the journey of the year

Things that convey learning activities (explicit and implicit artifacts from lessons)

Items that demonstrate students' best work to date

Things that show growth and change (skills, interests, extracurricular activities, attitudes)

Figure 6.5

The Artistry of Teaching For, With, and About Multiple Intelligences

BIBLIOGRAPHY

Feuerstein, R. 1980. *Instrumental enrichment*. Baltimore, MD: University Park Press.

Gardner, H. 1981. Do babies sing a universal song? *Psychology Today*.

———. 1982. *Developmental pscyhology: An introduction*. Boston: Little Brown.

———. 1983. *Frames of mind: The theory of multiple intelligences*. New York: Harper and Row.

———. 1987. *Developing the spectrum of human intelligences: Teaching in the eighties, a need to change*. Harvard Educational Review.

———. 1993. *Frames of mind: The theory of multiple intelligences—Tenth anniversay edition*. NY: Basic Books.

———. 1996. *Are there additional intelligences?* Cambridge, MA: Harvard Graduate School of Education.

Harman, W. 1988. *The global mind change*. Indianapolis: Knowledge Systems.

Harman, W., and H. Rheingold. 1985. *Higher creativity*. Los Angeles: J. P. Tarcher.

Houston, J. 1980. *Lifeforce: The psycho-historical recovery of the self*. New York: Delacourte Press.

———. 1982. *The possible human: A course in extending your physical, mental, and creative abilities*. Los Angeles: J. P. Tarcher.

———. 1987. *The search for the beloved: Journeys in sacred psychology*. Los Angeles: J. P. Tarcher.

Machado, L. 1980. *The right to be intelligent*. New York: Pergamon Press.

MacLean, P. 1977. On the evolution of the three mentalities. In *New dimensions in psychiatry: A world view* (Vol. 2), edited by S. Arieti and G. Chryanowski. New York: Wiley.

Masters, R., and J. Houston. 1972. *Mind games*. New York: Delacourte Press.

———. 1978. *Listening to the body: The psychophysical way to health and awareness*. New York: Delacourte Press.

Pribram, K. 1971. *Language of the brain: Experimental paradoxes and principles in neuro-psychology*. Englewood Cliffs, NJ: Prentice Hall.

———. 1974. *Holonomy and structure in the organization of perception*. Stanford, CA: Stanford University Press.

- Blacklines 6.1–6.8 list lesson planning ideas for all content areas for each of the eight multiple intelligences. Mentors and protégés can review these charts and discuss ideas appropriate for their classrooms and generate ideas of their own.
- Protégés can study the model lesson, A History Lesson with Musical/Rhythmic Intelligence, at the end of this selection and create their own multiple intelligences lesson for their mentors to review.
- Blacklines 6.9, 6.10, and 6.11 can be used by protégés when creating their own multiple intelligence lessons.

LESSON PLANNING IDEAS
Verbal/Linguistic

	HISTORY	MATHEMATICS	LANGUAGE ARTS	SCIENCE & HEALTH	GLOBAL STUDIES & GEOGRAPHY	FAMILY/CONSUMER SCIENCES, INDUSTRIAL TECHNOLOGY, & PE	FINE ARTS
	Play What's My Line? with figures from history	Write a series of story problems for others to solve	Teach concept mapping to help remember content	Write a humorous story using science vocabulary or formulas	Read stories, myths, and poetry from other cultures	Give verbal explanation of gymnastic routines	Listen to a piece of music and make up a story about it
	Debate important issues and decisions from the past	Explain how to work a problem to others while they follow	Write a sequel or next episode to a story or play	Create a diary on The Life of a Red Blood Cell	Hold Countries of the World spelling and pronunciation bee	Write instructions for use and care of shop machines	Verbally describe an object while a partner draws it
	Create limericks about key historical events	Make up puns using math vocabulary or terms	Create crossword puzzles or word jumbles for vocabulary words	Write steps used in an experiment so someone else can do it	Keep an Insights from Other Cultures for Us log	Tell another how to run a word processing program—then do it	Tell a partner the steps to a dance while they perform it
	Study poetry from different periods of history	Solve problems with a partner—one solves and one explains process	Play New Word for the Day game	Make up an imaginary conversation between parts of the body	Study a road map and give verbal instructions to get someplace	Pretend you are a radio sportscaster describing a game in progress	Turn a Greek or Shakespearean tragedy into a situation comedy
	Compile a notebook of history jokes	Create poems telling when to use different math operations	Practice impromptu speaking and writing	Give a speech on Ten Steps to Healthful Living	Learn basic conversation in several foreign languages	Play Recipe Jeopardy—make questions for answers given	Describe an emotion or mood and play music it suggests

LESSON PLANNING IDEAS
Logical/Mathematical

HISTORY	MATHEMATICS	LANGUAGE ARTS	SCIENCE & HEALTH	GLOBAL STUDIES & GEOGRAPHY	FAMILY/CONSUMER SCIENCES, INDUSTRIAL TECHNOLOGY, & PE	FINE ARTS
Find examples when history repeated itself	Find unknown quantities or entities in a problem	Predict what will happen next in a story or play	Use the symbols of the Periodic Table of Elements in a story	Play Follow the Legend map-reading games and exercises	Follow a recipe to make bread from scratch	Learn patterns of ten different dance steps
Compare and contrast different periods of history	Teach someone else how to use a calculator for problem solving	Create a 4x4x4 outline on a favorite hobby	Find five different ways to classify a collection of leaves	Play Guess the Culture based on artifacts in a time capsule	Find the relation of keyboard actions and computer performance	Compose a piece of music from a matrix
Ask fat and skinny questions about key historical decisions	Create number sequences and have a partner find the pattern	Learn to read, write, and decipher code language	Do a KWL goal-setting chart for a study of AIDS	Rank-order key socioeconomic factors that shaped a culture	Design a physical exercise routine using a matrix	Use a Venn diagram to analyze characters in a play
Create time sequence charts with titles for major eras of history	Mind-map proofs for geometry theorems	Analyze similarities and differences of various pieces of literature	Learn the pattern of successful and reliable scientific experiments	Predict what will happen in several current event stories	Create problem-solving scenarios for shop machines	Create a paint-by-numbers picture for another person to paint
Predict what the next decade will be like based on patterns of the past	Design classification charts for math formulas and operations	Use a story grid for creative writing activities	Practice webbing attributes of various systems of the body	Learn cause and effect relations of geography and geological events	Make a matrix on meanings of computer symbols	Analyze plays using the dramatic structure model

Blackline 6.2

Lesson Planning Ideas
Visual/Spatial

HISTORY	MATHEMATICS	LANGUAGE ARTS	SCIENCE & HEALTH	GLOBAL STUDIES & GEOGRAPHY	FAMILY/CONSUMER SCIENCES, INDUSTRIAL TECHNOLOGY, & PE	FINE ARTS
Have imaginary talks or interviews with people from the past	Do a survey of students' likes and dislikes, then graph the results	Play Pictionary with vocabulary words	Draw pictures of things seen under a microscope	Draw maps of the world from your visual memory	Draw pictures of how to perform certain physical feats	Watch dancers on video and imagine yourself in their shoes
Make visual diagrams and flowcharts of historical facts	Estimate measurements by sight and by touch	Use mind mapping as a notetaking process	Create posters or flyers showing healthy eating practices	Study a culture through its visual art—painting and sculpture	Create visual diagrams of how to use shop machines	Pretend you can enter a painting—imagine what it is like
Imagine going back in time—see what it was like back then	Add, subtract, multiply, and divide using various manipulatives	Draw pictures of the different stages of a story you are reading	Create montages or collages on science topics (e.g., mammals)	Make maps out of clay and show geographical features	Practice drawing objects from different angles (drafting)	Listen to music with eyes closed and create a sculpture from clay
Paint a mural about a period of history	Imagine using a math process successfully, then really do it	Learn to read, write, and decipher code language	Draw visual patterns that appear in the natural world	Make decor for the classroom on a culture you are studying	Learn a series of spatial games (e.g., horseshoes, ring toss)	Draw the sets for the various scenes of a play you are reading
Imagine and draw what you think the future will be like	Learn metric measurement through visual equivalents	Use highlight markers to colorize parts of a story or poem	Pretend you are microscopic and can travel in the bloodstream	Use a map to get around an unfamiliar place or location	Imagine your computer is human—draw how it works	Draw the visual and color pattern of a dance

Blackline 6.3

LESSON PLANNING IDEAS
Bodily/Kinesthetic

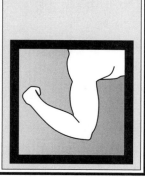

HISTORY	MATHEMATICS	LANGUAGE ARTS	SCIENCE & HEALTH	GLOBAL STUDIES & GEOGRAPHY	FAMILY/CONSUMER SCIENCES, INDUSTRIAL TECHNOLOGY, & PE	FINE ARTS
Perform and/or create dramas from a period of history	Use different parts of the body to measure things	Play the Parts of a Sentence charades	Role-play the parts and dynamics of the life of a cell	Learn folk dances of a culture being studied	Learn and perfect various multitracking routines	Create the dance equivalent for different inventions
Reenact great scenes or moments from history for today	Add and subtract members to and from a group to learn about fractions	"Embody" (act out) the meaning of vocabulary words	Create the rotation of planets with the class members acting as the solar system	Create gestures to represent the legend of a map	Invent something in shop class such as a new household tool	Create human sculpture tableau to express an idea
Hold an historical period, costume, and food day	Design something that requires applying math concepts	Act out a story or play that you are studying	Become and act out the different states of matter	Play physical movement games from another culture	Practice physical movements in your mind then with your body	Make up gestures for parts of a musical score
Play Great Moments from the Past charades	Create and act out a play in which the characters are geometric shapes	Learn the alphabet by body movements and physical gestures	Conduct a series of hands-on scientific experiments	Simulate going shopping using currency from another country	Make up a new kind of snack food, prepare it, and eat it	Design a "live painting" of a classical work
Learn dances from previous periods of history (e.g., minuet)	Make up a playground game that uses math concepts or operations	Make up a Parts of Speech folk dance	Study and try various biofeedback techniques or methods	Study body language from different cultural situations	Create and perform a drama on how a computer operates	Practice doing impromptu dramatic mime activities

Blackline 6.4

Lesson Planning Ideas
Musical/Rhythmic

HISTORY	MATHEMATICS	LANGUAGE ARTS	SCIENCE & HEALTH	GLOBAL STUDIES & GEOGRAPHY	FAMILY/CONSUMER SCIENCES, INDUSTRIAL TECHNOLOGY, & PE	FINE ARTS
Analyze different historical periods through their music	Learn mathematical operations through songs and jingles	Learn Morse Code and practice communicating with it	Learn to use music to reduce stress	Listen to music from different cultures	Perform physical exercise routines in sync with music	Play Guess the Rhythm or Guess the Instrument with musical pieces
Create a series of key dates in history raps	Learn addition and subtraction through drum beats	Use different kinds of music for different kinds of writing	Listen to sounds of things in the natural world	Play musical instruments from around the world	Learn to recognize shop machines through their sounds	Draw or paint a piece of music as it plays
Make musical instruments from the past and compose a piece	Play a rhythm game to learn multiplication tables	Learn and practice phonetic punctuation (a lá Victor Borge)	Experiment with the effect of vibration on sand in a metal plate	Create a sound- or tonal-based legend for a map	Record and recognize the varying sounds of a computer operating	Turn a nonmusical play into a musical
Teach songs that were sung in previous eras (e.g., Gregorian chant)	Break a set of tones into various groups to learn division tables	Create songs or raps to teach grammar and syntax	Try various humming patterns to see how they change mood	Learn characteristic rhythm patterns of different cultures	Experiment with the effect of different kinds of music on how you eat	Practice impromptu music composition
Watch films about the past and focus on the sounds of history	Make up sounds for different math operations and processes	Illustrate a story or poem with appropriate sounds	Assign sounds to systems you are studying such as the nervous system or circulatory system	Sing songs from nations or countries being studied	Use music to help improve keyboarding skills and speed	Make up a creative or interpretive dance to a piece of music

Blackline 6.5

LESSON PLANNING IDEAS
Interpersonal

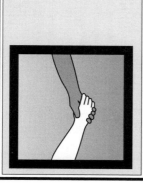

HISTORY	MATHEMATICS	LANGUAGE ARTS	SCIENCE & HEALTH	GLOBAL STUDIES & GEOGRAPHY	FAMILY/CONSUMER SCIENCES, INDUSTRIAL TECHNOLOGY, & PE	FINE ARTS
Do an historical period investigation jigsaw	Solve complex story problems in a group	Experiment with joint story writing—one starts then passes it on	Discuss Saying No to Drugs and create Say No strategies	Assume the perspective of another culture and discuss a news item	Teach and play a series of noncompetitive games	Learn a new dance and teach it to others
Role-play a conversation with an important historical figure	Do a statistical research project and calculate percentages	Analyze a story and describe its message—reach a consensus	Assign group research projects—groups design and implement plans	Find the relation of geography or climate to cultural values and customs	Assign teams to prepare and serve meals from foreign countries	Create a team cooperative sculpture from clay
Pass over into the lives of historical people and describe their feelings or thoughts	Each One Teach One new math processes or operations	Use a human graph to see where a group stands on an issue	Use lab teams for science experiments and exercises	Create scenarios of culture shock and analyze it for its causes	Use peer coaching teams for individual shop projects	Sketch your partner with different expressions
Make a case for different perspectives on the Revolutionary War	Describe *everything* you do to solve a problem with a partner	Read poetry from different perspectives and in different moods	Discuss controversial health topics and write team position papers	Brainstorm and prioritize ways to overcome "ugly Americanism"	Have students work in pairs to learn and improve sports skills	Practice Stop the Action and Improvise with a play
Discuss the impact of key historical decisions on today's world	Have teams construct problems linking many math operations, then solve them	Conduct language drill exercises with a partner	Describe the before and after of key scientific paradigm shifts	Learn to read different kinds of maps, then teach someone how to understand them	Create cooperative computing teams to learn computer skills	Learn to sing rounds and countermelody songs

Blackline 6.6

The Artistry of Teaching For, With, and About Multiple Intelligences

LESSON PLANNING IDEAS — *Intrapersonal*

HISTORY	MATHEMATICS	LANGUAGE ARTS	SCIENCE & HEALTH	GLOBAL STUDIES & GEOGRAPHY	FAMILY/CONSUMER SCIENCES, INDUSTRIAL TECHNOLOGY, & PE	FINE ARTS
Keep a journal about questions from your life that history might be able to answer	Track thinking patterns for different math problems	Write an autobiographical essay entitled My Life to Date	Design, implement, and evaluate a one-month Be Healthy project	Try awareness techniques from other cultures	Discuss how different physical exercises make you feel	Draw yourself from different angles in a mirror
Do a PMI analysis of famous historical decisions	Bridge math concepts beyond school using What? So What? Now What?	Write an autobiographical essay entitled My Life in the Future	Conduct silent reflections on pictures of the solar system	List criteria of your ideal geography or climate and find it on a map	List how things learned in shop can help in your future life	Dance the different stages of your life's journey
Discuss this question: If I could be any historical figure who would I be and why?	Use guided imagery to see complex story problems	Analyze literature for connections to our lives today	Write about: If I could be any animal what would I be and why?	Discuss this question: How would I be different if I had grown up in another culture?	Write down and analyze conversations using your computer	Create a series of sculptures to express your moods
Write an essay on mistakes from the past that you will not repeat	Evaluate your strengths and weaknesses in understanding math	Write a new poem each day for a week answering the question Who am I?	Lead a series of I Become What I Behold exercises	Learn focusing techniques and see how each culture uses them	Watch yourself fix a meal and note *everything* that goes on	Imagine yourself as *each* character in a play
Imagine people from the past giving advice for living today	Watch mood changes as you do math problems and note causes	Imagine being a character in a story or play— What would you do?	Practice techniques for achieving deep relaxation (e.g., breathing)	Keep a feelings diary as you read about current events	Imagine a skill and then try to do it *exactly* as you imagined	Carefully observe the effects of music on you

Blackline 6.7

LESSON PLANNING IDEAS
Naturalist

HISTORY	MATHEMATICS	LANGUAGE ARTS	SCIENCE & HEALTH	GLOBAL STUDIES & GEOGRAPHY	FAMILY/CONSUMER SCIENCES, INDUSTRIAL TECHNOLOGY, & PE	FINE ARTS
Recognize and interpret historical trends (à la Toynbee)	Work story problems based on or dealing with patterns in nature	Nature scene re-creations or simulations for literature and poetry	Classify different foods for healthy diet planning	Environmental representations for different cultures	Grow fruits, vegetables, and herbs and use them in preparing a meal	Compose using sounds from nature and the environment
Understand how natural events have influenced history	Use nature manipulatives in math problem solving	Poetic or descriptive essay writing based on nature experiences	Experience past scientific experiments firsthand (Do them!)	Grow and/or taste foods from various cultures	Experience (via field trips) the process of making cloth from natural materials	Recognize and re-create visual images of natural patterns
Create analogies between historical and natural events	Graph positive and negative influences on the environment	Learn and practice using the vocabulary of nature and the naturalist	Keep a diary of the natural processes of your own body	Study the influence of climate and/or geography on cultural development	Create useful objects for the home, classroom, or office using *only* natural products	Create dances which "embody" or demonstrate patterns in nature
Study how animals have affected history and historical trends	Understand the mathematical patterns of nature	Understand influences of climate and/or environment on authors	Use various naturalist taxonomies on nature field trips	Re-create multimedia experiences of the natural environments of different cultures	Play outdoor games that use natural objects and that are based on natural patterns	Design full-blown dramatic enactments of natural processes
Study the lives of famous naturalists and their impact on history	Calculation problems based on nature and natural processes	Creative story-writing using animal characters and their characteristics	Use cognitive organizers to explore and understand scientific processes	Study animals, insects, etc. from different parts of the world	Create virtual reality encounters with natural phenomena on a computer	Make montages or collages incorporating natural products

Blackline 6.8

MODEL LESSON

A HISTORY LESSON WITH

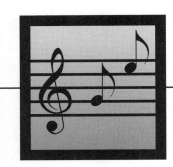

Musical/Rhythmic Intelligence

GUIDEBOOK

Lesson Palette: *Musical/Rhythmic* Emphasis

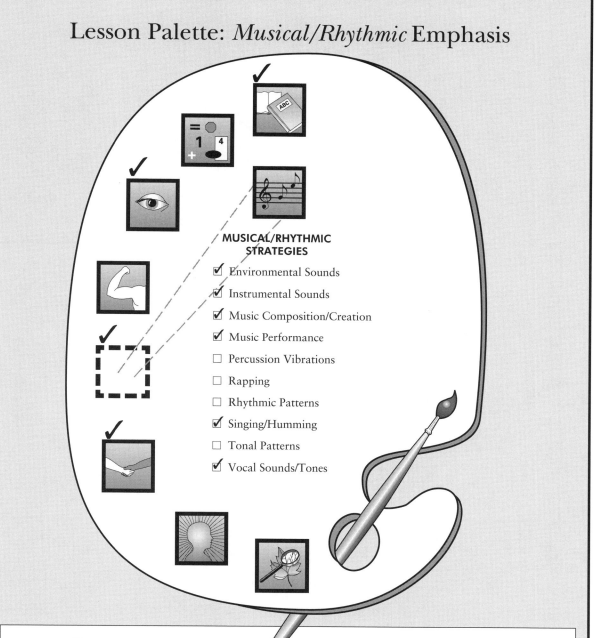

MUSICAL/RHYTHMIC STRATEGIES

- ☑ Environmental Sounds
- ☑ Instrumental Sounds
- ☑ Music Composition/Creation
- ☑ Music Performance
- ☐ Percussion Vibrations
- ☐ Rapping
- ☐ Rhythmic Patterns
- ☑ Singing/Humming
- ☐ Tonal Patterns
- ☑ Vocal Sounds/Tones

SUBJECT AREA: History

INTELLIGENCE EMPHASIS: Musical/Rhythmic

LESSON OBJECTIVE: To grasp an historical period as an unfolding, dramatic story that has a number of messages and much relevancy for our current world situation.

SUPPLIES/MATERIALS:
- written summary of key events of a period of history
- notebook paper
- pens or pencils
- a variety of instruments (drums, noise makers, etc.)
- Team Reflection Log

ROOM ARRANGEMENT: Desks arranged in groups of five around the room with the center of the room as the stage (like theatre in the round)

The Artistry of Teaching For, With, and About Multiple Intelligences

THE LESSON . . .

STAGE I
AWAKEN

Awaken musical/rhythmic intelligence with the resonance or vibrational effect of music and rhythm on the brain. Use such things as the human voice, sounds from nature, musical instruments, and percussion instruments.

MUSICAL/RHYTHMIC

INTELLIGENCE

STAGE III
TEACH

Teach for and with musical/rhythmic intelligence using the specific tools of this intelligence and applying them to help learn content, acquire specific knowledge, and achieve the lesson's goal and/or objectives.

STAGE IV
TRANSFER

Transfer musical/rhythmic intelligence to life by discussing the intelligence tools used, finding applications beyond the lesson to other curriculum areas, and finally integrating it into the task of living in the world outside of the classroom.

Amplify musical/rhythmic intelligence by practicing listening to music and other sounds, expressing feelings through tones, beats, and vibrations, creating songs or jingles to communicate thoughts, and using music, humming, and rhythm to alter moods.

AMPLIFY
STAGE II

The Model

...AT A GLANCE

STAGE I
AWAKEN

- Lesson Introduction: Teacher demonstrates that history is a story about students' lives and that history has meaning for students today.
- Students view pictures and make up stories to go with each.
- Students think of songs that could go with each picture.

MUSICAL/RHYTHMIC

INTELLIGENCE

STAGE III
TEACH

- Read about and discuss historical events.
- Write scripts for radio shows.
- Add special effects and songs to scripts.
- Perform the radio shows.

STAGE IV
TRANSFER

- Reflect on our approach to history in this lesson.
- Reflect on connections between past and present.
- Reflect on ways to use music and rhythm in learning.

- Play audiotapes of old-time radio shows and listen for sound effects.
- Guess how the sound effects were produced.
- Discuss the music involved.

AMPLIFY
STAGE II

The Model *Applied*

A History Lesson with

Musical/Rhythmic Intelligence

Introduction

History is a story about our lives—where we have come from and where we are going. In this lesson students will illustrate an event from the past with sound, music, and rhythmic patterns. First, they will learn about something that happened in American history, either by reading a short article or by hearing a teacher lecture. Then, in cooperative groups, they will create songs and sound effects for retelling the story as if it were an old-time radio show. Tell the students that this lesson will emphasize the musical/rhythmic way of knowing. Ask them to be aware of this as they work on the lesson.

In addition to the musical/rhythmic emphasis of this lesson, verbal/linguistic, visual/spatial, and interpersonal intelligences are involved. Verbal/linguistic intelligence tools are employed at several points: reading, answering questions, and writing about an historical event. Interpersonal intelligence is involved in working with a team. Visual/spatial intelligence is accessed through using pictures, both in the opening exercise and in the pictures of historical scenes.

Awaken

1. Begin by showing students a series of pictures from a magazine. Ask volunteers to tell what they think is happening in the pictures. (Note: Try for a variety of pictures, such as people relaxing on a beach, people involved in an argument, a family eating dinner, etc.)

2. Ask the class to imagine that these scenes are on television but something is wrong and they cannot see the pictures. Ask them how they could figure out what was happening. Make a list on the board or overhead of such things as the dialogue, the music being played, sounds effects, etc.

3. Now have them think of a kind of music that might be played for each picture which would help someone know what was happening. Prompt the class to hum or sing it.

4. Ask them to think of sounds and noises that would be necessary to help someone know what was happening if they couldn't see the picture. Encourage the class again to make some of the sounds.

Amplify

1. Give a short lecture on the old days of radio, before television. Remind students that people only had radios, so when a radio story was being told the story-tellers had to use special sounds, music, conversation between people, and different noises to help the listening audience understand the story. For example, they would often use wooden blocks to make it sound as if a horse were running, or they would rattle a bag of broken glass to make it sound as if a window had been broken.

2. Play several examples of different kinds of old radio shows so they get a sense of what this was like. (Note: You might try the *Lone Ranger, Fibber McGee* and

Molly, The Shadow or some other suspense or detective show. Make sure the segments you play illustrate the importance of sound and music in these productions.)

3. Ask the students the following:
   - How do you think the radio programs produced the different sounds?
   - How did the music help the story?

Teach

1. Divide the students into cooperative groups with four members in each group. For a musical way to break into groups, have everyone pull a song out of a hat. Then have the students start humming their songs and find their groups by identifying the students who are humming their song. Assign the roles of reader, encourager, recorder, and group organizer.

2. Pass out pictures, one picture per team, that depict important events from the early days of American history (e.g., Columbus landing on the shores of the New World, the signing of the Declaration of Independence, Abraham Lincoln at Gettysburg, etc.) On the back of each picture have one or two paragraphs that explain what is happening in the picture along with two or three discussion questions.

3. Assign teams to look at their pictures while the reader reads the paragraph on the back. After reading the paragraph, the group organizer is to ask the discussion questions while the recorder writes down the team's answers.

4. Ask the students to recall the radio shows they listened to earlier. Tell them they are to create a radio show about their pictures and the stories they tell. Each team will perform its program for the class just like the old-time radio shows.

GUIDEBOOK

5. In order to get ready for the show, each team will do the following:
   a. Write a simple script that tells the story of the picture and involves all members of the team with a speaking part.
   b. Create a song about the event and/or find a piece of music to start off and end the show. They can either make up the music themselves or find recorded music to play, or a combination of both!
   c. Decide on at least five special sound effects to be used during the show to help the audience understand what is happening.
      (Note: You will have to monitor the groups very closely to make sure they do not get stuck. You may have to become more actively involved with some groups than others. Also, this project could extend over several days with teams working on one part of the assignment each day.)
6. When they are ready, have the teams perform their show from another room using an amplification system to transmit the program to the main classroom (if possible). If you cannot do this, have them perform their shows from behind a screen so they are hidden from view and must rely only on sound to communicate their story. If you can, record each show so they can listen to it later.
7. After each team has completed its show, thank them for their work and ask the class some questions to check their understanding of the event that was portrayed.

Transfer

1. Ask the whole class to reflect on the radio programs:
   - What do you remember from these different radio programs?
   - What sounds are still ringing in your ears?
   - What lines of dialogue do you remember?
   - What music stands out for you?
2. Pass out the Team Reflection Log (see next page) to each individual. Post the names of the different shows on the board or overhead and have the teams write them in the appropriate columns.
3. For each show have the teams discuss the following questions and have each individual write down thoughts from the team:
   - What was the story being told? Can you remember its parts?
   - How did it make you feel?
   - What are your questions about this event?
   - Why is this story important for us today?

Spiral Adaptations of the Lesson

Middle School Level

1. Practice turning relatively simple information—parts of speech, multiplication tables, states, and capitals—into songs or raps.
2. Have students read material from their history textbook, then retell the story in their own words, illustrating it with songs or raps.
3. After creating several songs about history, turn them into a Broadway-style musical.

Team Reflection Log

	Show #1	Show #2	Show #3	Show #4
What was the story being told?				
How did it make you feel?				
What are your questions about this event?				
Why is this story important for us today?				

Secondary School Level

1. Focus the lesson on learning about the mood, feel, and temperament of a part of history through music, rhythm, and sound.
2. Learn to recognize patterns in music and rhythm that communicate such things as emotions, actions, and moods, as well as patterns that can evoke certain feelings in people.
3. Gather a series of examples of music from a period of history you have been studying (e.g., Gregorian chant, madrigal, minuet, waltz, cantata, etc.). Listen to the music and challenge students to describe what this period must have been like based on its music. Then discuss what today's music says about us! Compare students' impressions with textbook descriptions.

Assessment Tips

Portfolios

1. Ask students to include a copy of the script their teams wrote for the radio show.
2. Have students include a copy of the team's answers to the questions about their picture.

Journals

1. Prompt students to include the Team Reflection Log about the different radio shows.
2. Challenge students to write a brief log entry on what they liked or did not like about the lesson.

Look to the Future . . .

Think about a lesson you have coming up in the near future. How would you structure it to teach *for* and *with* musical/rhythmic intelligence?

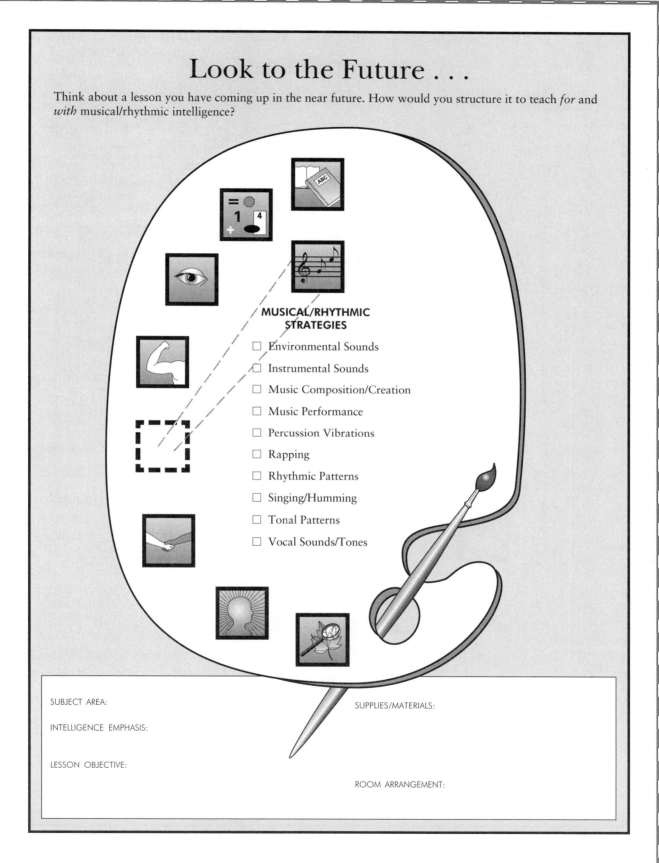

MUSICAL/RHYTHMIC STRATEGIES

☐ Environmental Sounds
☐ Instrumental Sounds
☐ Music Composition/Creation
☐ Music Performance
☐ Percussion Vibrations
☐ Rapping
☐ Rhythmic Patterns
☐ Singing/Humming
☐ Tonal Patterns
☐ Vocal Sounds/Tones

SUBJECT AREA:

INTELLIGENCE EMPHASIS:

LESSON OBJECTIVE:

SUPPLIES/MATERIALS:

ROOM ARRANGEMENT:

The Artistry of Teaching For, With, and About Multiple Intelligences

Look to the Past . . .

Rethink a lesson you have completed recently. How would you restructure it to teach *for* and *with* musical/rhythmic intelligence?

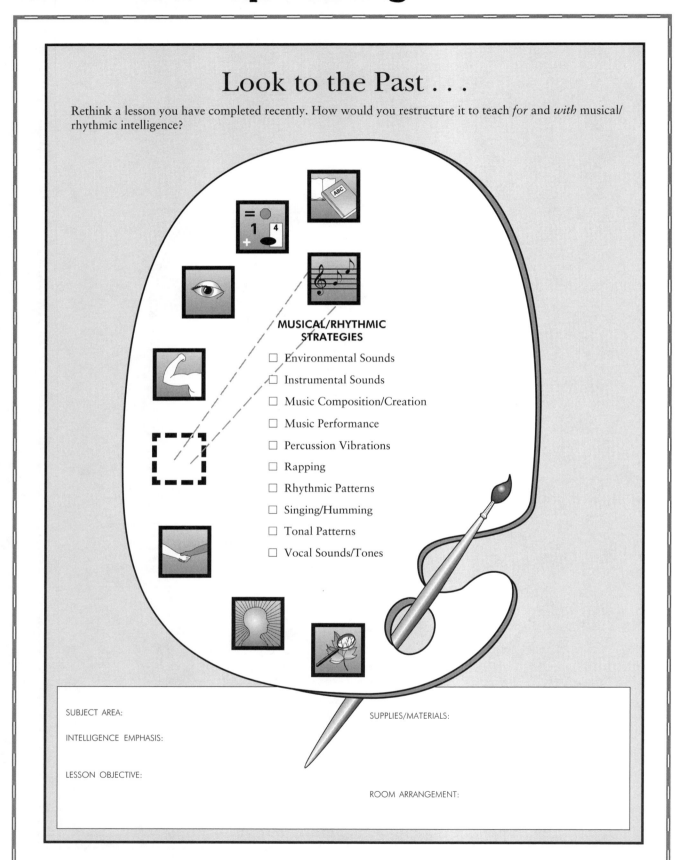

MUSICAL/RHYTHMIC STRATEGIES

- ☐ Environmental Sounds
- ☐ Instrumental Sounds
- ☐ Music Composition/Creation
- ☐ Music Performance
- ☐ Percussion Vibrations
- ☐ Rapping
- ☐ Rhythmic Patterns
- ☐ Singing/Humming
- ☐ Tonal Patterns
- ☐ Vocal Sounds/Tones

SUBJECT AREA:

INTELLIGENCE EMPHASIS:

LESSON OBJECTIVE:

SUPPLIES/MATERIALS:

ROOM ARRANGEMENT:

Eight Ways of Teaching Weekly Checklist

Have I taught for the eight ways of knowing this week? Check yourself by listing the specific strategies, techniques, and tools you have used in classroom lessons this week.

	MONDAY	TUESDAY	WEDNESDAY	THURSDAY	FRIDAY
Verbal/Linguistic					
Logical/Mathematical					
Visual/Spatial					
Bodily/Kinesthetic					
Musical/Rhythmic					
Interpersonal					
Intrapersonal					
Naturalist					

Note: This blackline is provided as a useful tool for teachers to think through their weekly multiple intelligences strategies.

Blackline 6.9

The Artistry of Teaching For, With, and About Multiple Intelligences

THE LESSON . . .

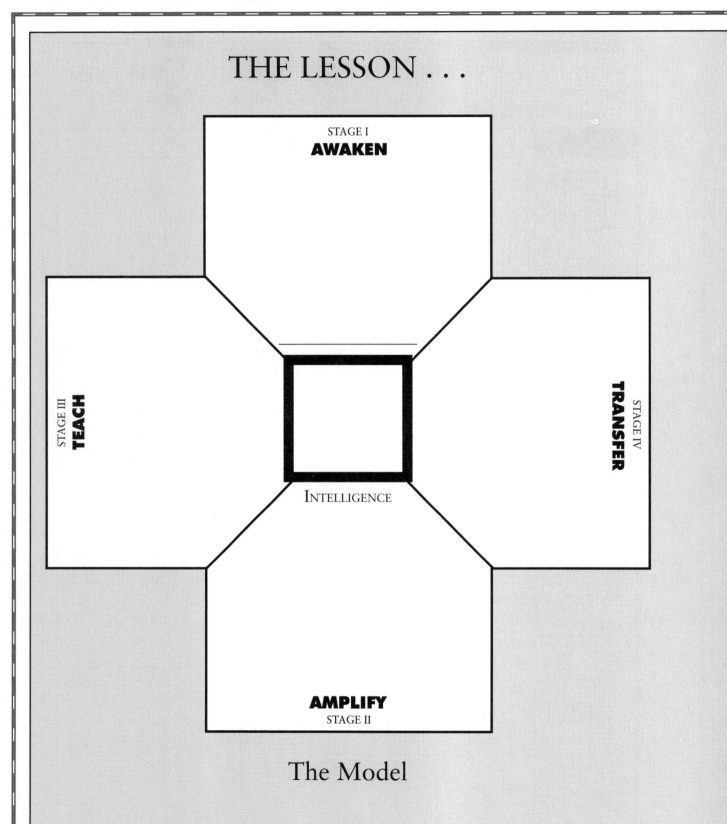

The Model

. . . AT A GLANCE

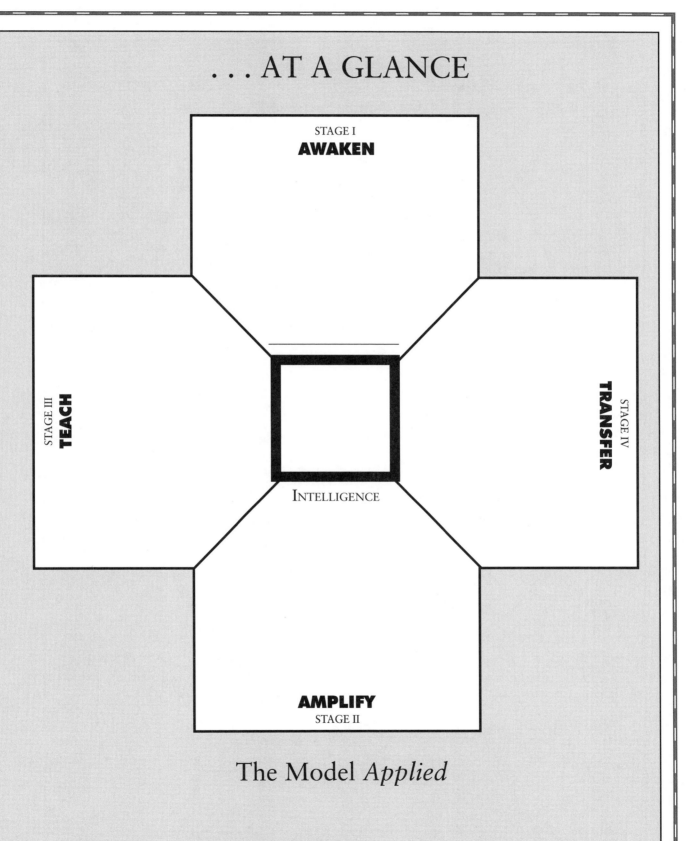

STAGE I
AWAKEN

STAGE III
TEACH

INTELLIGENCE

STAGE IV
TRANSFER

AMPLIFY
STAGE II

The Model *Applied*

The Artistry of Teaching For, With, and About Multiple Intelligences

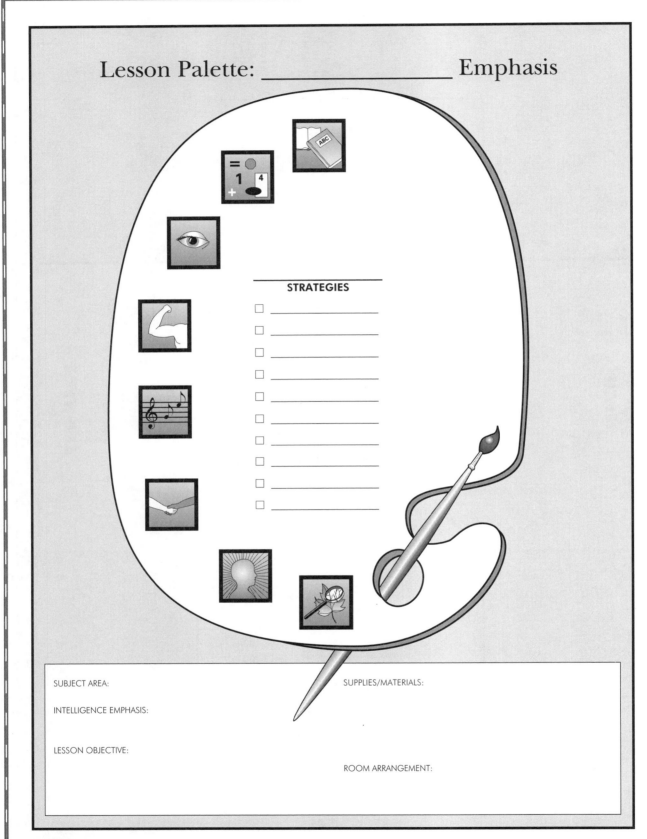

Lesson Palette: _____ Emphasis

STRATEGIES

☐ _____
☐ _____
☐ _____
☐ _____
☐ _____
☐ _____
☐ _____
☐ _____
☐ _____
☐ _____

SUBJECT AREA:

INTELLIGENCE EMPHASIS:

LESSON OBJECTIVE:

SUPPLIES/MATERIALS:

ROOM ARRANGEMENT:

Unit plans allow students to demonstrate their abilities through a variety of learning experiences and assessments. Mentors can guide protégés in development of these two- to three-week unit plans that allow students to demonstrate their ability to use their multiple intelligences.

Creating a Unit Plan Using the Multiple Intelligences

by **Kay Burke**

Teachers are experimenting with a variety of instructional methods and assessments to evaluate students' achievement and progress toward meeting standards. Some educators are also experimenting with planning integrated instructional units that include learning experiences from all of the multiple intelligences. Using a graphic organizer such as the grid on Blackline 7.1 (at the end of this selection) to devise the unit plan helps groups of teachers focus on standards, integrate their curricula, brainstorm learning experiences and assessments, and decide on the key whole-class assessments to capture important concepts in the unit. This approach, as detailed below, helps teams of teachers or individual teachers plan a unit that synthesizes cooperative learning, higher-order thinking, portfolios, and performance tasks as well as rubrics with the multiple intelligences. (See Figure 7.1 for learning experiences and assessments classified by multiple intelligences.)

Adapted from *How to Assess Authentic Learning,* 3rd edition, by Kay Burke, pp. 43–45, 47–50, 53. © 1999 by Corwin Press. Used with permission.

Creating a Unit Plan Using the Multiple Intelligences

Thirteen Steps to Develop a Unit Plan

The following format for developing a unit plan can be adapted to meet the needs of the teacher or a group of teachers. (Sample unit plans appear in Figures 7.2, 7.3, and 7.4.)

1. Decide on a unit or theme that will last at least two to three weeks. The unit could be on a specific topic (Oceanography or Greek Mythology), a book (Stephen Crane's *The Red Badge of Courage*), or a country (Egypt). Some teachers choose to work on a thematic or integrated unit that connects several content areas. Some thematic units might include:

   - Health and Wellness
   - Justice in America
   - Off to Work We Go
   - Crime and Punishment
   - A Decade—The 1920s
   - The Future
   - Heroes

2. Draw a grid on large pieces of newsprint or use a blank grid. (See Blackline 7.1 at the end of this selection for a blank grid.)

3. Decide on the standards and/or benchmarks that will be the major goals of the unit. What should the students be able to do at the end of the unit?

4. Distribute sticky notes to each participant. Ask participants to brainstorm ideas for learning experiences or assessments for the unit and write one idea per sticky note. (See Figure 7.1 for ideas for learning experiences.) Allow five minutes for individual thinking and writing. Remember to be specific. Don't say, "Read a book about oceans"—recommend *Chadwick the Crab*.

5. Read each idea and decide where it should go on the grid. Remember that many ideas cross over into other intelligences. For example, holding a mock trial to determine whether President Roosevelt suspected Pearl Harbor was going to be bombed could be

classified as interpersonal, bodily/kinesthetic, or verbal/linguistic. Just place the idea where you think it goes or where you need more selections.

6. Review the grid to make sure there are at least three learning experiences/assessments for each intelligence. Remember, many activities are assessments. For example, creating a Venn diagram to compare and contrast Hemingway and Faulkner is an activity; it is also an assessment.

7. Decide on four learning experiences from the grid that would benefit the whole class. Consider the following criteria for selecting each experience:

   - Does the experience help meet the standards?
   - Does it include several intelligences? (Does it meet the needs of more students?)
   - Is it worth the time to do it?
   - Can it be assessed?
   - Is it doable in my class? (time, resources, money, space)
   - Is it fun and motivating?
   - Will it meet the diverse needs of my students?

8. Write the four learning experiences in the boxes on the bottom of the grid (see Blackline 7.1). Remember that teachers on the team may select different whole-class experiences based upon their focus for the unit and the individual needs of their students.

9. Decide on how to assess the four learning experiences selected. Remember to combine traditional assessments (quizzes, tests, research reports) with performance assessments (logs, journals, portfolios, projects).

10. Create a culminating event to bring closure to the unit. The event should synthesize all the ideas and provide a showcase for the students to share their learnings with a wider audience. Examples of culminating events include mock trials, field trips, portfolio exhibitions, plays, costume days, medieval banquet, Renaissance fair, job fairs, and re-enactments.

11. Develop a portfolio that includes three to four teacher-selected items to show the students have met the standards. Allow students to select four or five other entries from the grid for their student choices.

12. Create rubrics to evaluate projects, group or individual performances, and the portfolio. Students can work in their groups to determine the criteria for each project. Teachers usually decide on four or five group projects and let students choose their groups. Groups could be divided as follows:

    - Research reports
    - Videotaped interviews
    - Simulations or performances
    - Newspaper stories
    - PowerPoint presentations

    Each group reviews samples of the product and determines the criteria that is necessary to create a successful product or performance. For example, the group creating the video could decide on three criteria regarding the sound element: loudness, dialogue clarity, and overall effect. They could then develop a rubric to help them prepare the video and to assess it for the final evaluation. The students and teacher may need to refine the rubric and add more focused descriptors as they work on the project, but it at least makes them aware of all the components they need to address.

13. Create a rubric to assess the portfolio. It could include criteria such as completeness, timeliness, understanding of content, visuals/graphics, reflections, mechanics, organization, etc. Many of the items included would have been graded previously; therefore, one grade using a weighted rubric could be used. The students should be a part of the discussion about criteria and should self-evaluate their own portfolio using the rubric.

Figure 7.1, on the following page, classifies learning experiences and assessments by multiple intelligences. Three samples of unit plans organized by multiple intelligences are also provided in Figures 7.2, 7.3, and 7.4.

REFERENCES

Gardner, H. 1983. *Frames of mind: The theory of multiple intelligences.* NY: Harper and Row.
———. 1993. *Frames of mind: The theory of multiple intelligences—Tenth anniversary edition.* NY: Basic Books.

Blackline 7.1 is provided at the end of this selection for use as a planning guide for creating a unit of study. (Mentors and protégés may also refer to the samples in Figures 7.1–7.4.) Protégés may use the blackline to plan their units. Mentors can help protégés design units by assisting them in filling out the blackline and suggesting activities and assessments for the multiple intelligences. Protégés can also work in teams to create units.

Learning Experiences

VERBAL/ LINGUISTIC	LOGICAL/ MATHEMATICAL	VISUAL/ SPATIAL	BODILY/ KINESTHETIC
Speeches	Puzzles	Artwork	Field trips
Debates	Outlines	Photographs	Role-playing
Storytelling	Timelines	Math manipulatives	Learning centers
Reports	Analogies	Graphic organizers	Labs
Crosswords	Patterns	Posters, charts	Sports/games
Newspapers	Problem-solving	Illustrations	Cooperative learning
Internet	Lab experiments	Cartoons	Body language
	Formulas	Props for plays	Experiments
		Use of overhead	

MUSICAL/ RHYTHMIC	INTERPERSONAL	INTRAPERSONAL	NATURALIST
Background music	Group video, film, slides	Reflective journals	Outdoor education
Songs about books, people, countries, historic events	Team computer programs	Learning logs	Environmental studies
Raps	Think-pair-share	Goal-setting journals	Field trips (farm, zoo)
Jingles	Cooperative tasks	Metacognitive reflections	Bird watching
Choirs	Jigsaws	Independent reading	Nature walk
	Conferences	Silent reflection	Weather forecasting
		Diaries	Stargazing
			Exploring nature
			Ecology studies
			Identifying leaves

Figure 7.1

Oceanography Unit

Subject Area: _Integrated Unit—Elementary_   Timeline: _3–4 weeks_

Major Goals of Unit:

1. _Know the major difference between fresh and ocean water_
2. _Know that an organism's patterns of behavior are related to the nature of that organism's environment_
3. _Know that the transfer of energy (e.g., through the consumption of food) is essential to all living organisms_

List at least three learning experiences/assessments under each intelligence.

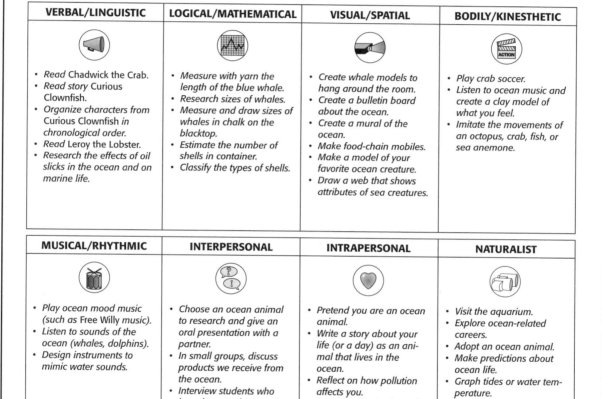

VERBAL/LINGUISTIC	LOGICAL/MATHEMATICAL	VISUAL/SPATIAL	BODILY/KINESTHETIC
• _Read_ Chadwick the Crab. • _Read story_ Curious Clownfish. • _Organize characters from_ Curious Clownfish _in chronological order._ • _Read_ Leroy the Lobster. • _Research the effects of oil slicks in the ocean and on marine life._	• _Measure with yarn the length of the blue whale._ • _Research sizes of whales._ • _Measure and draw sizes of whales in chalk on the blacktop._ • _Estimate the number of shells in container._ • _Classify the types of shells._	• _Create whale models to hang around the room._ • _Create a bulletin board about the ocean._ • _Create a mural of the ocean._ • _Make food-chain mobiles._ • _Make a model of your favorite ocean creature._ • _Draw a web that shows attributes of sea creatures._	• _Play crab soccer._ • _Listen to ocean music and create a clay model of what you feel._ • _Imitate the movements of an octopus, crab, fish, or sea anemone._
MUSICAL/RHYTHMIC	INTERPERSONAL	INTRAPERSONAL	NATURALIST
• _Play ocean mood music (such as_ Free Willy _music)._ • _Listen to sounds of the ocean (whales, dolphins)._ • _Design instruments to mimic water sounds._	• _Choose an ocean animal to research and give an oral presentation with a partner._ • _In small groups, discuss products we receive from the ocean._ • _Interview students who have been to the ocean._ • _Do a KWL chart before you begin the unit._	• _Pretend you are an ocean animal._ • _Write a story about your life (or a day) as an animal that lives in the ocean._ • _Reflect on how pollution affects you._ • _Write a reflective journal on the sounds of the ocean._	• _Visit the aquarium._ • _Explore ocean-related careers._ • _Adopt an ocean animal._ • _Make predictions about ocean life._ • _Graph tides or water temperature._

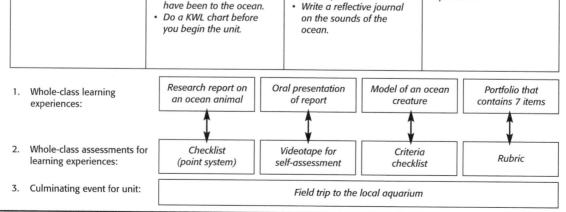

1. Whole-class learning experiences:

Research report on an ocean animal	Oral presentation of report	Model of an ocean creature	Portfolio that contains 7 items

2. Whole-class assessments for learning experiences:

Checklist (point system)	Videotape for self-assessment	Criteria checklist	Rubric

3. Culminating event for unit: _Field trip to the local aquarium_

Figure 7.2

Adapted from Training the Trainers workshop, Summer 1996, Chicago.

Creating a Unit Plan Using the Multiple Intelligences

Greek Mythology

Subject Area: *Integrated Unit—Middle School*   **Timeline:** *4–6 weeks*

Major Goals of Unit:
1. *Communicate ideas in writing to describe, inform, persuade, and entertain*
2. *Demonstrate comprehension of a broad range of reading materials*
3. *Use reading, writing, listening, and speaking skills to research and apply information for specific purposes*

List at least three learning experiences/assessments under each intelligence.

VERBAL/LINGUISTIC	LOGICAL/MATHEMATICAL	VISUAL/SPATIAL	BODILY/KINESTHETIC
• *Read* The Iliad. • *Read* The Odyssey. • *Read Edith Hamilton's Mythology.* • *Write an original myth to explain a scientific mystery.* • *Write poems about mythology.* • *Write a eulogy for a fallen Greek or Trojan warrior.*	• *Use a Venn diagram to compare the Greeks and the Trojans.* • *Create original story problems that can incorporate Pythagorean theorem.* • *Draw a family tree of the twelve Olympians and their children.* • *Complete a timeline of Odysseus' trip home from Troy.*	• *Draw the battle plan for the Greeks' attack on Troy.* • *Draw Mt. Olympus.* • *Sketch the Greek gods and goddesses.* • *Create a video of the Olympic games.* • *Draw items that relate to mythology.*	• *Act out a Greek tragedy.* • *Recreate some of the Olympic events.* • *Act out a myth.* • *Create a dance for the forest nymphs.* • *Reenact the battle scene between Hector and Achilles.*

MUSICAL/RHYTHMIC	INTERPERSONAL	INTRAPERSONAL	NATURALIST
• *Write a song for a lyre.* • *Pretend you are Apollo, God of Music, and CEO of Motown.* • *Select music that correlates with each god or goddess.*	• *Interview Helen about her role in the Trojan War.* • *Work in a group to create a computer crossword puzzle about mythology.*	• *Pretend you are a Greek soldier away from home for ten years. Keep a diary of your thoughts.* • *Write a journal about how you would feel if you were Prometheus chained to a rock.* • *Reflect on the effects of war on civilians.*	• *Using scientific data, predict how long it will take before anything grows after the Greeks destroy Troy and sow the fields with salt.* • *Describe the animals and plants on Mt. Olympus.*

1. Whole-class learning experiences:	*Read Hamilton's Mythology*	*Read excerpts from The Iliad and The Odyssey*	*Select a group project or performance*	*Portfolio that contains 7–10 items*
2. Whole-class assessments for learning experiences:	*Teacher-made test*	*Write a paper comparing the Greeks to the Trojans*	*Rubric to assess each one*	*Rubric created by class*
3. Culminating event for unit:	*Exhibition in the school gym—students and teachers dress up as favorite mythological characters. Invited guests view videos, portfolios, artifacts, and an original skit.*			

Figure 7.3

The Red Badge of Courage Unit

Subject Area: _American Literature—High School_   **Timeline:** _3 weeks_

Major Goals of Unit:

1. _Demonstrates competence in general skills and strategies for reading a variety of literary texts_

2. _Demonstrates competence in the general skills and strategies of the writing process_

3. _Demonstrates competence in speaking and listening as tools for learning_

List at least three learning experiences/assessments under each intelligence.

VERBAL/LINGUISTIC	LOGICAL/MATHEMATICAL	VISUAL/SPATIAL	BODILY/KINESTHETIC
• Read the novel The Red Badge of Courage. • Write a letter to President Lincoln about your feelings about the Civil War. • Interview a historian about the Battle of Chancellorsville.	• Graph the number of dead and wounded from major Civil War battles. • Compare the number of injured and dead in the Civil War to World War I, World War II, the Korean War, and the Vietnam War. • Create a Venn diagram comparing General Grant to General Lee.	• Draw a political cartoon about the Civil War. • Draw a mind map of the Civil War that contains major battles. • Draw a timeline of major events in the war. • Draw a book jacket for this novel.	• Act out one key scene from the novel. • Demonstrate marching drills used in the Civil War. • Visit a Civil War battleground, cemetery, or museum.

MUSICAL/RHYTHMIC	INTERPERSONAL	INTRAPERSONAL	NATURALIST
• Sing the songs the troops of the North and South sang while marching. • Learn the dances of the Civil War era. • Make up a ballad about Henry, the protagonist of the novel.	• Read other books about buddies during war time, such as All Quiet on the Western Front, Catch 22, and For Whom the Bell Tolls. • Write and act out a dialogue between two military buddies in either Vietnam, Korea, World War I, or World War II.	• Keep a daily diary of boot camp. • Write a poem about your feelings. • Write a last will and testament in case you die in battle. • Write a eulogy for a soldier who died in battle.	• Find specific passages where author Stephen Crane tells about how war destroys nature. • Write how the environment (weather, rivers, terrain) impacts battle decisions. • Research the effects weapons of destruction have on the environment.

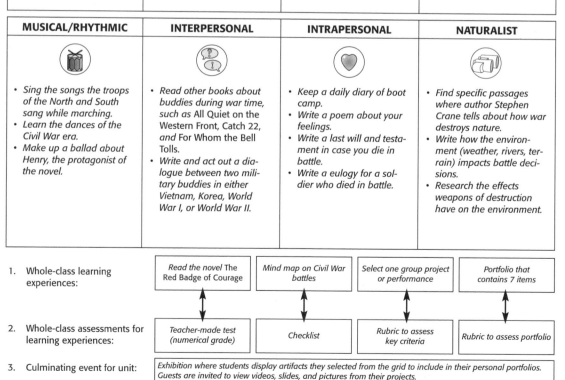

1. **Whole-class learning experiences:**

Read the novel The Red Badge of Courage	Mind map on Civil War battles	Select one group project or performance	Portfolio that contains 7 items

2. **Whole-class assessments for learning experiences:**

Teacher-made test (numerical grade)	Checklist	Rubric to assess key criteria	Rubric to assess portfolio

3. **Culminating event for unit:** Exhibition where students display artifacts they selected from the grid to include in their personal portfolios. Guests are invited to view videos, slides, and pictures from their projects.

Figure 7.4

Creating a Unit Plan Using the Multiple Intelligences

_____ **Unit**

Subject Area: _____   Timeline: _____

Major Goals of Unit: 1. _____

2. _____

3. _____

_____

List at least three learning experiences/assessments under each intelligence.

VERBAL/LINGUISTIC	LOGICAL/MATHEMATICAL	VISUAL/SPATIAL	BODILY/KINESTHETIC

MUSICAL/RHYTHMIC	INTERPERSONAL	INTRAPERSONAL	NATURALIST

1. Whole-class learning experiences:

2. Whole-class assessments for learning experiences:

3. Culminating event for unit:

Mentors can help novice teachers design performance tasks to assess students' ability to apply their learning. They can also discuss how rubrics provide the criteria for quality work and objective assessment.

Performance Tasks and Rubrics

by **Kay Burke**

Performance tasks are more than activities that teachers assign students. They encompass many skills and usually have a direct application to real tasks people are asked to do in everyday life. Lewin and Shoemaker (1998) feel that a performance task has the following key characteristics:

1. Students have some choice in selecting the task.
2. The task requires both the elaboration of core knowledge content and the use of specific processes.
3. The task has an explicit scoring system.
4. The task is designed for an audience larger than the teacher; that is, others outside the classroom would find value in the work.
5. The task is carefully crafted to measure what it purports to measure. (p. 5)

Adapted from *How to Assess Authentic Learning,* 3rd edition, by Kay Burke, pp. 78–93. © 1999 by Corwin Press. Used with permission.

Gronlund (1998) writes how performance tasks and the assessments that are built into them usually have the following four characteristics:

1. Greater realism of tasks (i.e., more like those in the real world)
2. Greater complexity of tasks (i.e., less structured problems that encourage originality and thinking skills and may have multiple solutions)
3. Greater time needed for assessment (due to the difficulty of designing tasks, the comprehensive nature of the tasks, and the increased time needed to evaluate the results)
4. Greater use of judgment in scoring (due to the complexity of tasks, originality of the responses, and, in some cases, the variety of possible solutions) (p. 136)

Types of Performance Tasks

Gronlund uses the designation *restricted performance* to refer to performance tasks that tend to be highly structured to fit a specific instructional objective (i.e., read aloud a selection of poetry or construct a graph from a given set of data). He uses the term *extended performance tasks* to refer to tasks that are so comprehensive that numerous instructional objectives are involved. Extended performance tasks tend to be less structured and broad in scope. One task could ask students to "assume you are investing $40,000 in the stock market for your college education. Select the stocks, make a record of their value for 30 days, then write a report describing your success and indicating what changes you would make in your portfolio of stocks" (Gronlund, 1998, pp. 136–137). Another extended performance task could ask students to bid on a job to landscape their school. Students could be told they have one week to prepare a written proposal, a diagram of the landscape design plan, and a three-minute videotape on the proposed plan to present to school officials

The extended performance task includes several smaller tasks that can be assessed separately, but they are all part of a bigger task that involves initial and creative problem solving.

Performance tasks appear in many different forms according to Gronlund (1998), but the majority of them fall into the following categories:

1. Solving realistic problems (e.g., how to reduce drug use in the United States)
2. Oral or psychomotor skills without a product (e.g., giving a speech, speaking a foreign language, using a microscope, repairing an engine)
3. Writing or psychomotor skills with a product (e.g., writing a theme, writing a lab report, typing a letter, building a bookcase) (p. 136)

From *Assessment of Student Achievement* by N. E. Gronlund, 6th ed. Copyright © 1998 by Allyn & Bacon. Reprinted by permission.

Probably the key characteristic of performance tasks involves using real-life applications to real-life problems. Performances require students to apply what they have learned—not just fill in a selected-response Scantron test. By demonstrating what they can do, students have a greater probability of transferring the skills they learned to life rather than merely reproducing knowledge for a test on Friday. See Figure 8.1 for an example of how performance tasks can be designed.

Why Performance Tasks?

Advocates of performance tests and performance assessment base their support on a number of factors. Mehrens (1992, as cited in Popham, 1999), a prominent educational measurement specialist, has identified descriptors of three influences he believes contribute to the support for performance assessment. A summary of those influences include:

- Dissatisfaction with selected-response tests—multiple-choice tests call for the students to only select a response that calls for recognition on the part of the student but fail to tap higher-order thinking skills like problem solving, synthesis, or independent thinking.

Creating Performance Tasks

Create a meaningful performance task for your subject area.

Subject Area: _Health_   Grade Level: _8th Grade_

Task Description: As part of the school's Health Fair Week, the Cancer Prevention Association has asked your class to develop a plan for eliminating all smoking areas from local businesses. The project will include: 1) a presentation; 2) a brochure; 3) a letter to the community newspaper; 4) a 5-minute video "selling" the students' ideas to the business owners. Be prepared to present your anti-smoking campaign to members of the Cancer Prevention Association at their monthly meeting.

Direct Instruction for Whole Class: The whole class will be involved in the following learning experiences:
• Guest lecture from the school nurse on the effects of secondhand smoke
• Lectures and discussions on the health risks related to smoking
• Reading from articles and textbooks
• Oral presentation techniques

Group Work: Students select one group project.

Group One	**Group Two**	**Group Three**	**Group Four**
Research facts and statistics related to smoking.	Prepare a brochure on health risks related to smoking.	Summarize the key research points in a letter to the editor of the local newspaper.	Prepare a 5-minute PowerPoint presentation for local business owners.

Individual Work: In addition to the group project, each student will complete the following individual assignments:
1) A poster that integrates the most essential facts, statistics, quotes, and visuals to argue for a smoking ban in all public businesses in the area; 2) A 5-minute speech persuading local businesses to eliminate smoking from their establishments.

Methods of Assessment:
• Teacher-made test on the health risks of smoking
• Checklist to assess each of the four group projects
• Checklist to assess individual poster
• Checklist and rubric to assess persuasive speech

Figure 8.1

- Influence of cognitive psychology—cognitive psychologists believe students must acquire both content knowledge and procedural knowledge since all cognitive tasks require both kinds of knowledge. Since certain types of procedural knowledge are not assessable via selected-response tests, many cognitive psychologists are calling for performance assessments to emphasize students' acquisition of procedural knowledge.

- The sometimes harmful instructional impact of conventional tasks—with the advent of high-stakes tests, teachers tend to teach to the test and the mastery of the domain of skills or knowledge on the test. Because many educators recognize that high-stakes tests will continue to influence what a teacher teaches, they argue that performance assessments would constitute more praiseworthy instructional targets by shifting teachers' instructional activities in more appropriate directions. (Mehrens, 1992 cited in Popham, 1999)

Performance tasks and assessments can help teachers focus their instruction on meaningful tasks and interactive methodology to help students prepare for life. They also provide a systematic way to evaluate skills and procedural knowledge that cannot be measured effectively with multiple-choice formats.

The outcomes, standards, and benchmarks in most courses need to be assessed on the basis of performance. As Gronlund (1998) states, "Although tests can tell us whether students know what to do in a particular situation, performance assessments are needed to evaluate their actual performance skills" (p. 138). Once again, it is evident that one type of assessment is not sufficient to evaluate all the content, knowledge, skills, growth, and performances required of students. The balanced assessment approach calls for a repertoire of assessment tools targeted to measure specific learnings and applications. The key for teachers is to determine which tools work best with which students in which situations.

Performance Tasks and Rubrics

How Should We Assess Performance Tasks?

Popham (1999) states "Performance assessment typically requires students to respond to a small number of more significant tasks rather than respond to a large number of less significant tasks" (p. 161). This characteristic of performance assessment could be a concern for educators. Since the students perform fewer but more in-depth tasks than they do with conventional paper-and-pencil testing, it is more difficult to generalize accurately what skills the student possesses. Instead of multiple assessments, a student's grade could be based on a single task. Psychometricians, according to Popham, have some difficulties with the "generalizability" of the performance to a student's ability. Because of this dilemma, it is important to choose tasks that optimize the likelihood of accurately generalizing a student's capabilities.

Popham (1999) offers seven evaluative criteria that educators might wish to consider when selecting from existing performance tasks or creating their own (Figure 8.2).

It is important to select or create performance tasks that are "rich" in terms of the criteria which meet and require an in-depth understanding of key concepts, knowledge, and skills. The philosophy of "less is more" threads through performance tasks. If there are fewer tasks, they need to be of the highest quality. "A few truly important criteria are preferable to a plethora of trifling criteria . . . go for the big ones." (Popham, 1999, p. 168). Parents and students are used to seeing hundreds of worksheets with smiley faces each quarter. It is a major paradigm switch for a teacher to go from assigning 30 grades a working period to assigning only 10 grades. Educators must justify the importance of fewer tasks that involve more in-depth learning and convey their rationale to students and parents. It is critical to design meaningful performance tasks that meet Popham's criteria if teachers want to make sure the evaluation is valid—measuring what they intend to measure and what was taught—and reliable; that is, the performance can be replicated with consistency on repeated measures.

Evaluative Criteria for Performance Tasks

1. **Generalizability.** Is there a high likelihood that the students' performance on the task will generalize to comparable tasks?

2. **Authenticity.** Is the task similar to what students might encounter in the real world as opposed to encountering only in school?

3. **Multiple foci.** Does the task measure multiple instructional outcomes instead of only one?

4. **Teachability.** Is the task one that students become more proficient in as a consequence of a teacher's instructional efforts?

5. **Fairness.** Is the task fair to all students—that is, does the task avoid bias based on such personal characteristics as students' gender, ethnicity, or socioeconomic status?

6. **Feasibility.** Is the task realistically implementable in relation to its cost, space, time, and equipment requirements?

7. **Scorability.** Is the task likely to elicit student responses that can be reliably and accurately evaluated?

From *Classroom Assessment: What Teachers Need to Know* by W. James Popham. Copyright © 1999 by Allyn & Bacon. Reprinted by permission.

Figure 8.2

Developing Criteria

Once the performance task is designed, the next very important step involves developing the criteria to determine the adequacy of the student's performance. Bear in mind that a standard dictionary definition for a *criterion* is a standard on which a judgment or decision may be based. Popham (1999) explains when teachers set criteria they are trying to make a judgment regarding the adequacy of student responses, and the specific criteria to be used will influence the way a response is scored. If a student is giving a speech, the criteria could include the following: eye contact, gestures, organization, visual aid, opening, closing, etc.

Scoring Rubrics

Popham (1999) states, "The evaluative criteria that are used when scoring students' responses to performance tests (or their responses to any kind of constructed-response item) really control the whole evaluative enterprise" (p. 166). Popham describes how performance assessment has at best three features (Figure 8.3).

Performance assessments usually focus on the application of knowledge to a real-life experience. Identifying the parts of a letter requires factual knowledge; writing a letter with a purpose and audience requires a real performance—the act of writing the letter.

The criteria for judging students' response identify the factors to be considered when determining the adequacy of a student's performance. Criteria are often referred to as rubrics, scoring guidelines, and scoring dimensions. The criteria are usually discussed with the students before they prepare their product or presentation. Criteria by themselves provide a guideline for students to follow when preparing their

Features of Performance Assessment

- **Multiple evaluative criteria.** The student's performance must be judged using more than one evaluative criteria. To illustrate, a student's ability to speak Spanish might be appraised on the basis of the student's accent, syntax, and vocabulary.

- **Prespecified quality standards.** Each of the evaluative criteria on which a student's performance is to be judged is clearly explicated in advance of judging the quality of the student's performance.

- **Judgmental appraisal.** Unlike the scoring of selected-response tests in which electronic computers and scanning machines can, once programmed, carry on without the need of humankind, genuine performance assessments depend on human judgments to determine how acceptable a student's performance really is.

From *Classroom Assessment: What Teachers Need to Know* by W. James Popham. Copyright © 1999 by Allyn & Bacon. Reprinted with permission.

Figure 8.3

performance, but the indicators of what constitutes a quality performance to attain the standard or earn the "A" or "B" are usually described in the rubric. See Figure 8.4 for Sample Criteria for Judging Performances.

Solomon (1998) states that rubrics are "a set of guidelines for distinguishing between performances or products of different quality. . . . They should be based on the results of stated performance standards and be composed of scaled descriptive levels of progress towards the result" (p. 120).

Typically, a numerical scale from zero to six is used for each criterion. Sometimes the scale points are accompanied by verbal descriptors and even visuals. Some scales contain only verbal descriptors with no numbers. Numerical scales assign points to a continuum of performance levels. According to Herman, Aschbacher, and Winters (1992), the length of the continuum or the number of scale points can vary from three

Sample Criteria for Judging Performances

Speech
- organization
- research
- opening
- eye contact
- gestures

Research Paper
- outline
- notecards
- rough draft
- thesis statement
- bibliography

Problem-solving
- identify problem
- brainstorm solutions
- analyze solution
- evaluate effectiveness

Videotape
- focus
- dialogue
- content
- activity

Portfolio
- cover
- table of contents
- evidence of understanding
- reflective comments
- goal setting
- self-evaluation

Journal entry
- use of examples
- dialogue
- grammar
- sentence structure
- figures of speech

Figure 8.4

to seven or more. However, a shorter scale will result in a higher percentage agreement and a larger scale will take longer to reach consensus if more than one person is evaluating the performance.

Most educators find that even-numbered scales 0–1–2–3, 1–2–3–4, 1–2–3–4–5–6 work best because odd-numbered scales 1–2–3 or 1–2–3–4–5 tend to cause people to select the middle number. The even-numbered scales force people to pick a side—either low or high—with no middle ground for compromise. (See Figure 8.5.)

Types of Scales

Numerical Scales

0	1	2	3	4
1	2	3	4	5

A Numerical Scale with Verbal Descriptors

1	2	3	4	5
Weak	Satisfactory	Very Good	Excellent	Superior

Verbal Descriptors

Novice	Adequate	Apprentice		Distinguished
Task not completed		Task partially completed		Task completed

Verbal Descriptors

Criterion: Eye Contact During Speech

No evidence	Minimal evidence	Partial evidence	Complete evidence
Does not look at audience	Looks some of the time at some of the audience	Looks most of the time at most of the audience	Looks all the time at all of the audience

Figure 8.5

A Fun Rubric

Creating a rubric to assess student performances could be difficult for teachers and students. It is recommended that, as a first step, teachers work with their students to create a fun rubric in order to understand the process of developing them. Topics for a fun rubric could include: school lunches, a pep rally, pizza, movies, a graduation party, a field trip, or any nonacademic topic that students know about. The object of the fun rubric is to practice setting brainstorming criteria and then to develop indicators for ratings. See Figure 8.6 for an example of a fun rubric created by students.

Using a Performance Rubric

Once students have become familiar with the format of a performance rubric, they will be better able to understand how to use the rubric to assess their products and performances. See Figure 8.7 for a performance rubric for assessing a speech.

Student Involvement

One of the most powerful instructional tools to help students internalize the criteria and recognize quality work is to have students develop the criteria for performance assessment with the teacher. The teacher can show examples of work from different levels and then ask the students to brainstorm the criteria that are essential to the performance task.

After the students identify the criteria and, in some cases, demonstrate or gather more examples to make sure every student understands the expectations, the class then selects four or five criteria at a time in order to focus on key elements. Criteria can expand as the students become more proficient or when new criteria replace ones that have been mastered. Students presenting their first persuasive speech cannot achieve the same level as a Martin Luther King, Jr. The expectations should correlate with the benchmarks of the

Performance Tasks and Rubrics

Rubric for Assessing a Birthday Party

Criteria	1	2	3	4
	"I need to go home and do my home-work!"	"Can't stay— I've got chores at home."	"Can I spend the night?"	"Will you adopt me?"
Food	Steamed Broccoli and Carrots	Mom's Tunafish and Potato Chip Casserole	McDonald's Happy Meal™ (free balloons)	Super Deluxe Supreme Pizza (deep dish)
Gifts	New Underwear (K-mart specials)	School Supplies (Mr. Eraserhead)	*Monsters, Inc.* DVD	Full Set of Harry Potter books— with DVD and action figures
Entertainment	My Sister's Poetry Readings (T.S. Eliot)	Lawrence Welk Polka Contest (accordion rap song)	Blues Clues	'N Sync
Games	"Go Fish!" and "Slap Jack"	Musical Chairs to Broadway Show Tunes	X Box and Playstation 2	"Full-Contact Twister" (no chaperones)

Adapted from *The Portfolio Connection Training Manual* by Kay Burke, Robin Fogarty, and Susan Belgrad. © 1995 by IRI/SkyLight Publishing, Inc. Reprinted with permission.

Figure 8.6

Rubric for Assessing a Speech

Performance Task: Students will present a five-minute persuasive speech.
Goal/Standard: Speak effectively using language appropriate to the situation and audience.

SCALE: Criteria:	0 Not Yet	1 Student Council Elections	2 The Senate Floor	3 Presidential Debates
Organization • Hook	None	Introduces topic	Grabs attention	Electrifies audience
• Transitions	None	Uses words to link ideas	Makes key connections between ideas	Smooth flow of ideas
• Closure	None	Lacks interest	Referred to introduction	Powerful and dramatic
Content • Accuracy	3 or more factual errors	2 factual errors	1 factual error	All information is correct
• Documentation	No sources cited	1 source cited	2 sources cited	3 or more sources cited
• Quotations	No quotes	1 quote to support case	2 quotes to support case	3 key quotes to prove case
Delivery • Eye Contact	Reads speech	Looks at some people some of the time	Looks at some people all of the time	Looks at all of the people all of the time
• Volume	Could not be heard	Could be heard by people in front	Could be heard by most people	Could be heard clearly by all people
• Gestures	None	Used a few gestures	Used some gestures appropriately	Used many appropriate gestures effectively
Visual Aid • Graphics	None	Minimal	Colorful	Creative graphics that enhance speech
• Appeal	None	Little visual appeal	Captures our attention	Visually stimulates audience
• Relevance	None	Minimal relationship to topic	Relates specifically to topic	Relates and reinforces topic

Figure 8.7

grade level. Educators need to progress at a speed that is developmentally appropriate and allows students to undertake a novel challenge that is neither too easy nor too difficult.

The reality of performance tasks is that they do represent an alternative to traditional paper-and-pencil tests, and that they often are more authentic—that is, reflective of the types of tasks students will be called upon to perform in the real world. The reality of performance tasks is also that they need to be rigorous and suitable tasks, and the scoring procedures need to isolate "appropriate evaluative criteria and spell out the scoring scale for each criterion" (Popham, 1999, p. 177).

Performance tasks take much more time to construct and score than a selected-response test—time well spent. The students' performances will demonstrate their in-depth learning. In addition, feedback provided from their self-assessment of their own work from using the rubric will provide valuable information to the teacher. Performance tasks and rubrics demonstrate the power of integrated instruction with evaluation. It is impossible to know where instruction stops and assessment begins. In fact, instruction and assessment are so closely correlated in today's classroom that they literally become the "intersection of learning."

BIBLIOGRAPHY

Burke, K. 2000. *How to assess authentic learning.* Thousand Oaks, CA: Corwin Press.

———. 1999. *How to assess authentic learning training manual.* Thousand Oaks, CA: Corwin Press.

Burke, K., R. Fogarty, and S. Belgrad. 1995. *The portfolio connection training manual.* Thousand Oaks, CA: Corwin Press.

———. 2002. *The portfolio connection: Student work linked to standards,* 2nd ed. Thousand Oaks, CA: Corwin Press.

Gronlund, N. E. 1998. *Assessment of student achievement,* 6th ed. Boston: Allyn and Bacon.

Herman, J. A., P. R. Aschbacher, and L. Winters. 1992. *A practical guide to alternative assessment.* Alexandria, VA: Association for Supervision and Curriculum Development.

Lewin, L., and B. J. Shoemaker. 1998. *Great performances; Creating classroom-based assessment tasks.* Alexandria, VA: Association for Supervision and Curriculum Development.

Mehrens, W. A. 1992. Using performance assessment for accountability purposes. *Educational Measurement: Issues and Practices* 11(1): 3–9.

Popham, W. J. 1999. *Classroom assessment: What teachers need to know,* 2nd ed. Boston: Allyn and Bacon.

Solomon, P. G. 1998. *The curriculum bridge: From standards to actual classroom practice.* Thousand Oaks, CA: Corwin Press.

- Mentors and protégés can review the sample rubrics shown in Blackline 8.1–8.10. The grade levels for each sample rubric are provided. Protégés can refer to their own performance tasks and use the examples as templates for creating their own rubrics.

- Protégés can use Blacklines 8.11 and 8.12 to create their own performance rubrics.

- Protégés can use the sample performance task in Blackline 8.13 as a guide when creating performance tasks. (See Figure 8.1 for another sample.) After they review the sample, they can use the template in Blackline 8.14 to design their own performance tasks. Mentors can review their protégés' completed forms and give feedback before the task is created.

- Protégés can use Blackline 8.15 to reflect on their feelings about creating rubrics. Once protégés have completed the reflection page, they can discuss it with their mentors.

MENTORING

KINDERGARTEN

Math Rubric

Mathematics Standard—Understands and applies basic and advanced properties of the concepts of geometry. K–2 Benchmark—Understands that patterns can be made by putting different shapes together or taking them apart.

Criteria	Nothing's happening. 1	I am getting ready to hatch. 2	I have started hatching. 3	I have arrived! 4
Counting Dinosaurs	Counts 0 dinosaurs.	Counts 5 dinosaurs.	Counts 10 dinosaurs.	Counts 20 dinosaurs. (Understands the concept of "10".)
Dinosaur Patterns	No dinosaur pattern.	Recognizes in her own setting or uses two attributes to pattern with dinosaur manipulatives.	Uses three attributes to pattern or doubles up with two attributes (e.g., ●○○●● or ○○●●● ○○○●●●)	Creates on his own with a wide variety of materials and uses four attributes or groupings.
Dinosaur Sorting	No evidence of dinosaur sorting.	Sorts dinosaurs by color or one attribute.	Sorts dinosaurs by finding ones that match (e.g., triceratops and another triceratops).	Sorts dinosaurs by plant eaters or creates a new way to sort that he can explain.

(Janelle VerMaas, Pershing Elementary, Lexington, Nebraska 68850)

From *The Mindful School: How to Assess Authentic Learning Training Manual*, 3rd Ed., by Kay Burke. © 2000 by SkyLight Training and Publishing. Used with permission.

Blackline 8.1

Simulation Game Rubric

Criteria	1	2	3	4
Clearly Stated Goal of Game	No goal	Vague goal	Goal stated, but difficult to reach	Clearly stated and attainable goal
Directions for Game	No directions	Directions are provided, but they are unclear	Clear directions provided	Clear and concise directions
Visuals for the Game	No visuals	Simple graphics provided	Clear diagram of game provided	Diagrams are clear and creative
Originality	Copied from another game	Ordinary idea	Ordinary idea with a different twist	Novel idea
Group Effort	Group members did not work well together	Members worked well some of the time	Members worked well most of the time	All members worked well together all the time

❏ Self Assessment

❏ Group Assessment

❏ Teacher Assessment

Grading Scale

18–20 points = A
15–17 points = B
10–14 points = C
9 or below = Not Yet

Total Points

_____
(20)

From *The Mindful School: How to Assess Authentic Learning,* 3rd ed., by Kay Burke. © 1999 by Corwin Press. Reprinted by permission.

Blackline 8.2

Journal Writing

State Goal: Write to communicate for a variety of purposes.

Academic Standard: Use correct grammar, spelling, punctuation, capitalization, and sentence structure.

Early Elementary Learning Benchmarks: Write passages with correct grammar, spelling, punctuation, and sentence structure.

Elements	I am getting ready to pop.	I have started popping.	I have popped and popped.
Spelling	I had trouble spelling the words.	I used letter sounds to help spell the words.	I knew how to spell a lot of words.
Spacing	I forgot to put spaces between words.	I put spaces between some words.	I put spaces between all of my words.
Punctuation	I forgot to use capitals and periods.	I used some capitals and periods.	I used capitals and periods correctly.

(Adapted from Lisha Linder)

Communication Skills Rubric

Criteria	Novice	In Progress	Meets Expectations	Exceeds Expectations
Sharing Important Information	Does not share information with anyone	Shares some information with close friends	Shares with small group	Shares information with large group
Effective Body Language	• Inappropriate facial expression • Poor posture • Negative attitude	• Blank facial expression • Good posture • Bored attitude	• Positive facial expression • Confident posture • Supportive attitude	• Expressive facial expression • Regal bearing • Encouraging attitude
Effective Listening	• Does not acknowledge speaker • Does not look at speaker • Does not ask questions	• Nods appropriately • Occasional eye contact • Asks low-level questions	• Gives complete attention • Full eye contact • Appropriate verbal responses • Asks thoughtful questions	• Gives complete attention • Full eye contact • Effective response • Asks higher-level questions

From *The Mindful School: How to Assess Authentic Learning*, 3rd ed., by Kay Burke. © 1999 by SkyLight Training and Publishing. Reprinted by permission of SkyLight Professional Development.

Blackline 8.4

Performance Tasks and Rubrics

Group Work Rubric

Self-assessment of my cooperative group skills for our team project.

1. I have participated in all tasks.   1   2   3   4 ☐
   - I performed my assigned role
   - I helped team members
   - I contributed to the group

2. I have used time appropriately   1   2   3   4 ☐
   - I stayed on task
   - I monitored my team's activities
   - I did not wait until the "last minute" to finish our project

3. I behaved appropriately   1   2   3   4 ☐
   - I was courteous to everyone
   - I did not use put-downs
   - I used appropriate language

Comments:

_____

_____

_____

_____

_____

Scale

11–12	points = A
9–10	points = B
6–8	points = C
7 or below	= Not Yet

Final Score	
Final Grade	

Signed: _____   Date: _____

Weighted Computer Literacy Scale

Name: _____ Date: _____

Topic: Hypercard

Type of Assessment: ☐ Self   ☐ Group   ☐ Teacher

Score
(1–5)

1	2	3	4	5
Low				High

Directions: Circle the score for each indicator.

Terminology   **Score:** _____ x 1 = _____
- Understands Key Functions   1 2 3 4 5   (25)
- Relates One Function to Others 1 2 3 4 5
- Used to Solve Problems   1 2 3 4 5
- Correct Spelling   1 2 3 4 5
- Appropriate to Level   1 2 3 4 5

Organization   **Score:** _____ x 2 = _____
- Easy to Complex   1 2 3 4 5   (50)
- Each Card Complete   1 2 3 4 5
- Uses Graphics   1 2 3 4 5
- Key Ideas Covered   1 2 3 4 5
- Supportive Data Included   1 2 3 4 5

Creativity   **Score:** _____ X 1 = _____
- Color   1 2 3 4 5   (25)
- Style   1 2 3 4 5
- Pattern   1 2 3 4 5
- Appropriate Use of Language   1 2 3 4 5
- Multiple Uses   1 2 3 4 5

Scale: 93–100 = A   78–86 = C   **Total Score:**   _____
         87–92 = B   70–77= D   (100)

Comments:

(Courtesy of Kathy Bartley and Jeanne Lipman, Gabbard Institute, 1994)

Blackline 8.6

Performance Tasks and Rubrics

Scoring Rubric for Letter to the Editor

Task: Write a letter to the editor of your local paper persuading readers to take a stand on a controversial issue.

Goal/Standard: Compose well-organized and coherent writing for specific purposes and audiences.

Scoring Criteria	1 Rejected by Church Bulletin Committee	2 Published in High School Newspaper	3 Published in Local Newspaper	4 Published in The New York Times	Score
Accuracy of Information	3 or more factual errors	2 factual errors	1 factual error	All information is accurate	___ x 5 ___ (20)
Persuasiveness • Arguments • Examples	• No logic • No examples	• Faulty logic • 1 example	• Logical arguments • 2 examples	• Logical and convincing arguments • 3 examples	___ x 5 ___ (20)
Organization • Topic Sentence • Support Sentences • Concluding Sentence	Missing 2 elements— fragmented	Missing 1 element— lacks coherence	Includes all organizational elements	Elements provide coherence and clarity	___ x 5 ___ (20)
Style • Grammar • Sentence Structure • Transitions	4 or more errors— distracts from arguments	2–3 errors— choppy style	1 error— style reinforces arguments	Fluid style that informs and convinces	___ x 5 ___ (20)
Mechanics • Capitalization • Punctuation • Spelling	4 or more errors	2–3 errors	1 error	100% accuracy	___ x 5 ___ (20)

Scale
A =
B =
C =
D =

Final Score: _____ (100)

Final Grade: _____

Note: To change a rubric to a traditional grade that students can understand, use a scale to convert the points to a percentage or, as in this example, multiply each score to arrive at a percentage that can be converted to a letter or number grade.

From *The Mindful School: How to Assess Authentic Learning Training Manual,* 3rd Ed., by Kay Burke. © 2000 by Corwin Press. Used with permission.

Rubric for Algebra Data Analysis Using Inequalities

Illinois State Math Goal 8: Use algebraic and analytical methods to identify and describe patterns and relationships in data, solve problems, and predict results.

Task Description: The music store you work for has asked you to recommend what kind of music they should order for next month. They need information on what types of music are preferred by different age groups (under 10 yrs., teen, adults). You are to take a survey, display your results in a chart, include 3 types of graphs (triple bar, stem and leaf, and box and whisker plot) and write up a recommendation for your boss after you analyze this data.

Criteria	Indicators	0–1 Not Yet	2 Almost	3 Meets Expectations	4 Exceeds Expectations	Score
Format	• Has name, period on cover • Turned in on time	• No name • Not on time	NA	• Has name, period • On time	NA _____	
Web page	• Color title • Related graphics • Working links • Sources cited	Text only, 3–4 errors, incomplete footer and sources	Title, 2–3 errors, unrelated graphic, some sources cited	Title with color graphics, easy to read, 0–1 errors, all links work, sources cited	Superior attractive design that enhances topic, creative links, sources properly cited	
Overheads	• Colorful title slide • Includes graphs • Readable, no errors • Bibliography	Title page, no graphics, more than 3 errors, inaccurate graphs, and no bibliography	Title, some graphics, 2–3 errors, inaccurate graphs and bibliography	Title, graphics, graphs, 0–1 errors, bibliography	Creative title, appropriate graphics, accurate graphs, no errors, bibliography	
Graphs	• Break-even Equation • Profit Equation • Line Graphs	Correct or partially correct display of only 1 of 3 types of equations/graphs	Partially correct display of 2 out of 3 types of equations/graphs	Visually appealing correct display of all 3 types	Sophisticated display of all 3 types of graphs	
Written	• Evidence of reason • Supporting statistics	Unclear recommendation, no supporting data	Recommendation made without supporting data	Clear recommendation using supportive statistics	Insightful recommendation using supporting data	

Comments:

Scale

A = D =
B = F =
C =

Total Score _____

Adapted from Jean Tucknott, Eisenhower Jr. High, Schaumburg District 54, IL and Margaret Novotny, St. Raymond School, Mount Prospect, IL. Used with permission.

Blackline 8.8

Performance Tasks and Rubrics

Problem-Solving Rubric

Criteria	Novice	In Progress	Meets Expectations	Exceeds Expectations
Identifies Real Problem	Problem? What problem?	Someone else points out there is a problem	Recognizes there is a problem	Identifies "real" problem
Gathers Facts	Does not realize the need to gather facts	Able to gather one fact on own	Knows where to look to obtain additional facts	Accesses information to obtain all necessary facts
Brainstorm Possible Solutions	Does not generate any solutions	Generates 1 idea with someone's assistance	Generates 2 or 3 solutions independently	Generates 4 creative solutions independently
Evaluates Effectiveness of Possible Solutions	Does not evaluate the effectiveness of possible solutions	Recognizes pluses and minuses of some of the solutions	Takes time to analyze effectiveness of each possible solution	Uses reflection to decide what to do differently next time

Blackline 8.9

Resume Rubric

Assignment: Evaluate a resume in terms of five criteria.

Criteria	No Chance 1	Try Again 2	Being Considered 3	Hired 4
Use of Correct Format	No form	Minimal form—three elements missing	Two elements of format missing	All elements of correct, format included
Sequential Job History	No job history listed	Not in sequence	Listed in reverse order	Correct sequencing
Career Goals Clearly Stated	No goal stated	Needs more explanation	Goal adequately stated but needs polishing	Goal clearly stated
Overall Appearance	Three errors in: • Margins • Spacing • Corrections	Two errors in: • Margins • Spacing • Corrections	One error in: • Margins • Spacing • Corrections	No errors
Mechanics	Three or more errors in: • Spelling • Grammar • Punctuation	Two errors in: • Spelling • Grammar • Punctuation	One error in: • Spelling • Grammar • Punctuation	No errors

Scale A = 18–20
B = 15–17
C = 12–14

Reprinted courtesy of Anita Zuckerberg, New York.

Blackline 8.10

Performance Tasks and Rubrics

Performance Rubric

Learning Goal: _____

Academic Standard: _____

Performance Task: _____

Criteria	1	2	3	4	5	Score
						$\frac{x}{[DM]} = \frac{}{*(\quad)}$ [FS]
						$\frac{x}{[DM]} = \frac{}{*(\quad)}$ [FS]
						$\frac{x}{[DM]} = \frac{}{*(\quad)}$ [FS]
						$\frac{x}{[DM]} = \frac{}{*(\quad)}$ [FS]
						$\frac{x}{[DM]} = \frac{}{*(\quad)}$ [FS]

*DM = difficulty multiplier
FS = final score

Scale

A =

B =

C =

D =

Final Score: _____ (100)

Final Grade: _____

Comments:

Rubric for _____

Standard(s) _____

Assignment _____

Criteria	Below Standards 1	Almost Meets Standards 2	Meets Standards 3	Exceeds Standards 4	Score
•					
•					
•					
•					
•					
•					
•					
•					
•					

(continued on next page)

Burke, K., R. Fogarty, S. Belgrad. 2002. _The Portfolio Connection: Student Work Linked to Standards,_ 2nd ed. Corwin Press, Thousand Oaks, CA. Reprinted with permission.

Blackline 8.12

Performance Tasks and Rubrics

Rubric for _____

Standard(s) _____

Assignment _____

Criteria	Below Standards 1	Almost Meets Standards 2	Meets Standards 3	Exceeds Standards 4	Score
•					
•					
•					
•					
•					
•					
•					
•					

Total Points _____

_____ = Exceeds Standards
_____ = Meets Standards
_____ = Almost Meets Standards
_____ = Below Standards

Comments:

Signed: _____ Date: _____

Burke, K., R. Fogarty, S. Belgrad. 2002. *The Portfolio Connection: Student Work Linked to Standards*, 2nd ed. Corwin Press, Thousand Oaks, CA. Reprinted with permission.

Blackline 8.12 (continued)

Performance Task
Design a Travel Brochure

Standards
1) Demonstrate competence in the general skills and strategies of the writing process.
2) Gather and use information for research purposes.

Benchmarks
Writes pieces that convey an intended purpose (to describe, to explain, to market).
Writes for an intended audience (tourists).

Travel Brochure for a Country
You work for the department of tourism for the country you selected for your research report. Your task is to design an informative brochure to attract tourists to your country. You must include the following:

- ❏ an attractive cover
- ❏ a brief history of the country
- ❏ major attractions
- ❏ weather information
- ❏ cost of the trip
- ❏ testimonials from visitors

Rubric to Assess Brochure

Criteria	0	1	2	3
Cover	None	• 1 color	• 2 color	• 3 color
History	None	• No graphics • Many inaccuracies • Poorly written	• Graphic • 1–2 inaccuracies • Written adequately	• Graphics • No inaccuracies • Well written
Attractions	None	• 1–2 attractions • Uneven descriptions	• 3–4 attractions • Adequate descriptions	• 5–6 attractions • Vivid descriptions
Weather	None	• No temperatures • Missing a season	• Temperatures for all seasons	• Temperatures for all seasons • Clothing recommendations
Cost	None	• Hotel only	• Hotel • Travel	• Hotel • Travel • Dining plus tip
Testimonials	None	• 1–2 quotes • Boring or nondescript	• 3–4 quotes • Motivating	• 3–4 quotes • Famous personalities

Performance Tasks and Rubrics

Creating Performance Tasks

Create a meaningful performance task for your subject area.

Subject Area: _____ Grade Level: _____

Learning Standard:_____

Task Description:

Direct Instruction for Whole Class: The whole class will be involved in the following learning experience:

Group Work: Students may select their group and their task.

Group One   **Group Two**   **Group Three**   **Group Four**

Individual Work: In addition to the group project, each student will complete the following individual assignments:

Methods of Assessment:

Performance Tasks and Rubrics Reflection Page

A rubric is a rubric is a rubric!

1	2	3	4
Show me the Scantron.	Rubrics are our friends.	Rubrics rock.	Rubrics are forever.

1. How do you rate your attitude toward rubrics on the scale above? Explain.

2. List both the advantages and disadvantages of using rubrics to score student work.

Advantages

-
-
-

Disadvantages

-
-
-

Level 1

MENTORING GUIDEBOOK

SECTION IV

Managing the Classroom

Many teachers enter the teaching field directly from university teacher preparation programs where they mastered minimal pedagogical knowledge or skills. Often they are not taught how to establish the positive, organized learning environment necessary for them to teach and for students to learn.

—Freiberg 2002

The profession of teaching is quite unique—first-year teachers are often expected to do the same things as veteran teachers who have been in the classroom for 30 years! Unfortunately, new teachers may be expected to teach the same academic content—yet teach it to the most challenging students. The seniority of the veteran teachers often allows them to receive assignments of advanced or accelerated classes, honors, and advanced placement where the class size may also be lower. In these advanced classes, students' behavior is generally better because students are more motivated and academic achievement is usually a priority. Beginning teachers, on the other hand, may be assigned basic skills courses with students with learning and behavior problems or with special needs. Another real challenge is the number of preparations the new teachers are assigned. At the middle school and high school levels, teachers could have four or five separate classes. One expert describes the teaching profession as a place where educators "eat their young." Instead of allowing time for new teachers to learn and grow, we throw them to the wolves to see if they will survive.

When I began teaching in 1970, I taught 9th grade composition (two sections), 9th grade grammar, advanced 10th grade American literature, and the 10th grade basic skills composition course. Keeping up with four different books, four different lesson plans, and writing four different tests, as well as grading all the compositions, overwhelmed me. Moreover, I didn't have to meet state standards or prepare my students for high-stakes exit exams like teachers today must do. Although I don't believe the practice of tracking was right for all students, it did make teaching easier because I could create one lesson and assessment to meet the needs of most of the class. Today's teacher, however, must "differentiate" all lessons and assessments in the inclusive classroom.

Most importantly, the behavior problems I faced 32 years ago were not nearly as challenging as those encountered today. Freiberg (2002) notes that today's teachers develop a repertoire of teaching strategies through trial and error. He believes that this "haphazard process of strategy development may take several years—by which time many struggling, unprepared new teachers have already left the classroom" (56).

Today's first-year teachers face an inclusive classroom with students of varying ability levels and behavior needs. They have to vary lesson plans, instructional strategies, and assessments. They have to meet district curriculum goals and state standards and prepare students to take a high-stakes test almost every year. And instead of "pulling out" students with specialized learning or behavior problems, first-year teachers have to include them and meet each of their needs as legally specified in an Individual Educational Plan (IEP). New teachers may be fortunate enough to have paraprofessionals to assist them, but budgetary cuts often eliminate aides. If they do have paraprofessionals, they need to know how to coordinate the duties to utilize them most effectively. Regardless of the number of paraprofessionals, parent volunteers, or aides, the teacher is the official person in charge of the classroom.

This last section, *Managing the Classroom,* offers suggestions to help novice teachers establish a classroom environment where students not only care about one another, but also take responsibility for their own behavior and learning.

In Selection 9, **Setting the Climate,** I discuss the importance of the beginning teacher establishing procedures, rules, and consequences, as well as developing specific strategies to address minor behavior problems.

In Selection 10, **Establishing a Cooperative, Responsible Classroom Environment,** I review proactive approaches that may prevent behavior problems before they start or at least diffuse them before they become major problems.

In Selection 11, **What Social Skills Do They Need?,** Bellanca and Fogarty provide strategies to teach students social skills to help them cooperate with one another to become more responsible for their own behavior. And finally, I offer problem-solving strategies for teachers to use when dealing with challenging students in Selection 12, **Students with Behavior Problems.**

The techniques introduced in this section could help mentors assist new teachers in developing a management plan and establishing a cooperative classroom that is conducive for learning. Correia and McHenry (2002) describe how classroom management is a common concern for beginning teachers. "They [beginning teachers] may find it difficult to maintain a balance of lessons that are motivating and interactive within an environment that is manageable and conducive to learning" (16). Teachers cite classroom management problems and student misbehaviors as the major reasons they leave the profession. It is imperative that mentoring programs and individual mentors spend time before the start of school and during the first critical months reviewing and sharing management techniques they have used successfully, as well as ideas in books and videos—all available resources—to help guide the protégé through the obstacle course to quality teaching. One of the keys to effective classroom management, however, is quality instruction. Mentors need to stress the importance of Section III, *Designing Lesson and Unit Plans*. Designing motivating lessons is critical—100 classroom management strategies will not work for very long without the support of meaningful, well-organized teaching. What comes first—instruction or classroom management? The answer: They need to come together! Instruction and management are linked and both must be developed, established, and implemented the first day of school.

REFERENCES

Correia, M. P., and J. M. McHenry. 2002. *The mentors handbook: Practical suggestions fot collaborative reflection and analysis.* Norwood, MA: Publishers.

Freiberg, H. J. 2002. Essential skills for new teachers. *Educational Leadership* (59)6: 56–60.

> Once instructional planning is in progress or completed, beginning teachers must also establish a classroom environment that is conducive for learning. Mentors should help the new teacher create procedures, rules, and consequences that provide clear expectations for student behavior and set the stage for a cooperative classroom.

Setting the Climate

by **Kay Burke**

Classroom Climate

Improved school climate is an ideal, a goal to pursue. A school that claims that it has a perfect school climate is myopic, for improved school climate is something that professional educators are working toward—always.
                                              —Hansen and Childs 1998

The climate of a classroom refers to the type of environment students are exposed to when they are learning. A person can get a feel for a school by walking in the halls, getting a view of the surroundings, and seeing how people treat one another. The climate of a school is often difficult to define, but it has a tremendous influence on learning.

Freiberg (1998) believes that school climate is an ever-changing factor in the lives of the students and teachers in a school, and states that "much like the air we breathe, school climate is ignored until it becomes foul" (p. 22). The school climate can either enhance learning or serve as a barrier to learning. Schools that have mandatory attendance at all school functions, lack of choice in curriculum, heavy emphasis on high-stakes testing and evaluation, and a litany of "not" rules ("students shall not chew gum") created and enforced by the faculty and staff isolate and separate the faculty from the students. Darling-Hammond (as cited in Hansen and Childs 1998) affirms that

Setting the Climate

"schools really are much alike, regardless of where they are. Mandates and regulations govern many school systems in ways that make schools impersonal, indifferent, and generally insensitive to the individuals within them" (p. 14).

In describing the climate of a classroom, educators should begin with a vision of what the classroom ought to be like. Kohn talks about the idea of climate as "one that promotes deep understanding, excitement about learning, and social as well as intellectual growth" (1996, p. 54). Kohn believes students need to play an active role in the decision-making process, teachers need to work with students to structure the curriculum to meet their needs and interests, and the environment needs to support children's desires to discover new ideas and their love of learning. A classroom where the teacher depends upon compliance from the students and uses a lock-step system of rewards and punishment to ensure their compliance does not foster an environment conducive to learning. Students need to construct knowledge for themselves and feel empowered to help make some decisions about their classroom environment and their own learning.

Classroom Management

Freiberg (1999) discusses the role behaviorist learning theory has played in classroom management. He says that the most common approach to classroom management in many schools is some form of behavior modification. The key ingredients of most teachers' discipline routines include "rules, consequences, and rewards" that have their roots in classical conditioning theory derived by Pavlov and operant conditioning described by B. F. Skinner. Operant conditioning is the reinforcement of behavior (candy, tokens, stars) and its relationship to specific consequences. This conditioning takes place when teachers try to stop a particular response by the student with a specific action. Teachers engaging in this conditioning use a contingency plan or action that is repeated to reinforce or shape a particular response by the student. However, it has been found that not all psychological lessons learned with rats and pigeons in the laboratory translate well to the classroom.

Freiberg says that even though cognitive learning theory, which focused on why people behave and think in certain ways, began to replace behaviorist learning theory in the 1970s, behaviorism began to flourish in the American classroom in the 1960s and '70s. Commercial programs such as Assertive Discipline focused on controlling student behaviors by using punishments (name on the board, removal of privileges) and rewards (stars, tokens, extra recess). In one study, researchers Emmer and Aussiker (as cited in Freiberg 1999) demonstrated that student attitude toward school was lower in the Assertive Discipline school. Freiberg concluded that, "Discipline programs that are highly behavioristic and focus on controlling student behaviors through punishment can diminish student self-discipline" (p. 8).

On the other hand, school programs that emphasize student self-discipline (the responsibility model), rather than external controlling factors (the obedience model) (see Figure 9.1), show greater promise in improving achievement and learning environments (Gottfredson, Gottfredson, and Hybl as cited in Freiberg 1999). Schools that improve the academic achievements of their students not only emphasize academics, but also emphasize an open environment and a healthy school climate (Hoy, Tarter, and Kottkamp as cited in Freiberg 1999).

Obedience Model vs. Responsibility Model

- External control
- Internal control

- Fear of getting caught
- Desire to do the right thing

- Authority figures
- Self-discipline

Figure 9.1

Setting the Climate

Person-Centered Classrooms

Freiberg (1999) advocates a person-centered classroom management program that emphasizes caring, guidance, cooperation, and the building of self-discipline. Person-centered classrooms encourage students to think for themselves and to help each other. Emphasis is also placed on self-discipline that is built over time and encompasses many different experiences: "It requires a learning environment that nurtures opportunities to learn from one's own experiences, including mistakes, and to reflect on these experiences" (Freiberg 1999, p. 13). Figure 9.2 shows how the traditional teacher-centered classroom differs from the person-centered classroom.

In the person-centered classroom, students self-regulate their learning and construct meaning for themselves. They initiate their learning, collaborate effectively with their peers, and self-evaluate their progress toward meeting their academic goals. They become prepared to function in a community of learners. Brophy (1999) believes teachers need to design their instructional and management methods to support this goal. This goal contrasts to the goal of the behaviorist model, which is to control students' behavior. As Brophy states: "Traditionally emphasized behavioristic management models, especially those designed to train students to follow unvaried routines and respond 'mindlessly' to cues, are not well suited to preparing them to fulfill today's more demanding roles" (p. 55).

A positive school and classroom climate is critical for learning. All the procedures, rules, consequences, metal detectors, and police support available cannot compensate for the absence of a school climate or culture that influences everything that goes on in a school. Peterson and Deal (1998) talk about how culture is the underground stream of norms, values, beliefs, traditions, and rituals that have built up out of time. They state: "This set of informal expectations and values shapes how people think, feel, and act in schools. This highly enduring web of influence binds the school together and makes it special. It is up to school leaders—principals, teachers, and often parents—to help identify, shape, and maintain strong, positive, student-focused cultures.

GUIDEBOOK

Teacher-Centered Classrooms Compared to Person-Centered Classrooms

TEACHER-CENTERED CLASSROOMS	PERSON-CENTERED CLASSROOMS
The teacher is the sole leader.	Leadership is shared.
Management is a form of oversight.	Management is a form of guidance.
Teacher takes responsibility for all the paperwork and organization.	Students are facilitators for the operations of the classroom.
Discipline comes from the teacher.	Discipline comes from the self.
A few students are the teacher's helpers.	All students have the opportunity to become an integral part of the management of the classroom.
Teacher makes the rules and posts them for the students.	Rules are developed by the teacher and students in the form of a classroom constitution or compact.
Consequences are fixed for all students.	Consequences reflect individual differences.
Rewards are mostly extrinsic.	Rewards are mostly intrinsic.
Students are allowed limited responsibilities.	Students share in classroom responsibilities.
Few members of the community enter the classroom.	Partnerships are formed with business and community groups to enrich and broaden the learning opportunities for students.

(Adapted from Rogers and Freiberg 1994, p. 240. Reprinted with permission of Prentice Hall, Upper Saddle River, NJ.

Figure 9.2

Setting the Climate

Without these supportive cultures, reforms will falter, staff morale and commitment will wither, and student learning will slip" (p. 28).

This selection explores ways in which teachers can create person-centered classrooms where students are involved in the decision-making process and encouraged to self-evaluate their behavior. By allowing students to make choices and by encouraging self-discipline, schools can create responsible, confident learners. Scenarios are presented throughout that represent ways teachers might facilitate implementation of classroom procedures with their students. Each scenario is followed by strategies, activities, and assignments to help teachers tackle the particular classroom issue outlined in the scenario.

Getting Started

"I feel it is very important that we always walk in the halls and enter the room slowly. Why do you think that procedure is important?" asks Mrs. Saunders.

"I saw a boy get hurt once when another boy was rushing into the room and knocked him into the doorknob," Mary replies.

"I don't like getting shoved by someone who is afraid of being late," adds John.

"So, you think we should all be courteous and enter the room walking rather than running or shoving?" Mrs. Saunders asks.

"Yes," says the class.

"All right, let's practice how we should all enter the room. Everyone file out quietly and stand by the drinking fountain down the hall. When I give the signal, you will all walk toward our classroom and enter the room the way we discussed."

[Students rehearse entering the classroom.]

"I really liked the way you took turns entering the room and going to your desks. Now, what do you think would be a consequence if someone forgot our procedure and ran into someone while running into the room?"

"I think that person should have to go back and practice walking into the room again," says Juan.

"He should also have to apologize to whoever he ran into 'cause no one likes to be pushed," Jack adds.

"Okay," says Mrs. Saunders, *"I think we all agree on the importance of this procedure. We'll add this to our list of classroom procedures and consequences."*

Setting Up the Classroom

Very few students function well in a chaotic environment. Even though students may pretend to enjoy having the freedom to do whatever they want, whenever they want, most of them prefer structures or routines so they know exactly what they are supposed to do. Structure can be implemented through the arrangement of the classroom, as well as through classroom procedures.

Room Arrangement

Before students walk into class on the first day of school, teachers should arrange the classroom to permit orderly movement, make efficient use of the available space, and keep potential disruptions to a minimum. This provides not only the students but also the teacher with an efficient and well-organized area in which to learn. Evertson, et al. (1997) suggest that teachers consider the following four guidelines:

1. Keep high-traffic areas free of congestion.
2. Be sure all students can be easily seen by the teacher.
3. Keep frequently used materials and teaching supplies readily accessible.
4. Be certain students can easily see whole-class presentations and displays.

Figure 9.3 shows one possible configuration of a room in which students sit in cooperative groups and everyone has a clear view of the teacher, blackboard, and screen.

Setting the Climate

Possible Room Arrangement

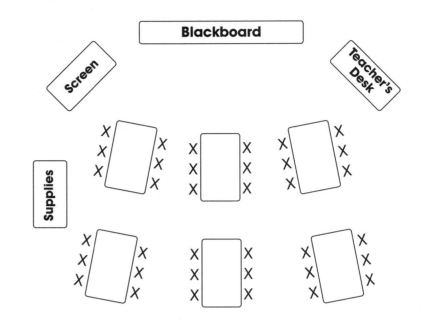

Figure 9.3

Procedures

Teachers can be creative and organize open-ended cooperative activities that allow students many options and choices while still providing them with structure. However, students need to walk before they can run, and it is essential that they know their boundaries the first week of class. Teachers should prepare a tentative list of procedures necessary for establishing the routines essential for classroom organization; however, the entire class should discuss the rationale for the procedures and have some input in their final adoption.

The most effective way for teachers to handle discipline problems is to prevent them. The proactive teacher anticipates potential management problems and establishes a positive classroom environment where students feel secure because they know what is expected of them. Researchers who have studied classroom management offer teachers the following tips:

- Proactive teachers help prevent discipline problems.
- Students who are actively involved in the lessons cause fewer behavior problems.
- Teachers who use instructional time efficiently have fewer management problems.

Good classroom management is primarily prevention, not intervention planning before the year begins, implementing on the first day of school, and maintaining consistently throughout the year. "Procedures are ways of getting class activities done. Their function is to routinize tasks for continuity, predictability, and time saving" (Evertson and Harris 1991, p. 2). Evertson and Harris recommend four steps in teaching classroom procedures:

1. Explain:
   - Give concrete definition of procedures.
   - Provide the reason or rationale.
   - Demonstrate the procedure.
   - Present the task step by step.
   - Explain and demonstrate cues.
2. Rehearse the procedure.
3. Provide feedback to individuals and the class.
4. Re-teach procedures as necessary. (1991, p. 2)

The procedures in a class should relate to the important principles that permeate the classroom climate. If students are expected to be prepared, on time, courteous, and respectful of others' rights, the procedures should support those principles. Courteous and responsible behavior builds cooperation and teamwork. When this behavior is the standard, students feel obliged to treat other students the way they would like to be treated.

Teachers need to decide on the types of procedures that are needed for their students and be prepared to discuss the procedures during the first few days of school. Some procedures may be negotiable, and some procedures will be nonnegotiable.

Some of the procedures may have consequences if they are violated (see the Consequences section later in this selection). The teacher and the students should discuss the necessity of the procedures offered by the teacher, vote on their adoption, and post them in the room.

Many of the procedures should be rehearsed or role-played, and the teacher should gently remind students of the procedures by standing close to the student who is violating the procedure and pointing to the list of procedures posted in the room.

The key to effective procedures is consistency. If a procedure isn't working, it should be discussed and changed. But if the procedure is necessary and it is on the list, it should be enforced. A breakdown in classroom management doesn't usually start with a bang—it starts with a whimper!

Teachers can use Figure 9.4 to discern which procedures are important to implement in their classrooms. Teachers can prepare their own procedures with Blackline 9.1 provided at the end of this selection.

Classroom Procedures—
Do Students Know What Is Expected of Them for Routine Operations?

Directions: Review the following procedures and check the ones your students will need to know and practice.

A. Beginning the class
- ❏ How should students enter the room?
- ❏ What constitutes being late? (in the room, in the seat)
- ❏ How and when will absentee slips be handled?
- ❏ What type of seating arrangements will be used? (assigned seats, open seating, cooperative group seating)
- ❏ How will the teacher get students' attention to start class? (the tardy bell, a signal such as a raised hand, or lights turned off and on)
- ❏ How will students behave during public address (PA) announcements?
- ❏ Others:

_____

_____

_____

_____

_____

B. Classroom Management
- ❏ How and when will students leave their seats?
- ❏ What do students need in order to leave the room? (individual passes, room pass, teacher's permission)
- ❏ How will students get help from the teacher? (raise hands, put name on board, ask other group members first)
- ❏ What are acceptable noise levels for discussion, group work, seat work?
- ❏ How should students work with other students or move into cooperative groups? (moving desks, changing seats, noise level, handling materials)
- ❏ How will students get recognized to talk? (raised hand, teacher calls on student, talk out)
- ❏ How do students behave during presentations by other students?
- ❏ How do students get supplies?
- ❏ How and when do students sharpen pencils?
- ❏ How will students get materials or use special equipment?
- ❏ Others:

_____

_____

_____

_____

_____

Figure 9.4

(continued on next page)

C. Paperwork

❏ How will students turn in work? (put in specific tray or box, pass to the front, one student collects)

❏ How will students turn in makeup work if they were absent? (special tray, give to teacher, put in folder, give to teacher's aide)

❏ How will students distribute handouts? (first person in row, a group member gets a copy for all group members, students pick up as they enter room)

❏ How will late work be graded? (no penalty, minus points, zero, "F", use lunch or recess to finish, turn in by end of day, drop so many homework grades)

❏ How and when will students make up quizzes and tests missed? (same day they return to school, within twenty-four hours, within the week, before school, during lunch or recess, after school)

❏ How will late projects such as research papers, portfolios, and artwork be graded? (no penalty, minus points, lowered letter grade, no late work accepted)

❏ Others:

_____

_____

_____

_____

_____

D. Dismissal from Class or School

❏ How are students dismissed for lunch?

❏ When do students leave class for the day? (when bell rings, when teacher gives the signal)

❏ Can students stay after class to finish assignments, projects, tests?

❏ Can the teacher keep one student or the whole class after class or school?

❏ What do students do during fire and disaster drills?

❏ Others:

_____

_____

_____

_____

_____

E. Syllabus or Course Outline

❏ How are students made aware of course objectives?

❏ How are students made aware of course requirements?

❏ Are students given due dates for major assignments several weeks in advance?

❏ Are students told how they will be evaluated and given the grading scale?

❏ Others:

_____

_____

_____

_____

_____

Figure 9.4 (continued)

(continued on next page)

F. Other Procedures

You may need to introduce procedures related to recess, assemblies, guest speakers, substitute teachers, field trips, fire drills, teacher leaving the room, etc. List other procedures that are needed.

❑ _____
❑ _____
❑ _____

Recess

❑ _____
❑ _____
❑ _____
❑ _____

Assemblies

❑ _____
❑ _____
❑ _____
❑ _____

Guest Speakers

❑ _____
❑ _____
❑ _____
❑ _____

Substitute Teachers

❑ _____
❑ _____
❑ _____
❑ _____

Field Trips

❑ _____
❑ _____
❑ _____
❑ _____

Fire Drills

❑ _____
❑ _____
❑ _____
❑ _____

Figure 9.4 (continued)

Who Makes the Rules?

"Okay class," begins Mrs. Baker. "One of the rules on our web is 'Students should raise their hands to speak!' Let's talk about that rule before we vote on it."

"I don't like that rule," Mary offers. "When I get an idea, I have to blurt it out quickly or I'll lose it."

"Yeah," Sam agrees. "I hate holding my hand up."

"All right, Mary and Sam have some legitimate concerns about the rule. Let's role-play a situation and get a handle on this problem. I'll start talking about the Middle Ages, and we'll allow students to talk without raising their hands."

"One of the major problems confronting the people in the Middle Ages was the Bubonic Plague. Researchers estimate that as many as one-third of the population of Europe died because of the plague. One interesting thing about . . ."

"Is that like AIDS today?" Jimmy interrupts.

"Didn't rats spread the plague?" wonders Susan.

"Oh yuck, I hate rats!" shouts Juanita.

"Hey, my sister has a pet rat!" Susan cries.

"My next-door neighbor has a pet snake. I bet it eats rats!" yells Jimmy.

Finally, Mrs. Baker says, "Let's see. Yes, Jimmy, we are going to talk about how the plague compares to AIDS, and yes, Susan, the plague was spread by fleas on rats. We'll be talking about that more tomorrow. Let's see, what else?"

"Stop!" yells Mary. "I understand why we need to raise our hands to speak. When people blurt things out, we get off track. Also, it's rude to interrupt the teacher."

"I'm glad you can see how easy it is to get off track when somebody talks in the middle of my idea," says Mrs. Baker.

"I agree," Sam says. "I don't like people interrupting me. You need to finish your idea and then call on someone. I'll vote for it!"

"Let's take a vote. All those in favor of passing the rule to raise our hands to get recognized before we speak, please raise your hand!" says Mrs. Baker. "Great, 32 in favor; 3 opposed. We hereby pass Rule #1."

GUIDEBOOK

Discussing Classroom Rules

If classroom procedures form the framework for a classroom climate conducive to students and teachers working together cooperatively, the classroom rules form the heart and soul of caring, cooperative classrooms. If students are going to buy into the system, they must be part of the rule-making process. Classroom rules that are fair, reasonable, and enforceable play an important role in creating and maintaining a positive learning environment.

Terminology

Jones and Jones (1998) have some concerns about using the term *rules*. They believe the term suggests compliance to classroom management. Therefore, they suggest instead using terms such as *behavioral standards, norms, expectations, or principles* to "describe the agreements teachers and students make regarding the types of behaviors that help a classroom be a safe community of support" (p. 241).

Guidelines

According to Kohn (1991), "an immense body of research has shown that children are more likely to follow a rule if its rationale has been explained to them . . . Discipline based on reason is more effective than the totalitarian approach captured by the T-shirt slogan 'Because I'm the Mommy, that's why'" (p. 502).

Curwin and Mendler (1988) feel that effective rules describe specific behavior. They also believe that effective rules should be built on characteristics such as honesty, courtesy, helpfulness, and the like. Evertson and Harris (1991) offer eight guidelines for writing classroom rules.

Rules should be . . .

1. Consistent with school rules
2. Understandable
3. Doable (students able to comply)
4. Manageable

5. Always applicable (consistent)
6. Stated positively
7. Stated behaviorally
8. Consistent with teacher's own philosophy of how students learn best (p. 2)

Clearly stated rules that describe specific behavior enable students to understand what is expected of them. However, if rules are too specific, too many rules are needed. For example:

Too general: "Students shouldn't bother other students."

Too specific: "Students should not grab, push, shove, or trip other students."

Better rule: "It is best that students keep their hands off other people."

Other rules that could be developed include:

1. Respect other people's property.
2. Listen and be polite to other people.
3. Raise your hand to be recognized.
4. Obey all school rules.
5. Bring all materials to class.

A set of five rules should be sufficient to cover most classroom behaviors, but teachers sometimes may need to add a new rule to cover a situation not mentioned in the rules.

It is imperative that students get an opportunity to discuss the proposed classroom rules and understand the rationale behind the rules. A class meeting is the perfect opportunity to have a frank discussion of the rules, role-play situations, and come to a class consensus about the rules the students and teacher will adopt to ensure a positive and organized classroom environment.

It is important to note that some rules are nonnegotiable. Students must understand that the school district or the school sets down some rules that are not subject to a vote. Rules related to fighting, damage to property, injury to self or others, and weapons are absolute because they set parameters for all students to ensure their health and safety. It is important that teachers review school rules and the discipline policies with all students the first day of class.

After class members and the teacher have come to a consensus on their classroom rules, they should discuss and agree on the logical consequences students will face if they violate the rules. The old-fashioned punishment paradigm of teachers dictating all the rules and threatening students with punishments is not effective. As Kohn (1991) states, "reliance on the threat of punishment is a reasonably good indication that something is wrong in a classroom, since children have to be bullied into acting the way the teacher demands" (p. 500). Student ownership of the classroom encourages students to become stakeholders in the democratic process.

Consequences

If teachers are to establish an atmosphere of cooperation where students assume responsibility for their actions, the old obedience model of "spare the rod, spoil the child" is ineffectual. Kohn (1991) notes that "isolating a child from his peers, humiliating her, giving him an F, loading her with extra homework, or even threatening to do any of these things can produce compliance in the short run. Over the long run, however, this strategy is unproductive" (p. 500).

Many educators, however, feel that the role of consequences in breaking a rule is controversial. Even though many researchers feel that consequences are not punishment, Kohn (1996) calls them "Punishment Lite." He contends that the line between punishment and logical consequences is thin at times and even though the students have a "pseudochoice," as Kohn calls it, they are still being punished. Some discipline programs describe logical consequences as punitive revenge on students. If a student bites other students, he has to wear a sign saying "I bite people." If a student writes notes, she has to read them in front of the class. If a student misbehaves, he cannot go to lunch or the library or he must write an essay in the principal's office. If a student talks, he must stand in the corner and miss recess. If a student talks back to the teacher, she must write "I will not talk back to my teacher," 500 times.

Consequences, however, should relate directly to the rule violation and seem more logical than just punishments. Curwin and Mendler (1988) warn, however, that "a consequence can become a punishment if it is delivered aggressively" (p. 65). According to Curwin and Mendler consequences work best when they:

1. Are clear and specific
2. Have a range of alternatives
   - Reminder
   - Warning (or second reminder)
   - Conference with student
   - Conference with parent and/or administrator
3. Are not punishments
4. Are natural and/or logical
5. Are related to the rule

For example, if a student violates the rule about homework by not completing it, the consequence would not logically be to send that student to the principal. The consequence would more logically involve having the student turn in the homework before the end of the day, stay in from recess or lunch to finish it, or lose points. Consequences relate directly to the rule violation. Across-the-board punishments such as "sit in the corner," "go to the office," or "miss the field trip" are punitive and don't necessarily "fit the crime."

In addition, punishment often diminishes the dignity of the student as well as breeds resentment and resistance. Kohn (1991) says that punishment teaches nothing about what a student is supposed to do—only about what he or she is not supposed to do. Curwin and Mendler (1988) feel that if students are only motivated by a reward-and-punishment system, they will only behave out of fear of getting caught rather than out of a sense of social responsibility. And Glasser (1990) warns that students will not be coerced into doing anything. Students must see the rationale behind the rules and they must be a part of the process.

Some effective generic consequences include those outlined in Figure 9.5.

Offenses and Consequences

First offense — Reminder (many students simply forget the rule)

Second offense — Second reminder

Third offense — Conference with student

Fourth offense — Social contract with student

Fifth offense — Conference with parent and administrators

Figure 9.5

Other consequences should be specifically related to the rule (see Figure 9.6).

Examples

Rule
Students will be in their seats when the bell rings.

Consequences
1. Reminder
2. Second reminder
3. Student must make up time after school
4. Conference with student
5. Social contract
6. Conference with parent

Rule
Students will hand in homework on day it is due.

Consequences
1. Reminder
2. Conference with student
3. Student must stay in from recess or after school to complete homework
4. Points subtracted from grade
5. Conference with parent
6. Conference with counselor or administrator

Figure 9.6

If students have some input in the establishment of consequences, they are more likely to recognize fairness and logic in their implementation. Furthermore, teachers need to administer the consequences calmly and fairly and remind students that they still like and respect them—it is their actions that are unacceptable. Students who accept their consequences, realizing they have not fulfilled their responsibility or obligation, are likely to learn from their mistakes as long as they are treated with respect, confidentiality, and caring.

Blackline 9.2, at the end of this selection, restates Evertson's and Harris's (1991) criteria for creating effective classroom rules and lists a series of rules that may or may not meet their criteria. Blackline 9.3, at the end of this selection, asks teachers to create five age-appropriate rules and determine logical consequences that could be administered if students violate the rules.

Behavior Checklists

Hopefully, most students will accept the rule and consequence paradigm, internalize their own responsibilities, and model the positive behavior of their peers and teachers. The need still exists, however, for teachers to chronicle the behavior of those who choose not to cooperate. It is imperative that the documentation of all violations remains private and confidential.

Teachers can use a grade book, checklists, or any type of written format to monitor disruptive behavior. However, writing the names of misbehaving students on the blackboard and adding checks after their names for repeat offenses is not conducive to establishing classroom trust, nor does it build the self-esteem of students.

No teacher wants to take time away from teaching to be an accountant whose job is to debit and credit discipline violations, but there are ways teachers can monitor student behavior efficiently. A checklist may help teachers keep track of violations without embarrassing students or losing instructional time. It is suggested that teachers record specific dates under each rule violation to determine which consequence applies and to document persistent discipline problems in case more formal referrals or follow-up actions are required later. A behavior checklist (Blackline 9.4) is provided at the end of this selection.

Attitude Versus Skill Issue

Regardless of the terms or methods used to handle violations of rules, teachers sometimes tend to respond to student disruptions in a punitive way rather than trying to reinforce and redirect students to the correct behavior. Jones and Jones (1998) feel that school personnel have too often viewed inappropriate behavior as an attitude rather than a skill issue. In many cases, they assume the student's error is premeditated, deliberate, and threatening, when in fact, the student could be unaware of the violation, the disruption was accidental, or the student didn't know the skill. Social skills and behavior norms need to be taught and reinforced as much as math skills. Good behavior just doesn't happen—it has to be taught and reinforced. Figure 9.7 is an example of a brainstorming web teachers can use to get the class thinking about the rules needed. A Blackline master (Blackline 9.5) is provided at the end of this selection.

Brainstorming Web

Example: This web graphic organizer shows areas where rules may be needed.

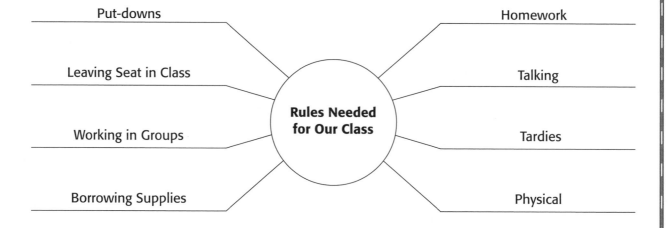

Figure 9.7

REFERENCES

Brophy, J. 1999. Perspectives of classroom management: Yesterday, today and tomorrow. In *Beyond behaviorism: Changing the classroom management paradigm,* edited by H. J. Freiberg. Boston: Allyn & Bacon

Curwin, R. L., and A. N. Mendler. 1988. *Discipline with dignity.* Alexandria, VA: Association for Supervision and Curriculum Development.

Evertson, C. M., Emmer, E. T., Clements, B. S., and Worsham, M. E. 1997. *Classroom management for elementary teachers,* 4th ed. Boston: Allyn & Bacon

Evertson, C., and Harris, A. 1991b. *Components of effective classroom management: Materials selected from the NDN-approved classroom organization and management program (COMP).* Nashville, TN: Vanderbilt University.

Freiberg, H. J. 1998. Measuring school climate: Let me count the ways. *Educational Leadership* 56(1): 22–26.

———, ed. 1999. *Beyond behaviorism: Changing the classroom management paradigm.* Boston: Allyn & Bacon.

Glasser, W. 1990. *The quality school.* New York: Harper Perennial.

Hansen, J. M. and Childs, J. 1998. Creating a school where people like to be. *Educational Leadership* 56(1): 14–17.

Jones, V. F., and Jones, L. S. 1998. *Comprehensive classroom management: Creating communities of support and solving problems,* 5th ed. Boston: Allyn & Bacon.

Kohn, A. 1991. Caring kids: The role of the schools. *Phi Delta Kappan* 72(7): 496–506.

———. 1996. *Beyond discipline: From compliance to community.* Alexandria, VA: Association for Supervision and Curriculum Development.

Peterson, K. D., and Deal, T. E. 1998. How leaders influence the culture of schools. *Educational Leadership* 56(1): 28–30.

Rogers, C., and Freiberg, H. J. 1994. *Freedom to learn,* 3rd ed. Upper Saddle River, NJ: Prentice-Hall.

Five Blackline masters are provided in the pages that follow:
- Classroom Procedures Form
- Creating Effective Rules
- Classroom Rules and Consequences
- Behavior Checklist
- Brainstorming Web

Mentors can help protégés complete the Blacklines and choose procedures and rules that promote a positive classroom climate.

Classroom Procedures Form

Directions: Write the specific procedures you will implement with your students.

Teacher:_____   **Grade Level:**_____   **Class:**_____

A. Beginning the Class

- ❑ _____
- ❑ _____
- ❑ _____
- ❑ _____
- ❑ _____
- ❑ _____

B. Classroom Management

- ❑ _____
- ❑ _____
- ❑ _____
- ❑ _____
- ❑ _____
- ❑ _____

C. Paperwork

- ❑ _____
- ❑ _____
- ❑ _____
- ❑ _____
- ❑ _____
- ❑ _____

(continued on next page)

Blackline 9.1

D. Dismissal from Class or School

❑ _____
❑ _____
❑ _____
❑ _____
❑ _____
❑ _____

E. Syllabus or Course Outline

❑ _____
❑ _____
❑ _____
❑ _____
❑ _____
❑ _____

F. Bringing Books, Notebooks, and Supplies to Class

❑ _____
❑ _____
❑ _____
❑ _____
❑ _____
❑ _____

G. Other Procedures

❑ _____
❑ _____
❑ _____
❑ _____
❑ _____
❑ _____

Blackline 9.1 (continued)

Creating Effective Rules

Guidelines for effective rules (Evertson and Harris 1991, p. 2):

1. Consistent with school rules
2. Understandable
3. Doable (students able to comply)
4. Manageable

5. Consistent
6. Stated positively
7. Stated behaviorally
8. Consistent with teacher's own philosophy of how student's learn best

Directions: Review the above guidelines. Then check to see if the seven rules listed below meet the guidelines for classroom rules. If so, mark the rule "Yes." If not, mark it "No" and rewrite the rule to make it a "Yes."

Rules	YES	NO
1. Don't talk out of turn. *Rewrite:* _____	❏	❏
2. Be considerate of others. *Rewrite:* _____	❏	❏
3. Do not hit others. *Rewrite:* _____	❏	❏
4. Respect the property of others. *Rewrite:* _____	❏	❏
5. Do not use profanity. *Rewrite:* _____	❏	❏
6. Listen quietly while others are speaking. *Rewrite:* _____	❏	❏
7. Obey all school rules. *Rewrite:* _____	❏	❏

Blackline 9.2

Setting the Climate

Classroom Rules and Consequences

Directions: Develop five rules and logical consequences for violating the rules that are appropriate for your students.

Teacher:_____ **Class/Grade:**_____ **Date:**_____

Rule #1: _____
Consequences   1.
2.
3.
4.
5.

Rule #2: _____
Consequences   1.
2.
3.
4.
5.

Rule #3: _____
Consequences   1.
2.
3.
4.
5.

Rule #4: _____
Consequences   1.
2.
3.
4.
5.

Rule #5: _____
Consequences   1.
2.
3.
4.
5.

Blackline 9.3

Behavior Checklist

Teacher:_____ **Class:**_____ **Date:**_____

Rules:		Consequences:
Rule #1	_____	1. _____
Rule #2	_____	2. _____
Rule #3	_____	3. _____
Rule #4	_____	4. _____
Rule #5	_____	5. _____

Write the dates of all violations in boxes under rule numbers.

Class Roll	Rule 1	2	3	4	5	Comments
1.						
2.						
3.						
4.						
5.						
6.						
7.						
8.						
9.						
10.						
11.						
12.						
13.						
14.						
15.						
16.						
17.						
18.						
19.						
20.						

Blackline 9.4

Setting the Climate

Brainstorming Web

Teacher:_____ Class:_____ Date:_____

Directions: Draw a web on the blackboard or on newsprint. Ask students to brainstorm a list of areas where rules are needed in order to ensure a cooperative climate.

Brainstorming Web

Rules Needed for Our Class

B eginning teachers may not realize that some of their actions or comments could be causing behavior problems. Mentors can help new teachers become sensitive, proactive teachers who prevent many potential disturbances by establishing a comfortable classroom environment. If students feel valued and safe, they can focus on their learning.

Establishing a Cooperative, Responsible Classroom Environment

by **Kay Burke**

"I hate doing these geometry problems," groans Chuck. "Why do we need to know this for life? We spend half the class working on these theorems!"

"What's the problem, Chuck?" asks Mrs. Nordstrom.

"Math is boring," Chuck explodes.

"Now, Chuck," Mrs. Nordstrom replies. "Things are not boring— people who don't understand them just think they're boring."

"I understand the problems," shouts Chuck. "I just don't give a damn!"

"If you understand so much," says Mrs. Nordstrom through gritted teeth, her voice rising, "Why did you score a 54 percent on your last test?"

"Because I wanted to flunk—it was my personal best."

Mrs. Nordstrom angrily shouts, "All right, young man. You can just march yourself down to the principal's office right now."

"Great, I'd rather sit in the office all day than sit in this stupid room!"

Adapted from *What to Do with the Kid Who. . . : Developing Cooperation, Self-Discipline, and Responsibility in the Classroom* by Kay Burke, pp. 89–95. © 2000 by Corwin Press. Used with permission.

Establishing a Cooperative, Responsible Classroom Environment

Creating the Climate

The climate of a classroom refers to the teacher-student and peer relationships. A positive climate is established when a teacher not only "engages students' imaginations but also convinces them that they are people of worth who can do something in a very difficult world" (Kohl as cited in Scherer 1998, p. 9).

Kohl (as cited in Scherer 1998) believes that the first big thing that makes a difference is respect. If teachers don't feel that their students have equal value to themselves, then they won't teach them much. Kohl also believes that humiliation is absolutely a sin. He feels that teachers need to deal with students who defy them, but humiliation has to go. Lyrics from the song "The Wall" by Pink Floyd represent this point: *We don't need no education / We don't need no thought control / No dark sarcasm in the classroom / Teacher leave the kids alone.* Kohl feels we do need some education, "but dark sarcasm has to be removed from the teacher's repertoire of strategies" (Kohl as cited in Scherer 1998, p. 9).

Publicly humiliating or embarrassing students does not help students learn from their mistakes. It could, however, make them try harder not to get caught and cause them to devise clever ways to get revenge on whomever embarrassed them.

Dealing with disruptive students in private, in a fair and consistent manner, and in a manner that maintains their dignity and self-esteem helps them develop an "internal locus of control" and responsibility. Students with an internal locus of control feel guilty when they misbehave, learn from their mistakes, are able to accept the consequences for their actions, and know they can control their actions in the future.

Dealing with disruptive students in front of their peers in an emotional outburst of frustration and anger lowers the students' self-concepts, decreases their desire to cooperate and succeed, and prevents them from developing their own sense of responsibility. They learn how to become defensive and use an "external locus of control" to blame others for their problems. Consequently, these students rarely accept responsibility for their own actions. Public reprimands, moreover, eventually

GUIDEBOOK

destroy the positive climate in any classroom. Students do not feel free to engage in interactive discussion, contribute ideas, or share experiences if they are never sure when they will incur the teacher's wrath or become the object of the teacher's sarcasm or anger. Respecting the dignity of each and every student is essential for effective classroom management.

Teacher Behaviors

If students perceive that the teacher is treating them unjustly, they may label that teacher "unfair" or "the enemy." The seeds of insurrection may then be planted, causing a small behavior incident to escalate into a major discipline problem.

Teachers need to be careful in their enforcement of classroom rules and consequences. Sometimes the message can be fair, consistent, and positive, but the delivery system can be sarcastic, punitive, and negative.

The "Dirty Dozen" (see Figure 10.1) describes the types of teacher behaviors that can erode a positive classroom climate and undermine any discipline program—no matter how democratic. Teachers can send signals to individual students and to the whole class in both subtle and blatant ways that jeopardize the caring, cooperative classroom. It is remarkable how many people remember an incident from school in which they were treated unjustly. These incidents often become a "defining moment" in shaping their own character. Educators can use Blackline 10.1 (at the end of this selection) to analyze and process critical incidents that they remember from school.

Establishing a Cooperative, Responsible Classroom Environment

---

Burke's "Dirty Dozen"

Teacher Behaviors That Can Erode the Classroom Climate

1. **Sarcasm**

   Students' feelings can be hurt by sarcastic put-downs thinly disguised as humor.

2. **Negative tone of voice**

   Students can "read between the lines" and sense a sarcastic, negative, or condescending tone of voice.

3. **Negative body language**

   A teacher's clenched fists, set jaw, quizzical look, or threatening stance can speak more loudly than any words.

4. **Inconsistency**

   Nothing escapes the students' attention. They are the first to realize the teacher is not enforcing the rules and consequences consistently.

5. **Favoritism**

   "Brown-nosing" is an art and any student in any class can point out the "teacher's pet" who gets special treatment.

6. **Put-downs**

   Sometimes teachers are not aware they are embarrassing a student with subtle put-downs or insults.

7. **Outbursts**

   Teachers are sometimes provoked by students and they "lose it." These teacher outbursts set a bad example for the students and could escalate into more serious problems.

8. **Public reprimands**

   No one wants to be corrected, humiliated, or lose face in front of his or her peers.

9. **Unfairness**

   Taking away promised privileges; scheduling a surprise test; "nitpicking" while grading homework or tests; or assigning punitive homework could be construed as "unfair."

10. **Apathy**

    Students do not want to be ignored. Teachers who forget students' names or appear indifferent will lose students' respect.

11. **Inflexibility**

    Teachers who never adjust homework assignments or test dates to meet the needs of their students appear rigid and uncaring.

12. **Lack of humor**

    Teachers who cannot laugh at themselves usually don't encourage students to take risks and make mistakes. Humorless classes lack energy.

Figure 10.1

Proactive Teachers

The effective classroom teacher engages in the "professional response" to a student's inappropriate question or comment by anticipating the types of problems that could occur in the classroom and developing a repertoire of strategies for solving these problems. This type of proactive approach to preventing discipline problems before they occur is far less time-consuming than the reactive approach where teachers expend all their energy trying to solve problems after they occur. Teachers can utilize the following procedures to engage in a proactive approach.

1. **Anticipate Potential Behavior Problems**

   - Don't allow potential problem students to sit together or work together in groups.
   - Arrange seating patterns so teacher can see and be close to all students.
   - Give both verbal and written directions to eliminate confusion and frustration, which often lead to behavior problems.
   - Structure assignments that are relevant, motivating, and developmentally appropriate.
   - Allow enough time for students to complete assignments.
   - Scan the class frequently to notice or respond to potential problems.
   - Make allowances for students with learning disabilities or physical handicaps so they are not frustrated and overwhelmed.
   - Encourage peer tutoring to help weaker students complete their work without becoming frustrated.
   - Conference with students prone to behavior problems to find out if they have some personal or family problems that might be causing them to be upset or uncooperative.
   - Talk with counselors or support personnel to find out about any previous behavior problems students might have experienced and get suggestions about how to best meet the individual needs of students.

2. Diffuse Minor Problems Before They Become Major Disturbances

Proximity

- Move close to students when you sense a problem developing.

Student-Selected Time-Out

- Allow students to select a time-out from the class or the group. Let the agitated student go to a desk or chair in the corner of the room to collect his or her thoughts or calm down.

Teacher-Selected Time-Out

- Ask the student to go to the time-out area to complete work when his or her behavior is disrupting the group's activity.

3. Address Disruptive Behaviors Immediately

- Ask to speak with the student privately in the hall, after class, or after school.
- Ask the student to explain what he or she thinks the problem is.
- Send "I-messages" telling the student how his or her behavior affects you. For example, "I feel upset when I see you arguing with your group members."
- Try to identify the real problem.
- Remind students of the procedures or rules.
- Handle the problem quickly and calmly.
- Don't create a bigger disruption when attempting to solve problems.
- Don't "lose it" by overreacting and becoming angry.
- Remove the offender(s) from the class so the other students are not an audience.
- Provide students with choices, if possible. For example, "If you choose to work alone rather than with your group, you must complete the entire project by yourself."

The Last Resort: The Principal

Even if teachers provide quality lessons that stimulate students' ideas and relate to real-life situations, and even if they are proactive, there will always be that hard-core group of students who choose to disrupt the rest of the class because the class does not satisfy their needs or because their desire for attention, power, or recognition supersedes their need to learn.

It is the teacher's responsibility to make sure these disruptive students do not destroy the positive atmosphere of the class and cooperative spirit of the learning teams. If teachers do their best to anticipate potential behavior problems, diffuse minor problems before they become major disturbances, and address disruptive behaviors immediately, they should be able to counteract most problems. However, once the teacher has done everything possible to solve the problem and to control the student's negative behavior, he or she must resort to outside help—the administration. Sending the student to the principal is not a cop-out, unless, of course, it is done at the first sign of a problem.

Teachers should never relinquish their position of authority early on in a problem situation with a student or they will lose the respect of that student, and possibly the respect of the whole class. Once the teacher contacts the administrator, he or she is no longer in control; the administrator is. If, however, the teacher has exhausted his or her repertoire of strategies, the student's behavior has not improved, and the disruptive behavior is negatively influencing the entire class, the last resort becomes the next step. The student may also have to be referred to the school counselor, psychologist, special education coordinator, or social worker. It is important that teachers have accurate documentation of the student's behavior (dates, incidents, actions taken). It is also important for teachers to engage in a variety of problem-solving strategies to try to determine the real problem that might be causing the misbehavior.

Blackline 10.2 (at the end of this selection) is an agree/disagree chart where teachers can read the statement about setting the classroom climate and decide whether they agree or disagree. Establishing a comfortable classroom climate is the first step toward effective classroom management.

REFERENCE

Scherer, M. 1998. A conversation with Herb Kohl. *Educational Leadership* 56(1): 8–13.

T wo Blackline masters are provided on the pages that follow:
- Reflecting on the Dirty Dozen
- Agree/Disagree Chart

The mentor can ask the protégé to complete both blacklines. The mentor can discuss the dirty dozen and the protégé's experience with the problem behaviors—encouraging the protégé to avoid the dirty dozen when teaching. The mentor can also help the protégé review his or her ideas about setting a good classroom climate and discuss the best way to create a positive climate for the protégé's students.

Reflecting on the Dirty Dozen

Directions: Review the Dirty Dozen list of teacher behaviors and select one behavior that happened to you when you were a student. Write a short description of the incident.

Behavior: _____

Description: _____

_____

_____

_____

_____

_____

_____

Select one behavior that you may have used with your own students. Write a short description.

_____

_____

_____

_____

_____

_____

_____

_____

_____

Suggest another way either one of these incidents could have been handled. _____

_____

_____

_____

_____

_____

_____

_____

_____

_____

Blackline 10.1

Establishing a Cooperative, Responsible Classroom Environment

Agree/Disagree Chart

Directions: Review the following statements about classroom climate and check if you "agree" or "disagree" with a statement.

Setting the Classroom Climate

	Agree	Disagree
1. The term *rules* sounds too dictatorial. It should be replaced with *expectations* or *principles.*		
2. Logical consequences are the same as punishments.		
3. Writing students' names on the board improves their behavior.		
4. A "time-out" area should be designated in a classroom.		
5. Sarcasm is effective in introducing humor to the classroom.		
6. Classroom management is basically behavior problem solving.		
7. Students should be sent to the principal for violating a rule.		
8. Teachers need to create the rules.		

Select one statement and provide the rationale for either agreeing or disagreeing with it.

Statement #:_____ **Rationale:** _____

_____

_____

_____

_____

_____

_____

Blackline 10.2

Once behavior expectations have been established, teachers must also design lessons to teach the skills students need in order to meet those expectations. Mentors can guide new teachers in creating social skills lessons to help students engage in positive social interactions in whole-class, cooperative groups, and individual learning activities.

What Social Skills Do They Need?

by James Bellanca and Robin Fogarty

Lots of times you have to pretend to join a parade in which you are really not interested in order to get where you're going.

—Christopher Morley

In this selection, the goal is to create a cooperative classroom. To accomplish this goal, the teacher must develop each student's social skills. In short, she teaches them how to cooperate with each other to achieve their shared goal. Cooperative groups are the primary mechanism for students to improve their social skills.

Some students respond to the informal social skills woven into the classroom expectations, roles, and guidelines. Others require more formal direction in acquiring the cooperative social skills.

It is especially helpful to give more formal attention to social skill instruction with younger students and with students in "low tracks." These are the students who can profit most with direct instruction, guided practice, and constructive feedback.

Adapted from *Blueprints for Achievement in the Cooperative Classroom*, 3rd edition, by James Bellanca and Robin Fogarty. © 2002 by Corwin Press. Used with permission.

Deciding on Social Skills

How does a teacher decide which cooperative social skills to teach formally? Which ones are best done informally? The answers to these questions depend on the cooperative skill levels found in each classroom. Students who enter with strong interpersonal skills, either because they developed those at home or in a previous class, need less time on the basics and can advance to the more sophisticated skills.

Informal Instruction

For the informal instruction in social skills, the teacher will reinforce previously learned cooperative skills: roles (e.g., encourager, recorder); rules (e.g., 6-inch voices, one person talks); expectations (e.g., work on your attentive listening), processing (e.g., "Select a cooperative skill to practice and describe how you are improving"), and feedback (e.g., "I'm glad to see how quietly you moved into your teams"). Every activity, every lesson can be heightened by including informal, cooperative skill development within it.

Formal Instruction

For the formal instruction of cooperative skills, it is important that students

- understand the need and value of the skill,
- know the chief behavior indicators of the skill,
- know when to use the skill,
- practice the skill,
- reflect on improved use of the skill, and
- persist in refining the skill until it is automatic.

A Focus on Forming Skills

What Skills Are Best Taught?

In the forming stage, individuals learn how to contribute to and benefit from teamwork. This stage includes learning

- how to move into a group,
- how to move out of a group,
- who talks in a group,
- who listens,
- how to help the group, and
- how to keep on task.

See Figure 11.1 for a chart to use to assess your class.

Assessing Your Class

THE FORMING SKILLS

Skill	Needed	Have	Comments
Move into a group			
Move out of a group			
One person talks at a time			
Stay with group			
Control volume of talk (3", 6", 12")			
Practice all roles			
Keep hands and feet to self			

Figure 11.1

What Social Skills Do They Need?

How to Move Into Groups

Let's consider how you might teach one of the basic forming skills—moving into groups. With a permanent seating arrangement for the groups there is little to worry about in moving desks. If, however, desks are moved in and out of rows, then teach, practice, reinforce, and reflect on these model procedures:

1. Say, "Pick up your books and set them against the wall. Sit down." (Do one row at a time.)
2. Give each student a group assignment:
   - Who Is In Which Group? (Use cards with colored dots, group names, or another group assignment method.)
   - Who Has Which Role? (Assign roles appropriate for the lesson and the students: calculator, reader, encourager, etc.)
   Display the desired group pattern on the overhead or blackboard.
3. Say, "Move your seats so you are sitting with your new group." Invite the students to form their groups quietly. If the class is too noisy, stop the activity until all students are quiet; reinforce the class's quiet expectation and begin again.
4. Give positive reinforcement for a completed, quiet move and invite the students to gather their books or to get their work materials for today's task.
5. After the task is done, instruct students to put their materials back, to rearrange their desks (put diagram on overhead or blackboard), and to sit until they are dismissed.

Teaching Other Forming Skills

Determine which of the other forming skills on the list (Figure 11.1) will help your students work on task in a group. For instance, if you have a low tolerance for noise or a particular class is noisy, use a direct-instruction lesson to reinforce your expectations for quiet. Use your signal to get the class's attention. When all are quiet, give your expectation (speak in voices you can hear no more than six inches away); sit in a group and demonstrate a six-inch voice; guide practice until you can say "Great! You have it." When the class strays, repeat the cycles at the "teachable moment."

A Focus on Norming Skills

Every teacher deserves the norms of student-to-student interaction to be positive and encouraging. Unfortunately, the norms learned from TV's humor, sports figures, and the playground may be negative and discouraging. To change the norms from negative put-downs, disrespectful slurs, and inattention to good social skills, explicit attention from the teacher is needed.

One skill most practical to initiate in any classroom is encouraging. In the TV-saturated world of students, the art of the comic put-down makes peer encouragement a highly needed "basic" skill for the cooperative classroom.

Preparation

Solid formal instruction of a social skill requires the same careful preparation found in any procedural lesson (see Figure 11.2). To teach a social skill, first use a "hook." A hook, is usually a role play, a structured group experience, or a story that illustrates the social skill lesson. (See the IALAC lesson at the end of this selection. Other hooks include people searches, agree/disagree statements, or think-pair-share). After the hook, create a T-chart that includes the words and behaviors common to the social skill (see Figure 11.3 for a sample). The T-chart, applicable to every cooperative social skill, helps students understand the specific behaviors that make up a chosen social skill. Instead of dealing with abstract words such as *encouragement* or *attentive listening*, the students work with specific behaviors. What does encouragement sound like? What does it look like?

What Social Skills Do They Need?

Teaching Social Skills

Hook The hook lessons lay the groundwork. For the younger students and other students who lack the cooperative skills or thrive in a peer culture that reinforces negative social skills, more time and more energy on practice, reinforcement, and recognition of the essential cooperative skills are necessary. All students need some form of encouragement to develop these skills.

Teach Use a T-chart or web with the students. This will enable them, after the hook lesson, to generate the specific behaviors of the social skill. Do charts for both the acceptable behaviors (i.e., listening) and for the non-acceptable behavior (i.e., non-listening). Add behaviors the students miss from your preparation charts. Post the charts on the bulletin board or provide a copy for each student's notebook.

Practice Guided skill practice, massed in short bursts, is a necessary step after presenting the hook and teaching the basics. For instance, active listening pairs can practice with each other in three- to five-minute segments. Student A listens as student B shares an idea, explains a selected concept or describes an event. After the practice, A self-evaluates his or her listening practice. On the next day, they reverse roles. As the pairs develop their listening skills, begin to focus more and more on using course content as the subject for practice.

Extended practices give students a chance to reinforce the listening skill. Build a listening component into each lesson. In the criteria for lesson success, tell the students what is expected with the skill: (e.g., "I want to see at least five listening behaviors from each group" or "On your group evaluation, I expect you to report five examples of active listening").

Observe As students practice the desired social skills, the teacher or designated student observers watch for examples. To help with the observations, some teachers keep a checklist. While the groups work on task, the teacher records samples of the specified social skills. After the groups process their work, the teacher recognizes the positive examples he or she observed and encourages continued practice of the skills by all students.

Practice should continue until the social skill becomes automatic. This takes time. When the skill is first introduced with the hook, the students enter the first stage of change: awareness. If the hook catches them, they will perceive the need for the skill and increase commitment to improvement. After positive feedback they refine and refine until the skill becomes automatic.

Reflect Self-reflection helps students develop intrinsic motivation.

Figure 11.2

After creating the T-chart, you may choose to prepare a display. A large bulletin board celebrating encouragement with words and pictures, a model T-chart on the wall, or a T-chart handout provides a daily reminder.

As needed, practice the behaviors with a role play, simulation, or imbedded group task. Observe and record examples of students using the behaviors in practice. Conclude with a reflection using a stem (I like encouragement because . . .; encouragement is most helpful when . . .).

At some point in the putting together of cooperative groups, take time to give feedback on progress being made in becoming effective groups. This will help the class stay focused on setting the norm for positive interactions.

Obviously, students who already have the forming and norming skills well in hand do not need to spend time on these basics of cooperation. Share the expectations and unite the group teams with them—they will be ready to wade into the course content and to learn the more advanced social skills.

T-Chart

ENCOURAGEMENT

Sounds Like	Looks Like
Keep at it.	thumbs up
Atta girl, Atta boy!	pat on back
Way to go!	smile
Here's another way to look at it . . .	head nodding
Great idea.	beckoning hand
Keep trying.	
You're getting close.	

Figure 11.3

What Social Skills Do They Need?

A Focus on Advanced Social Skills

The forming and norming social skills are only the start. If students turn these skills into habits in a flash, as many do, they are ready to tackle the more advanced social skills. The more advanced the class becomes in its collaborations, the more opportunities appear for infusion of social skills into lesson designs. The more skilled students become with the social skills, the more productive and on-task the groups will function. The more "time on task" caused by skillful group work, the better the achievement results.

As explained earlier, social skills do not develop without deliberate, specific, and repeated attention. In teaching social skills, the explicit model outlined has proven most beneficial for the introduction of a skill. Integration of a skill and reflection on its use are the two keys most likely to open the door to groups best able to monitor their own behavior. Figure 11.4 outlines the six phases of the small-group process. Coupled with each phase is a listing of suggested social skills appropriate for explicit attention during the instruction of that phase.

For example, it seems appropriate (and probably necessary) to teach students how to disagree with ideas, not people, as groups show evidence of storming. Similarly, as groups show signs of exquisite performance and become high-functioning teams, it is appropriate to target the more sophisticated skill of reaching consensus.

Although the charted skills are probably somewhat developmentally listed, individual situations dictate the depth and/or sequence of the actual teaching of social skills. Each teacher must decide on the final design of the social skill introductions. Reference to the chart is suggested only to help plan explicitly for the wide range of social skills needed.

As the social skill instruction develops throughout the year, explicit inclusion of skills from each of the categories is important. Thus, when trying to choose which social skills to teach, how many skills to include, and when to teach which skills, the categories may be helpful for picking the actual menu of items.

GUIDEBOOK

Phases of Introduction of Social Skills

PHASE	SOCIAL SKILLS Communication (C), Trust (T), Leadership (L), Conflict Resolution (CR)	
Forming *to organize groups and establish behavior guidelines*	Use a 6" voice. (C) Listen to your neighbor. (C) Stay with the group. (C)	Heads together. (C) Do your job. (L) Help each other. (L)
Norming *to complete assigned tasks and build effective relationships*	Include all members. (L) Encourage others. (L) Listen with focus. (T)	Let all participate. (L) Respect each other's opinions. (T) Stay on task. (L)
Conforming *to promote critical thinking and maximize the learning of all*	Clarify. (C) Paraphrase ideas. (C) Give examples. (C)	Probe for differences. (CR) Generate alternatives. (CR) Seek consensus. (CR)
Storming *to function effectively and enable the work of the team*	Sense tone. (C) Disagree with idea not person. (CR) Keep an open mind. (T)	See all points of view. (CR) Try to agree. (CR) Contribute own ideas. (L)
Performing *to foster higher-level thinking skills, creativity, and intuition*	Elaborate on ideas. (C) Integrate ideas. (L) Justify ideas. (CR)	Extend ideas. (C) Synthesize. (L) Reach consensus. (CR)
Re-forming *to apply across curriculum and transfer into life beyond the classroom*	Begin cycle of social skills again—each time: • New group is formed. • New member joins the group. • Member is absent from group. • New task is given. • Long absences occur.	

Figure 11.4

What Social Skills Do They Need?

The most successful teachers of cooperative learning are natural modelers of the cooperative social skills. These teachers go beyond modeling social skills in a "demo" lesson. They model positive social skills in all interactions with students. They speak softly, often with a "six-inch voice"; they establish eye-contact and focus their listening on what is said; they probe for differences in ideas, not the person. They avoid shouting at students, arguing, or dominating discussions. Most important, the students experience this high level of social skills in action and more easily copy what the teacher is doing. Thus, these teachers put in place the axiom, "Do as I do and as I say."

The caveat to all: Do not COVER social skills. Each skill is meant to be modeled, practiced, and used throughout the students' time in the classroom. One social skill mastered by the class each semester is more helpful than 20 "covered"! Less is more.

If teachers are under inordinant pressure to cover curriculum, it is sometimes difficult for them to see where social skills "fit." Let us say only this: whether a teacher takes the time to introduce the forming skills because those are needed for basic classroom management, or takes time to teach the more complex skills at the performing or norming stage, the pay off is always greater mastery of content. Sometimes it is necessary for a teacher to throw out miniscule facts in order to find the time. More likely, the improved social skills will enable more on-task, on-focus, concentrated student effort. The results of such effort and such increased student responsibility to learning are obvious not only for increased achievement, but also for an increase in the lifelong skills of collaborating with others.

Conclusion

Because cooperative learning teaches students by word and by example how to work well with others, it promotes higher student achievement. As a result of learning how to develop the social skills necessary for learning from the notion that "many hands together are better than one hand alone," students have increased support and assistance to meet the challenges of the curriculum, overcome obstacles to learning, and benefit from multiple points of view.

For the teacher, there are benefits beyond student achievement. When a teacher lays the foundation of a less stressful, more positive classroom culture, students help each other without bullying, violent interaction or annoying distractions. When the teacher builds the groups and works them through the stages of development, she expands the students' capabilities to work successfully in family and work collaborations throughout life.

What Social Skills Do They Need?

BIBLIOGRAPHY

Barell, J. 1998. *Problem-based learning: An inquiry approach.* Thousand Oaks, CA: Corwin Press.

Bellanca, J., and R. Fogarty. 1986. *Catch them thinking: A handbook of classroom strategies.* Palatine, IL: IRI/SkyLight Training and Publishing.

Caine, R., and G. Caine. 1994. *Making connections: Teaching and the human brain.* New York: Addison-Wesley/Innovative Learning Publications.

Costa, A. L. 1985. *Developing minds.* Alexandria, VA: Association for Supervision and Curriculum Development.

Feuerstein, R. 1980. *Instrumental achievement.* Baltimore, MD: University Park Press.

Johnson, D., and R. Johnson. 1978. Social interdependence within instruction. *Journal of Research and Development in Education.* 12(1): 1–152.

———. 1986. *Circles of learning: Cooperation in the classroom.* Alexandria, VA: Association for Supervision and Curriculum Development.

Three sample lessons are provided on the pages that follow:

• Tell/Retell (elementary)

• IALAC (middle)

• The Nonlistening Challenge (secondary)

All three give ideas for teaching social skills. Protégés may adapt any of these lessons to their classrooms with guidance from their mentors. Mentors may also encourage protégés to create their own lessons for teaching specific social skills.

BLUEPRINT: ELEMENTARY LESSON

Tell/Retell

SETTING UP THE SCAFFOLDING

To teach about attentive listening, prepare a bulletin board with an attentive listening theme. Show pictures of (a) a class attending to the teacher, (b) group members attending to each other, (c) a class attending to a visitor, and (d) a class attending to a student speaker.

Make and display a T-chart on the bulletin board.

ATTENTIVE LISTENING	
Sounds Like	**Looks Like**
1. "uh huh"	1. eyes alert and focused on talker
2. "I see."	2. mirroring emotions
3. clarifying questions	3. leaning forward or toward speaker
4. silence	4. head nods at right time
5. paraphrasing	5. taking notes
6.	6.
7.	7.
8.	8.

WORKING THE CREW

Gather students around and explain the bulletin board and chart. Have volunteers share how it feels to have someone's full attention. Solicit several answers. Demonstrate with the principal, another teacher, or a volunteer what attentive listening looks and sounds like.

Divide students into pairs. Instruct one student to share a fun adventure. Instruct the other to attend closely so he or she can repeat the story. Walk among the pairs and give a thumbs-up to each child seen listening.

Use this monitoring time to be aware of misbehaving students, especially during these times when interpersonal skills and social behavior are the focus. Be aware of "the kid who..." seeks attention, feels inadequate, makes the power play, is looking for revenge, or shows signs of emotional disturbances.

When a misbehaving student exhibits a deficit in a social skill, take time to address the social skill with clear, directed, and effective action. Say, for example, in this "Tell/Retell" lesson, one student is causing a lot of distraction during the partner interaction by clowning around and seeking the attention of the students around him or her. This is the teachable moment. You could begin with the strategy recognizing a student who is modeling the proper behavior. For example, standing near the attention seeker who is faking falling out of his chair to get attention from his partner and others, the teacher might say to a nearby pair: "I like the way you're positioned for good listening. Eye-to-eye, knee-to-knee is how attentive listening partners often sit."

By focusing on the desired modeled behavior and by telling explicitly what it looks like, the teacher cues the misbehaving student about two things: (1) modeling desired behavior gets the attention of the teacher, and (2) the desired behavior looks like this.

Although these actions seem like simple classroom management, by addressing the incident within the context of learning, the teacher adds power to the reinforcement strategy. Additionally, the teacher can talk about the incident or use the groups' reflection time to lead discussion on the idea of "seeking attention" as "clowning around."

REFLECTING ON THE DESIGN

To process affectively, conduct a brief sharing, then let several listeners tell the class what they heard in their partner interactions. Praise them for good listening. Have them tell how it felt to have someone listen so carefully.

To process the social skill of active listening, ask students to tell about someone they think is a good listener.

To process cognitively, continue to practice on succeeding days. Begin each practice with a review of the T-chart. End it with praise to the attentive listeners.

After several short practices, have a discussion in which the class talks about (a) why listening attentively is a good idea and (b) what times in class and at home are important for attentive listening. This metacognitive talk helps students transfer the social skill beyond the lesson.

BLUEPRINT: MIDDLE SCHOOL LESSON

IALAC

SETTING UP THE SCAFFOLDING

Use Sidney Simon's IALAC (I Am Lovable And Capable) strategy or tell the students a unique version of the IALAC story using the following sample. Hold the IALAC sign.

(Name) , age _____ , woke up one school morning looking at _____ pajama top. _____ saw a giant, neon sign. It flashed on and off, IALAC. _____ knew at once this meant "I Am Lovable And Capable." _____ dressed and ran quickly to the kitchen. _____ was very excited. Before _____ could speak, _____ sister said, "You pea-brain, (rip off a corner of the sign) what did you do with my new jacket?" "Nothing," _____ said. "Man," whined _____ sister, "_____ is a jerk." (rip) "_____," said _____ unhappy mother. "You oughta know better. Why can't you use your brain (rip) once in a while. Your big brother would never do nothing so stupid." (rip) "But Mom," _____ said, "I . . . ." "Don't sass me back," said _____ mother. "You are such a smart mouth." (rip) _____ saw _____ sister smurking. "Smart mouth, smart mouth." (rip, double rip)

By the time _____ left for the school bus, one-half of IALAC was ripped. On the school bus, George Burns said _____ was an idiot (rip), cry baby, and jerk (rip). _____ sister laughed each time. (triple rip)

In the first class period, Mrs. Smartzolla asked to put _____ homework problem on the board. _____ forgot a (name item) in the formula. "_____," she moaned, "how slow can you be? I've told you a thousand times." (rip)

In language arts, Mr. Thomas barked at _____ for getting the lowest score on the vocabulary quiz. (rip) He read how _____ had misspelled _____ to the whole class and said sarcastically, "I guess no one could ever accuse you of a gorgative brain." (rip) Everyone laughed. (rip)

By the end of the day, _____ went home with a very small IALAC sign. _____ was very upset.

The next day, _____ woke to find IALAC on _____ pajamas, but very small. _____ hoped that today would be better. _____ wanted to keep _____ IALAC so much.
(Continue this story with additional IALAC demolition.)

WORKING THE CREW

After the story, place students into groups of five, each group with one piece of 3" x 5" newsprint and a marker. Appoint a recorder in each group to write down all the different ways they have their IALACs ripped. After five minutes, ask several recorders to share samples.

Instruct the groups to make a second list: What things can they do or say to increase people's IALACs? After five minutes, ask for samples.

Ask each group to pick the three best IALAC builders from its list. Make an unduplicated class list to hang in the classroom.

REFLECTING ON THE DESIGN

To process affectively, have students finish this statement: It feels good when . . . .

To process socially, ask students to take time today to use positive statements with a family member.

To process cognitively, post the encouragement T-chart (Figure 11.3) and discuss how the class can use it to build each other's IALACs.

To process metacognitively, ask students to discuss what they did well in the groups, and what they would do differently next time to help their groups.

BLUEPRINT: SECONDARY SCHOOL LESSON

The Nonlistening Challenge

SETTING UP THE SCAFFOLDING

Divide the class into pairs. Ask students to think of a recent time when someone important paid close attention to them. As they tell you how they knew they were getting attentive listening, make a T-chart for attentive listening.

ATTENTIVE LISTENING	
Sounds Like	**Looks Like**
1. "uh huh"	1. eyes alert and focused on talker
2. "I see."	2. mirroring emotions
3. clarifying questions	3. leaning forward/toward speaker
4. silence	4. head nods at right time
5. paraphrasing	5. taking notes

Identify the oldest student in each pair. Those students are As. The younger student in each pair is B. Invite A to listen to the first instructions. Each A is to think of a time in the past year when someone did not listen. What happened? How did it feel? The As are to prepare their stories while the Bs are given instructions.

WORKING THE CREW

Invite the Bs to review the T-chart. Now say, "Now that you have reviewed how to behave when you listen with attention, you are to do your 100 percent, absolute, total best NOT to listen to your partner's story! You are to model non-listening behaviors." Require these guidelines: (1) all must stay in the room; (2) speakers do their best to tell the story; (3) don't hurt each other; and (4) stop when the teacher gives the signal (e.g., lights off, hands up).

What Social Skills Do They Need?

Move around the room and note the students' behavior. Be aware of genuine misbehavior in students, especially during these times in which interpersonal skills and social behavior are the focus. Be aware of "the kid who..." seeks attention, feels inadequate, makes the power play, looks for revenge, or shows signs of emotional disturbances. When a misbehaving student exhibits a deficit in a social skill, take time to address the social skill with clear, directed, and effective action.

Even better, in the "Non-listening" lesson activity you have asked students to deliberately demonstrate poor listening skills. Now, take advantage of this activity. Find the student who takes over the partner interview as the dialogue becomes very one-sided. This is the teachable moment to address the question, "What do you do with the kid who...takes over?"

Moving this student into a leadership role seems to be an applicable strategy for this situation. For example, in the midst of this partner interaction, tell the class to "freeze frame." Suggest that to reinforce the roles of each partner, one pair will model or role play an interaction. Select the pair with the partner who has "taken over" and have them model the desired actions. Surprisingly, the misbehavior disappears instantly and the desired behavior is modeled in true leadership style. However, since the non-listening activity is intentionally set up to focus on misbehavior, this "power play" might be tried by others.

By designating a leadership role for the "offender" in front of the class, the "power play" in the small group is no longer as interesting to the misbehaving student. So be sure to highlight the reason the strategy of giving a leadership role works. In addition, this same student has actually modeled the very behavior he or she was lacking. Although this may be simple classroom management, by addressing this incident within the context of social skill instruction, the teacher adds power to the situation with positive reinforcement. She or he also can talk about the incident or use the groups' reflection time to lead discussion on the idea of power plays as taking over the group.

After two minutes, stop the activity. Have each pair shake hands, with the Bs apologizing to the As.

REFLECTING ON THE DESIGN

For affective processing, conclude with a discussion of the positive effects on a speaker and a listener when attention goes both ways.

To process the social skill of listening, have students describe a TV character who is a good listener.

To process cognitively, put a double T-chart for non-listening on the board. What did non-listening look like, sound like, and feel like?

For metacognitve processing, discuss with the class instances when they may have experienced the same negative feelings caused by non-listening.

Mentors can help new teachers recognize the cause of many behavior problems and develop a repertoire of problem-solving strategies. Since classroom management problems cause so many teachers to leave the profession, it is critical that protégés recognize potential discipline problems and address them appropriately.

Students with Behavior Problems

by **Kay Burke**

Addressing Behavior Problems

When students display inappropriate behavior, they do so because they have the mistaken goal that it will get them the recognition and acceptance they want.

> —Dreikers et al. as cited in Vaughn, Bos, and Schumm 2000

Behavior problems constitute student behaviors that cause disruptions in the class. This type of behavior can be directed at other students or the teacher, and can include student behaviors such as talking when another student or the teacher is talking, name calling, fighting, arguing, throwing things, or getting up out of one's seat. Although any of these behaviors is enough to disrupt a classroom, they can be controlled by a proactive teacher.

Curwin and Mendler (1988) proposed the 80-15-5 model where they estimated that 80 percent of students in most classes never or rarely break the classroom rules and cause disruptions. They estimated that about 15 percent of students break rules on a regular basis

Adapted from *What to Do with the Kid Who. . .: Developing Cooperation, Self-Discipline, and Responsibility in the Classroom* by Kay Burke, pp. 200–235. © 2000 by Corwin Press. Used with permission.

and 5 percent are chronic rule breakers. However, Walsh (as cited in Levin and Nolan 1996) reports that some teachers spend as much as 30 to 80 percent of their time addressing discipline problems. It is evident that the successful teacher of the twenty-first century needs to be able to manage students in order to maximize the time spent on learning. With the increased emphasis on high-stakes standardized tests, standards, and accountability, teachers must increase time-on-task to prepare students to meet rigorous academic goals.

Ripple Effect

Teachers are concerned not only with addressing student disruptions, but also with the "ripple effect" (Kounin as cited in Levin and Nolan 1996). The ripple effect results from the initial misbehavior, the methods the teacher uses to curb the misbehavior, and the resultant behavior of the targeted student. "Studies have shown that rough and threatening teacher behavior causes student anxieties, which lead to additional disruptive behaviors from on-looking students. However, students who see that disruptive students comply with the teacher's control technique rate their teacher as fairer and are themselves less distracted from their classwork than when they observe unruly students defying the teacher" (Smith as cited in Levin and Nolan 1996). There are, therefore, many complex dynamics that come into play when a teacher addresses even a minor behavior disruption.

At-Risk Students

Educators often use the term *at risk* to describe a particular category of students. Slavin (as cited in Manning and Baruth 1995), referring only to academically at-risk learners, defines *at risk* as referring to students who, on the basis of several risk factors, are unlikely to graduate from high school. Yet, educators are also confronted with children and adolescents who have other at-risk factors due to "health problems, substance use, disabilities, socioeconomic status (SES), attempted suicides, and other behaviors such as experimenting with drugs and sexual activity" (Manning and Baruth 1995, p. 6).

The difficult challenge is labeling students, because at-risk conditions are not clear cut and what causes one student to be at risk may not affect other students the same way. Short, Short, and Blanton (1994) discuss how students who are low achievers in school activities are described as at-risk students. Some of the characteristics they describe for an at-risk child include students who have not mastered basic skills, have been retained, are below grade level on test scores, have a poor attendance record, have a record of suspensions, qualify for free or reduced lunch, or have a history of high mobility. In addition, at-risk students could have experienced child abuse or neglect; abused substances; have experienced racial, cultural, or gender bias; or come from a dysfunctional family. "A large proportion of school-age children either are or will be poor, multicultural/minority, and from nontraditional homes—all characteristics that have been related to school and social failure" (Short, Short, and Blanton 1994, p. 75).

Even though the characteristics of at-risk students are mostly extrinsic to the child, they still have a profound effect on the development and performance of the student in school. Moreover, at-risk students often display characteristics that distinguish them from the rest of their peer group. This difference can cause tremendous social pressures that result in their not fitting in with the social structure of the class and exhibiting recurrent discipline problems in school (Short, Short, and Blanton 1994).

Teachers have to be aware of the "baggage" many students bring to school each day. They need to be as fair and consistent as possible with maintaining high expectations for all students and enforcing classroom procedures, rules, and consequences. They must also, however, be aware of students' situations and the philosophical idea that "fair is not always equal," and each student should be handled with some consideration, respect, and flexibility, if possible.

Identifying Antecedents

The events or conditions that immediately precede instances of problem behavior are called antecedents (Kauffman, et al.

1993). Teachers can keep an anecdotal record or written notes to describe a pattern of when, where, and under what conditions the behavior most often occurs.

For example, if Jimmy usually becomes rude and obnoxious right before a major test, the teacher might have a private conference with him to find out why. Maybe he can't read the directions or he feels inadequate. Maybe he can't handle the time constraints of a test and would like more time. Maybe he can't understand the multiple-choice format and would do better on a performance task that demonstrates what he actually knows rather than how well he guesses.

Effective teachers look for patterns to identify specific events, times of the day, or activities that cause students to act out. One event that often causes disruptions is assigning students to groups. If Kathy hates Jenny because of a problem with an old boyfriend, she may cause a disruption to avoid working with Jenny in a cooperative project. Obviously, teachers cannot anticipate every potential problem, but the proactive teacher can diffuse potential problems before they become major problems.

Coercive Interaction

Kauffman, et al. (1993) discuss the typical situations that occur when a student finds a teacher's expectations and demands aversive or unpleasant. The teacher, in turn, finds the student's refusal to follow his or her order also aversive and therefore restates the demand and adds a threat or punishment as an "incentive." The student then feels challenged in front of his or her peer group and becomes even louder, more obnoxious, and more threatened, causing the teacher to respond with more severe threats of punishment. This type of coercive interaction continues until the teacher "wins" and the student backs down, which sometimes is temporary, and then the student continues to seek revenge on the teacher for "beating" him or her in public. Another typical situation results in the teacher backing down and not following through with the threat, in which case the student wins. In this case, sometimes

Coercive Interaction

Teacher asks student to complete page of math problems.

Student says, "I don't know how to do this crap!"

Teacher says, "Yes you do, we just did some problems like these yesterday. Get started now."

Student slams book closed, saying "Ain't doin' it!"

Teacher goes to student's desk, opens book, hands student pencil, says in angry tone, "Get started now!"

Student shoves book off desk.

Teacher squeezes student's shoulder, growls, "Pick that book up, young man!"

Student jumps to feet, says, "Get your hands off me, bitch! You pick it up! You can't make me do nothin'!"

Teacher yells, "That's it! I've had enough of this! Pick that book up and get to work now or you're outta here to the office!"

Kauffman, et al. 1993, p. 31. Reprinted with permission.

Figure 12.1

the teacher is "out to get the student" the rest of the year because he or she lost face in front of the class. The best situation that can occur is a win-win situation where both parties compromise, save face, and address the real cause of the problem and possible solutions in private. Figure 12.1 represents a typical coercive classroom interaction. Skillful teachers can avoid coercive interactions and recognize when students are baiting them to seek attention or engage in a power struggle.

Students Who Seek Attention

Glenn gets up from his desk and slowly walks down the aisle to the pencil sharpener and starts sharpening a long pencil. Each time he finishes sharpening, he puts the pencil inside again until it becomes a stub.

"Sit down," yells Mrs. Martinez. "We're trying to work here and you're not supposed to be out of your desk."

"I'm just trying to sharpen my pencil," Glenn announces loudly to the entire class. "Is that a crime? Excuse me for living!"

Mrs. Martinez walks over to Glenn and whispers quietly, "Glenn, the class is working on their group art project and your group really needs your help."

Glenn reluctantly rejoins his group and proceeds to draw a happy face on the back of Mary's black sweater with a piece of hot-pink colored chalk.

"You jerk," shrieks Mary. "When are you going to grow up?"

Glenn laughs and looks around the room to see all the students and Mrs. Martinez staring at him.

Mrs. Martinez walks over and taps Glenn on the shoulder and they both walk into the hall.

Solving the Problem

Many misbehaving students are seeking extra attention. Albert (1989) says that all people need a certain amount of attention to feel like they belong and are an important part of the social group. "In contrast, students who misbehave for attention are never satisfied with a normal amount. They want more and more, as if they carry around with them a bucket labeled 'attention' that they expect the teacher to fill" (p. 26).

Attention seekers are students who seek independence, but spend a great deal of their time complaining to others that they cannot control what is happening in their lives. "They see themselves as victims of circumstance and strive to gain attention by keeping adults busy with them" (Dinkmeyer, McKay, and Dinkmeyer 1980, p. 252).

Many attention seekers are discouraged students who may become obnoxiously loud and silly or may resort to immature acts like pushing books off a desk or trying to trip someone to get noticed. Attention seekers are like stage performers; they require an audience. They do get noticed, but many of them eventually get rejected by their peers and their teacher, who grow tired of their attempts to always be in the limelight. The attention seeker's idea of success is to be on stage, even if their actions violate the dignity and rights of other students and earn him or her the hostility of those who feel attacked or violated (Dinkmeyer and Losoncy 1980). In the elementary grades, attention seekers usually gear their performance towards the teacher, but as they move to upper grades, they prefer a wider audience that includes their classmates, guidance counselors, administrators, and sometimes the entire school community (Albert 1989).

Appropriate Attention

The origins of attention-seeking behavior can range from students not receiving enough attention at home to students not knowing how to ask for attention in an appropriate manner. The greatest challenge for teachers is to change the behavior of the attention seeker by giving him or her as little attention as possible when the misbehavior occurs. Bellanca and Fogarty (1991, p. 73) recommend the following strategies to teachers:

- Highlight students who are behaving appropriately.
- Move the student out of the spotlight by giving him an errand to run.
- Distract the student with a question.
- Attend to the attention seeker positively when he is on task.

By encouraging attention seekers to succeed in individual or group work and by noticing and encouraging their accomplishments, teachers and students can reinforce appropriate behavior with positive attention. The goal is to encourage attention seekers to strive for positive attention from peers and teachers rather than resort to negative attention to fulfill their needs.

Since one method to prevent students from seeking attention is to identify the goal of the misbehavior, teachers should help students to analyze their own behavior. The Newspaper Model (see Figure 12.2) allows attention seekers to analyze their actions and reflect on the causes and effects of their behavior. (A Blackline master of a Newspaper Model that teachers can use with their students is provided at the end of this selection [Blackline 12.1]). Teachers should work with students to fill out the form in order to discuss and reflect on the process.

The Newspaper Model

Ask the student to state what he or she thinks the problem is, and describe his or her take on who is involved, what usually happens, when the problem occurs, where it occurs, and why it happens. The attention seeker should write a paragraph about the situation and share the paragraph with others involved in the problem, taking steps to stop the problem.

Name: _Glenn_   Date: _Feb. 3_

Problem: _I got in trouble for sharpening my pencil and drawing on Mary's sweater._

Who	What	When	Where	Why
(me) Glenn	Caused a disturbance by sharpening my pencil and drawing on Mary's sweater	Tuesday Feb. 3 during 5th period	In Mrs. Martinez's art class at Oak School	Because I was mad that the teacher and Mary yelled at me

Write a paragraph describing your view of what happened.

I got mad because John and Mary think they are better than me. They never use my ideas when we meet in groups. They are always calling me names and putting me down. I went to sharpen my pencil to get away from the group. Then I got mad when Mary laughed when I got in trouble. I showed the class who got the last laugh.

Signed: _Glenn_

Have another group member write a paragraph about the situation.

I called Glenn a jerk because he is always fooling around instead of helping. I know I shouldn't call him names, but I get real frustrated with him. I laughed at him when Mrs. Martinez yelled at him because I told him not to do it. I get very angry at him.

Signed: _Mary_

Figure 12.2

Educators must remember that the number of students seeking attention will probably increase commensurate with the lack of attention students may be experiencing in their families and the large sizes of classes and schools. When students have to compete for attention each day, they may resort to more violent ways to capture the attention of their parents, teachers, classmates, and the media.

Other Strategies Teachers Can Use with Students Who Seek Attention

- Help the student find an area where she can shine. Find a specific interest or strength she has so that she can get attention in a positive way.
- Find the student a study buddy. Sometimes a student who lacks friends tries to compensate by acting out.
- Give the student an option of a short time-out period. He can go to a corner of the room and cool down or write in a journal about his feelings.
- Analyze the newspaper model to see when, where, and why most incidents occur. Remember to review the antecedents or context. If incidents usually arise from the student being involved with certain people or situations, try to avoid placing the student in those situations.
- When a student does something well, encourage her.
- When a student raises his hand, call on him quickly to give him positive attention for an answer or for trying to answer a question.
- Give the student legitimate positive attention by allowing her to run errands, lead the pledge, clean the board, collect papers, or take part in other positions of responsibility and honor. Be careful to rotate these privileges so the other students don't resent her.
- Have a secret signal to give the student from across the room to remind him when he is doing something to get attention.

MENTORING

Students with Behavior Problems

Students Who Seek Power

Mrs. Bradley returns the students' English tests and then asks if there are any questions.

"This sucks!" exclaims Brian. "You can't take off points for misspellings. We weren't allowed to use dictionaries!"

"You should know how to spell the words you write. I take off five points for every error."

"You can't do that!" Brian yells, moving forward in his desk. "This test was on short stories and we were supposed to describe the plots. Who cares if we misspelled a few words. You missed the point of the test! We didn't get to use spell check!"

"Excuse me, young man," Mrs. Bradley shrieks as her face turns red. "This is my class and I will be the one who decides what I will and will not grade!"

"This sucks," mutters Brian. "I want to go to my counselor to get transferred to Mrs. Brown's English class."

"You're not getting a pass from me," counters Mrs. Bradley.

"I don't need a pass—I'm outta here." Brian grabs his backpack and kicks his desk before he bolts from the room.

The other students glare at Mrs. Bradley in silence.

Solving the Problem

> I believe that the need for power is the core—the absolute core—of almost all school problems (Glasser as cited in Gough 1987, p. 658).

Students who seek independence sometimes engage in power conflicts with adults because they are determined not to do what adults want. Curwin and Mendler (1988) warn teachers not to get caught in a power trap: "Commit yourself to avoiding power struggles, even if it means initially backing down. Remember that continuation of a power struggle makes you look foolish and out of control. You must be prepared to see long-term victory (a cooperative, positive classroom climate) as more important than short-term winning" (p. 105).

Glasser (1986) feels that students, even good students, don't feel important in school because no one listens to them.

Moreover, students who receive poor grades and are considered discipline problems cannot feel important from the standpoint of academic performance and acceptance. Glasser asserts that students would work harder in school if they had more freedom and fun. Mendler (1997) says "it is estimated that 70 to 80 percent of challenging student behavior in school is primarily attributable to outside factors such as dysfunctional families, violence in our culture, the effects of drugs and alcohol, and fragmented communities" (p. 4). Yet, teachers cannot abrogate their responsibility for controlling student behavior in their classrooms by blaming it on outside forces. The challenge is to teach all students.

Most often, the power base in schools is tilted in favor of the teachers. Teachers have the power to threaten students and are able to back up those threats with minus points, minutes in the time-out area, detention, notes to parents, suspensions, expulsion, and the ultimate weapon—failure. Despite all the power teachers have, Glasser (1986) says that half the students still won't work because they don't feel they have any control over their lives. They are discouraged because they have so little to say about what they learn, when they learn it, and how they learn it. Students are discouraged and they don't have the patience to wait it out until teachers and the school system give them more say in their education. Power seekers vent this frustration through the use of temper tantrums, verbal tantrums, and quiet noncompliance (Albert 1989).

More and more schools are recognizing the need to empower students by allowing them to be involved in setting classroom rules and having some choice in what they study and how they will be assessed. "Students also need to learn to look for more effective behaviors while they wait, but they have less power over their lives than adults and little confidence that the school will change for the better. If we can restructure schools so that they are more satisfying, we can expect many more students to be patient when they are frustrated" (Glasser 1986, p. 55). The following tactics (see Figure 12.3) can be used by teachers to avoid getting pulled into a power struggle.

Tactics Teachers Can Use with Power Seekers

- Don't grab the hook. Teachers should not fall into the power trap, especially in front of the class.
- Avoid and defuse direct confrontations.
- Listen to the problem in private.
- Recognize the student's feelings.
- Privately acknowledge the power struggle.
- Do not embarrass students publicly.
- Give the students choices in their academic work.
- Place the power seeker in a leadership role.
- Encourage independent thinking, but not anarchy!

Figure 12.3

Students who seek power often try to dominate the entire class and their groups. If they cannot control the class, the teacher, or the school, they might consider their cooperative group as their personal power base. Teachers should monitor the roles assigned to group members and make sure power seekers are fulfilling their assignments without trying to take control of the entire group.

Another strategy teachers can use is to review the specific roles assigned to each group member and the responsibilities of each of these roles. Teachers can also remind students that group roles are rotated so everyone can get a chance to be the organizer or the group leader. If the tasks are structured so that they allow a great deal of choice, creativity, and freedom, power seekers should be satisfied that they do, in fact, have some control over their lives. This can help them to learn how to develop positive leadership qualities rather than negative dictatorial traits.

Figure 12.4 shows the phases in a power struggle.

Phases of a Power Struggle

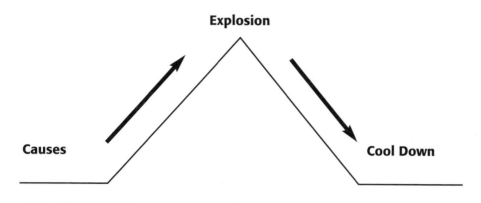

Explosion

Causes

Cool Down

Figure 12.4

Figure 12.5 shows how the student and the teacher in this scenario analyze what they could have done differently to prevent a power struggle. (A Blackline master of a form teachers can use with their own students is provided at the end of this selection [see Blackline 12.2]). This graphic organizer (developed by B. Wiedmann of SkyLight Professional Development), can help teachers and students analyze the "hot points" or "key words and actions" that can cause a minor comment or incident to escalate into a full-scale power struggle from which neither the teacher nor the student can emerge victorious.

Power-seeking students constantly challenge teachers by trying to prove they are in control of issues such as tardiness, incomplete work, making noises, gum chewing, or muttering under their breath. Albert (1989) reminds teachers, "Often power-seeking students don't act out until they're assured of an audience. We [teachers] fear that if we lose a public battle, we'll be labeled a 'loser' by the entire class until school is out in June. The pressure of having to handle such a difficult situation with so much at stake in front of an audience adds greatly to our discomfort."

Students with Behavior Problems

Phases of a Power Struggle

The teacher and the student involved in an altercation should fill out the form to find out what they did to provoke the struggle and what they can do in the future to prevent or resolve the problem.

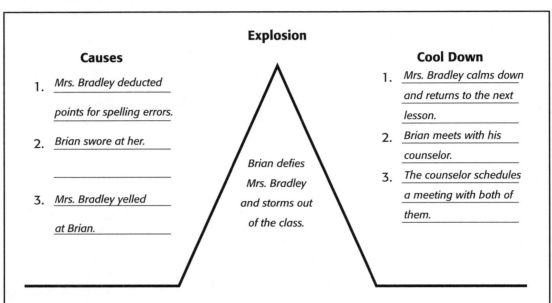

Explosion

Causes

1. Mrs. Bradley deducted points for spelling errors.

2. Brian swore at her.

3. Mrs. Bradley yelled at Brian.

Brian defies Mrs. Bradley and storms out of the class.

Cool Down

1. Mrs. Bradley calms down and returns to the next lesson.

2. Brian meets with his counselor.

3. The counselor schedules a meeting with both of them.

What the teacher could have done to prevent the problem:
I should have told the students my criteria for grading before the test. I should have taken Brian out in the hall when he blew up.

What the student could have done to prevent the problem:
I should have asked to speak to Mrs. Bradley after class in private. I should not have lost my temper in class.

Resolution to problem:
Both Mrs. Bradley and Brian will talk to the class. Mrs. Bradley will promise to share her grading procedures prior to the test. Brian will apologize for his language and behavior. He will serve two detentions for violating school policy. Both will make an effort to conduct all disagreements in private—not in front of the class.

Teacher: _Mrs. Bradley_   Student: _Brian_   Date: _Oct. 4_

Figure 12.5

Other Strategies Teachers Can Use with Students Who Seek Power

- Keep cool and remain calm. The power-seeking student often tries to excite and anger the teacher and fellow students.

- Isolate the student from other group members or classmates. Don't allow a confrontation to erupt where people say and do things they later regret.

- Allow the student some time to cool down and get herself together. Let her go to a private area (office, media center, counselor, time out) so she can compose herself.

- Defuse his anger by saying, "I see your point" or "I know how you must feel," but then state what you think is necessary.

- Delay the issue by saying, "You can stay in your seat now and I'll consider giving you a pass later."

- Conference with the student to find out if any personal or family problems are making her anxious or belligerent. Sometimes the blow-up is not caused by the minor incident that precipitated it; it is because of personal problems.

- Write a contract with the student to brainstorm alternative ideas he might try when he is upset and wants to take control of the class or the group.

- Try to give him a leadership position in one of the next class activities. He can then exercise his leadership role in a positive way, rather than a negative way.

- Reinforce anything the student does that is positive. Encourage her actions when she maintains her cool.

- Have the student keep a Power Problem Journal to record what specific things upset him. The student will get time to process his feelings and reflect on his behavior. Self-analysis is a powerful tool in redirecting behavior.

Students with Behavior Problems

Students Who Seek Revenge

Coach Carden passes out the history test papers and proceeds to lecture the class.

"You must not care about passing this class and getting into college. These tests are pathetic! Did anyone here bother reading the chapter on the Civil War?" he asks sarcastically.

Rick stares at his 62 percent score and doesn't say a word. Then he suddenly crumbles his paper into a ball and tosses it towards the garbage can. It misses!

"Some basketball player you are," scoffs Coach Carden. "I'm glad I'm not your coach."

"I might not be a basketball player after I get my grade for this class. This sucks!" yells Rick.

"What did you say? You know I don't tolerate that kind of language in this class. See me after school today for an hour detention. We'll practice polite conversation."

"You can go to hell!" Rick shouts. "I have practice after school. You can't make me stay."

"Oh yeah, we'll see about that. You'll stay or you'll be suspended and miss a few games!" replies Coach Carden.

"That's not fair. You can't flunk the whole class and you can't make me stay in this sorry excuse for a class. I'm out of here."

Rick storms out of the room shouting, "We'll see what my parents and my coach say when they hear about this. My dad's a lawyer! We'll see you in court!"

Solving the Problem

Sometimes power seekers who never satisfy their need for power become revenge seekers to get back at the person or persons who thwarted their quest for power. Usually the revengeful student is trying to retaliate for something hurtful said by a parent, teacher, or peer, or for some injustice or unfair deed. Albert (1989) says these students often sulk or scowl even when not lashing out. They put teachers on edge because teachers are never sure when these students will retaliate.

The most important thing teachers can do for students who are seeking revenge is to help them rebuild positive relationships with the teacher or the class. It may be difficult for teachers to build a caring relationship with someone who has announced to the whole class that they "suck," but it is important. The social skill of encouragement needs to be emphasized, and teachers should monitor group activities to make sure the revenge seeker is included. The student who seeks revenge should be taught how to express his or her hurt or anger appropriately by talking to the teacher or his or her peers to resolve the problem. Teachers themselves can use the following tactics (see Figure 12.6) with revenge seekers to encourage positive behavior and to reduce power struggles.

Tactics Teachers Can Use with Revenge Seekers

- Avoid sarcasm or put-downs.
- Do not confront the student in front of her peers.
- Don't seek revenge on revenge seekers.
- Listen carefully to his problems (probe for causes).
- Form a positive relationship with the student.
- Encourage the student when she behaves appropriately.
- Ask the student to keep a journal to process feelings and analyze the causes for his anger.
- Admit mistakes.
- Use frequent teacher-student conferences to monitor behavior.

Figure 12.6

Revenge seekers need to be defused or else their hidden agenda may torpedo the class. When this happens, the other students can become resentful and distrustful of the revenge seeker. As a result, the revenge seeker compounds his or her personal problems by alienating peers as well as the teacher.

The revenge seeker's hidden agenda can snowball into a personality problem that can serve to brand the student as a "bully," "incorrigible," or a "loner" for the rest of the year or the rest of his or her schooling. Teachers need to take time from the textbook and curriculum to allow students to process their emotions. Teachers can do this by conferencing with the student, calling in a counselor or another teacher to talk to the student, having the student keep a diary or journal to record events that trigger an outburst, and analyzing different responses.

If students are not happy, satisfied, and accepted in the classroom, they will continue to disrupt learning and interfere with group interactions until their personal needs are met—sometimes at a very extreme level. For example, the violence across American schools, especially in Columbine, Colorado, in 1999, can be linked to students who were enraged. When enraged students kill, they are trying to extort revenge on the person or persons who enraged or embarrassed them or treated them disrespectfully, or anyone else who happens to be in their path. There is a strong link between student revenge seekers and school violence.

Teachers can use a Divided Journal (see Figure 12.7) to allow both themselves and students to reflect on what they may have said or done in anger and propose another way they could approach the problem if it occurs again. (A Blackline master at the end of this selection offers a blank Divided Journal form teachers can use with their students [see Blackline 12.3]). Sometimes these journals help teachers learn more about the inappropriateness of their actions and how their actions could have escalated a minor incident into a showdown in which both parties try to save face with the rest of the class. The ultimate revenge a teacher can retaliate with is failure, but students should not suffer academically for their poor behavior. The problem needs to be addressed so it doesn't distract from learning.

Reflection, which is the focus of the Divided Journal, is a powerful tool to help adults, teenagers, and even young children process their feelings and analyze their actions in private.

Other Strategies Teachers Can Use with Students Who Seek Revenge

- Use I-messages: "When I see you losing your temper, I feel upset because . . .".
- Ask for a conference with the student and ask to have a counselor present as an objective observer.

Divided Journal

The teacher and the student need to process what happened by describing the incident and reflecting on what they would do differently. They should discuss their reactions and try to arrive at a mutually beneficial compromise.

Student: _Rick_ **Date:** _April 5_	**Upon Reflection** **Date:** _April 6_
Description of What Happened	**What I Would Do Differently**
I was angry because I studied hard for the test and Coach was yelling about how we weren't going to get into college. *I freaked out and threw my test away. It upset him, but I was upset that I might get kicked off the basketball team. Basketball means everything to me.*	*I realize that Coach was trying to motivate us to study harder. I should have talked to him after class about what I could do to bring up my grade. Then I would have been calmer and wouldn't have tried to save face with the class. I should never have threatened him with a lawsuit!*
Student: _Coach Carden_ **Date:** _April 5_	**Upon Reflection** **Date:** _April 6_
Description of What Happened	**What I Would Do Differently**
I passed out the tests and talked to the class about their poor performance. Rick was upset and threw his test away. *I was upset because I had planned to review the test and discuss the right answers. He tried to get back at me in front of the class.*	*I should not have passed out the test that way because kids saw each other's papers. I think Rick was embarrassed because one of the cheerleaders saw his 62 percent.* *I shouldn't have made fun of him when he missed the trash with his wadded-up test. I hurt him and he reacted the only way he could—to save face with his peers.*

Figure 12.7

Students with Behavior Problems

- Encourage students who have questions or concerns about assignments or grades to see you privately after class.
- Build in some down time during class while students are working when you are available to discuss problems (especially for students who cannot come in after school).
- Fold over test papers and return them personally to students to preserve confidentiality.
- Don't take the hook. Teenagers are often not in control of their emotions, but teachers should try to be in control of their emotions.

Students with Aggressive Behaviors

Ms. Cox divides the class into cooperative groups and posts the directions for their projects on the board.

Domingo groans when he sees that Jimmy is in his group. "I don't want to work with him," Domingo says to Ms. Cox. "Get him out of my group!"

Ms. Cox walks over to Domingo and asks him, "What is wrong? You know we respect everyone in the class and we try to get along."

"He stole my lunch money," Domingo blurts out. "I don't want to be near that thief!"

"You can't prove that," Jimmy mumbles as he grows more and more red.

"I don't have to prove it," retorts Domingo. "I have three witnesses that saw you take it from my book bag."

Jimmy stands up menacingly and begins walking toward Domingo.

"Sit down," yells Ms. Cox as she runs towards the phone in the room.

Domingo turns to face Jimmy as the rest of the class begins to move their desks away from the impending fight.

Jimmy pulls an Army knife from his pocket and flashes it in front of Domingo's nose. Domingo does not back down and Jimmy inches closer.

One of the boys in the class holds out his foot and trips Jimmy.

Just as Jimmy begins to scuffle with the student who tripped him, the coach in the next room who has heard the scuffle runs into the classroom. He grabs Jimmy, Domingo, and the student who stuck his foot out and hauls them all down to the principal's office.

Solving the Problem

Students who display aggressive behavior are often trying to gain control over their lives. When students constantly utilize anger in an attempt to dominate other students or the group, they are incapable of finding a workable solution to their problems. Their inability to communicate causes them to try to overpower, intimidate, or hurt others. If students are taught to disagree with the idea and not the person, to negotiate, to discuss, and to compromise, aggressive behavior can be prevented. Anger can either be talked out or acted out. When students act out anger, aggression is the result.

> A disinterested student rarely has a satisfying picture of school in his head; perhaps he has the picture of spending his days on the street 'hanging out.' But if his parents are able to force him to go to school, he may choose the angry behavior of disrupting to the extent that he is suspended. Now, out on suspension, he is satisfied. In school he was frustrated and he disrupted to get closer to the picture that he wants. On the street he is in control; in school he has almost no effective control at all (Glasser 1986, p. 53).

Jones and Jones (1998) recommend that teachers do not become emotional or display visible anger when dealing with a student who is demonstrating aggressive behavior. When a teacher begins turning red, speaking louder and faster, and getting upset, the student is so busy thinking about the teacher that he or she cannot think about his or her own mistake or make a new plan of behavior.

Jones and Jones recommend that teachers use the eight strategies and procedures (see Figure 12.8) to protect themselves and their students from violent behavior.

Handling Violent Student Behavior

Teachers should:

1. Remain calm and in control.
2. Send a student for assistance (teacher next door, administrator, school security guard).
3. Guard against confrontational methods because they increase chances of violent reactions from students.
4. Acknowledge the student's feelings, offer assistance, suggest alternatives.
5. Talk in a calm, gentle, yet firm, voice.
6. Give the students adequate space.
7. Remove the audience by asking the rest of the class to go to the library or to another teacher's classroom.
8. Continue to talk to the student about resolving the conflict before the administrator comes.

Adapted from Jones and Jones 1998, pp. 287–288. Reprinted with permission.

Figure 12.8

Of course, all the steps listed in Figure 12.8 can help diffuse the immediate aggressive situation, but the next steps involve meeting with the student, and perhaps the counselor and/or the parents. The behavior needs to be analyzed as to what provoked it, and some form of behavioral interventions, checkpoints, or conferences need to be set to monitor the student's ability to prevent future disturbances. In many cases, the aggressive outburst was merely a symptom of a more complex issue that needs to be articulated and addressed before the aggressive behavior stops.

Violent behavior problems cannot be handled with a detention or names on the board. Teachers need to work with students to develop a long-term action plan. When a student uses a weapon or attempts to use a weapon, he or she is usually suspended or expelled, depending upon the school rules. Other aggressive behaviors, however, include students threatening others, using their fists, or using their books or a desk in a violent fashion. The teacher needs to react quickly to protect the other students, and then work toward solving the long-term problem of the student's aggressive behavior when or if the student returns to class. Figure 12.9 shows a sample Action Plan for the scenario described, and a Blackline master at the end of this selection offers a form teachers can use to help their students (see Blackline 12.4).

Other Strategies Teachers Can Use with Students with Aggressive Behaviors

- After the student returns from suspension or expulsion, talk privately with him to find out why he behaves so aggressively with other students. Try to get to the cause of the problem by asking what personal issues may be causing the problem. Perhaps a counselor needs to be involved if the home problems involve abuse or parental problems.

- Call the student's parents and find out if she has displayed any aggressive tendencies at home or in other school situations, discuss possible solutions, and schedule follow-up conferences.

- Talk with the school counselor to see if there are any previous behavior problems on the student's record. See if a special education class or special counseling is warranted.

- Give the student the option of going to the time-out or satellite area to work on his own when the pressure builds. He should be responsible for all work, but he should do it individually, without assistance from the group.

- Set up a verbal or nonverbal signal that gives the student a warning that she is losing control. For example, one hand across another showing she has "crossed the line."

- Review the behaviors of the other students in the class to see if he is particularly aggravated by one of them and is, therefore, acting out because of a personality conflict.

Action Plan

Analyze the problem and create an Action Plan for the incident.

Students: *Jimmy, Domingo, Paul*

Problem: *Jimmy pulls an Army knife on another student.*

Quick-Recovery Actions

1. *I can separate the students (unless it poses a danger for me or other students).*
2. *I can call for help (or send a student for help).*
3. *I can talk calmly to Jimmy to see if he'll drop the knife.*
4. *I can tell the rest of the students to leave the classroom (remove the audience).*

Next-Step Actions

1. *Conference with both students to find out what caused the problem.*
2. *It may be better to talk to students separately to get both sides of the story.*
3. *Talk to the boy who tripped Jimmy.*
4. *Find out about the lunch money incident.*
5. *Get separate statements from all students involved.*

Long-Term Solutions

1. *Ask a peer mediator or counselor to mediate the conflict about the lunch money.*
2. *Reteach social skills dealing with conflict resolution to whole class.*
3. *Carefully select groups for a while to avoid personality conflicts.*
4. *Refer Jimmy to counseling when he returns from suspension or expulsion.*

Teacher: *Ms. Cox*　　　　Date: *Sept. 25*

Figure 12.9

- Build a personal relationship with the student by talking with her and discovering her special interests.
- Evaluate his academic status to see if he feels inadequate and is resorting to aggressive behavior to compensate for his inability to keep up with the rest of the group.
- Change the cooperative group frequently so she doesn't build up a long-standing feud.
- Have students make a checklist to keep track of their own antisocial behaviors—conference with them at the end of the period, day, or week about how they did and what strategies could help them.
- Videotape or audiotape a class and play it back to the student to let him see how other people perceive his behavior.
- Have the student keep a journal or log where she writes about how she feels when she is upset or angry.
- Assign him a task in which he will succeed to increase his self-esteem.
- While reviewing social skills, role-play a simulated incident involving an aggressive situation and have a discussion about how students should handle the problem.

Students Who Feel Inadequate

Mr. Williams' world history class is studying Greek mythology. The students all have their books open as Mr. Williams calls on various students to read the myths.

"Jamie, will you please read the myth about Aphrodite and Cupid for the class?" Mr. Williams asks.

Jamie turns three shades of red and starts to read slowly and haltingly.

"Aph-ro-dite was very vain. She spent a lot of time primp-ing and gazing in a mirror. On Mount Olymp-us (pause) she lived in a gold palace with her . . .

"I can't pronounce the next word," Jamie mumbles under her breath.

"Protégé," offers Mr. Williams.

"Can somebody else read," begs Jamie. "I don't feel well."

"Sure," Mr. Williams answers. "Lucas, will you please take over where Jamie left off?"

Jamie puts her head down on the desk for the rest of the class.

Solving the Problem

Students often play the "I can't" game because they feel they cannot accomplish a task perfectly. Some "inadequate" students need to realize that it's okay to be imperfect. They can still cooperate with others, perform tasks reasonably well, and produce products that are acceptable.

Dinkmeyer and Losoncy (1980) say that inadequate students often say "I can't" when what they really mean is "I won't." "I can't" is a form of passive resistance, whereas "I won't" is a form of active resistance that usually provokes a power struggle or challenge to teachers. According to Dinkmeyer and Losoncy, "The 'I can't' phrase suggests helplessness and can serve the following purposes:

1. One believes others should serve him or her and puts others in service by proclaiming inadequacy.
2. One believes that he or she is an inadequate person and protects himself or herself from possible failure by 'copping out'—avoiding facing life's challenges.
3. One believes that he or she is unable, helpless, and should be excused from being expected to function." (1980, p. 55–56)

Often students who feel inadequate lack confidence in their ability and perceive life as unfair because they may try very hard, but their efforts still lead to failure. These students become discouraged and develop negative self-concepts. In some cases, these students totally withdraw and give up completely (Dinkmeyer and Losoncy 1980). Teachers often let these quiet and withdrawn students slip through the cracks because they are too busy devoting their attention to the noisier students who are seeking attention or power. Unfortunately, the discouraged and inadequate block of students is much larger than most people realize, and these quiet students often become dropout statistics. In more cases than not, the roots of the problem can be traced to learning problems. Students who cannot read would rather refuse to read or appear uninterested rather than read in front of the class and embarrass themselves in front of their peers. Bellanca and Fogarty (1991) offer tactics to help inadequate students feel confident and in control (see Figure 12.10).

Tactics Teachers Can Use with Students Who Feel Inadequate

- Assign tasks that the student can successfully complete.
- Talk with the student to analyze why he or she feels inadequate.
- Pair the inadequate student with another empathetic student who can help.
- Lower the student's anxiety about mistakes.
- De-emphasize grades and emphasize a love of learning.
- Break larger tasks into smaller chunks.
- Encourage-encourage-encourage!
- Remind students of past successes.
- Keep high expectations for all students.
- Use team-building activities to build trust among group members.
- Give extra recognition for individual contributions to the group.
- Arrange for homework buddies so the student gets additional help and support.
- Give positive feedback.
- Give specific praise for an action when appropriate.
- Help the student remediate specific learning deficiencies that may be causing feelings of inadequacy.
- Listen empathetically to the student's concerns, fears, and frustrations.
- Structure highly motivating group activities so the student is working toward a goal.

Adapted from Bellanca and Fogarty 1991. Reprinted with permission.

Figure 12.10

Students with Behavior Problems

Some students who feel inadequate come to teachers with pessimistic expectations that have been ingrained in them since early childhood. Teachers will not always be able to lift the heavy weight from their shoulders after only one or two conferences. Persistence is the key to helping the student who feels inadequate feel successful, become a valuable member of the group, do well on whole group activities, and succeed on individual tasks. These students try to avoid anything that could cause them to fail; therefore, it's the role of the teacher to structure activities that will make the student succeed, gain confidence, and develop a positive self-concept.

One strategy teachers can use is to read between the lines to determine the real cause of a problem. A student could be acting out or withdrawing to cover a real problem that is causing him or her to feel insecure or inadequate. Sometimes a one-on-one private teacher-student conference can help teachers discover how best to help the student.

The key to effective problem solving in a conference is reflective listening. Teachers who use "closed questions" that call for a "yes-or-no" answer and begin with the word "why" tend to cut off true communication.

Closed Questions

"Closed questions" can sound accusatory, somewhat sarcastic, and negative. They antagonize students and put them on the defensive. The smart responses students sometimes give the teacher are in retaliation for the teacher embarrassing the students in front of their peers. Even if students say nothing or reply courteously, they have suffered humiliation and their self-esteem has been lowered. It is doubtful that "closed questions" will motivate students to shape up. Some sample closed questions are given in Figure 12.11.

GUIDEBOOK

Sample Closed Questions

Question: "Are you just going to sit there or are you going to get busy?"

Answer: "Yes, I'm going to sit here—what are you going to do about it?"

Question: "Do you really think you're funny?"

Answer: "Yes, I do think I'm funny!"

Question: "Why don't you stop fooling around and get on task?"

Answer: "Because, I'm not quite finished fooling around yet."

Figure 12.11

Open Questions

"Open questions" invite further conversation and many possible responses. They also help establish a rapport between teacher and student because they convey to the student a sense of caring and fairness (see Figure 12.12).

Sample Open Questions

Question: "Why do you think you get nervous when you read out loud?"

Answer: "I am embarrassed I might make a mistake and the kids might laugh."

Question: "Hmm. How can I help you feel more confident when you read in front of the class?"

Answer: "Maybe you could work with me after school to help me learn to pronounce the words."

Figure 12.12

As the teacher listens to the student talk about the problem, he or she may want to listen for and draw out the following "subtexts."

- Could it be the student would like other students to notice her more?
- Could it be other students tease her about reading out loud?

- Could it be she has a language problem that embarrasses her?

Dreikurs recommends that during such a discussion, teachers look carefully at the student for what he calls a "recognition reflex," or an involuntary sign that the guess is correct. The reflex could be a shift in posture, a change in eye contact, or a nonverbal cue that indicates the underlying reason for the problem. Often, the student is not aware of what the real problem is and it's the teacher's job to bring it to the surface (cited in Dinkmeyer, McKay, and Dinkmeyer 1980, p. 114).

As shown in the focus strategy in Figure 12.13, teachers may want to include parents in the plan for solving the problem and bolstering the student's self-esteem. (A Blackline master of a Teacher-Student Conference form teachers can use with their students is at the end of this selection [see Blackline 12.5].)

Even though teachers are extremely busy and teach many students each day, the one-on-one conference accomplishes a great deal. First, the teacher devotes individual attention to the student. Second, the teacher can focus on the problem without the distractions of the rest of the class. Third, the teacher gets to know the student on a more personal basis. The interpersonal touch goes a long way in helping students gain confidence and overcome inadequacy.

Other Strategies Teachers Can Use with Students Who Feel Inadequate

- A student may increase his self-esteem by succeeding at an extracurricular activity.
- Work out a secret system with the inadequate student. Promise the student that you will only call on her if you are standing right next to her. That way the student does not have to worry about being called on at other times and can concentrate on the lesson.
- Give the inadequate student a great deal of wait time when you ask questions. Also, try to ask questions you know he can answer to build his confidence.

Teacher-Student Conference

After the teacher asks the student a series of open questions, both the teacher and the student fill out this form.

Student: _Jamie_   Teacher: _Mr. Williams_   Date: _Sept. 9_

Teacher's concern: _I am concerned because you don't participate in class discussions_
and you always seem to get sick or have some other excuse whenever I call on
you in class to read or answer a question.

Student's concern: _I am really shy and I don't like to talk in class because I'm afraid I_
might say something stupid and the other kids will laugh at me. I also hate to
read out loud. I get really nervous and I don't understand one thing I read
because I'm thinking about pronouncing things wrong or not knowing the words.

Possible options:

1. _Mr. Williams will not call on Jamie unless she has her hand raised._

2. _Mr. Williams will not call on students to read in front of the whole class. He'll either_
   put students in groups of 2 or 3 to read together or allow them to read silently.

3. _Jamie will go to the reading teacher to get tested to see if she needs extra help._

Parent involvement:
I will have Jamie read out loud to me every night to help her feel more comfortable
with pronouncing words and reading out loud. I will also buy some audiotapes of
stories for her to listen to as she reads.

Parent's signature: _Mrs. Hansen_

Date of next conference: _Sept. 22_

Figure 12.13

- Give specific encouragement for the student's accomplishment. In other words, don't just say, "Great speech." Tell the student the speech was great because she used good eye contact, effective gestures, and appropriate humor. Be specific.
- Make sure to allow enough time for each activity. Inadequate students often feel rushed, and they become frustrated when the teacher and the class are moving faster than they are.
- Leave some time between activities so students can make the transition. Inadequate students may also suffer from learning disabilities, and they have a difficult time changing their mindset quickly from one task to another.
- Make sure all the homework assignments are realistic. Do not give excessive amounts of homework because inadequate students get very frustrated when they cannot complete all the work. It takes them longer to complete assignments than other students.
- Do not give new material for homework since students might not understand the new concepts. The homework should be a review of concepts already studied.
- Provide rubrics for all major assignments so that students know the expectations for quality work.

With the strategies outlined in this selection, teachers can provide students who demonstrate behavior problems with the appropriate direction and guidance needed to avoid major classroom and learning disturbances.

REFERENCES

Albert, L. 1989. *A teacher's guide to cooperative discipline: How to manage your classroom and promote self-esteem.* Circle Pines, MN: American Guidance Service.

Bellanca, J., and Fogarty, R. 1991. *Blueprints for thinking in the cooperative classroom.* Thousand Oaks, CA: Corwin Press.

Curwin, R. L., and Mendler, A. N. 1988. *Discipline with dignity.* Alexandria, VA: Association for Supervision and Curriculum Development.

Dinkmeyer, D., and L. E. Losoncy. 1980. *The encouragement book. Becoming a positive person.* New York: Prentice-Hall.

Dinkmeyer, D., G. D. McKay, and D. Dinkmeyer, Jr. 1980. *Systematic training for effective teaching.* Circle Pines, MN: American Guidance Service.

Glasser, W. 1986. *Control theory in the classroom.* New York: Harper & Row.

Gough, P. B. 1987. The key to improving schools: An interview with William Glasser. *Phi Delta Kappan* 68(9): 657–658.

Jones, V. F., and L. S. Jones. 1998. *Comprehensive classroom management: Creating communities of support and solving problems,* 5th ed. Boston: Allyn & Bacon.

Kauffman, J. M., D. P. Hallahan, M. P. Mostert, S.C. Trent, and D. G. Nuttycombe. 1993. *Managing classroom behavior: A reflective case-based approach.* Needham Heights, MA: Allyn & Bacon.

Levin, J., and J. F. Nolan. 1996. *Principles of classroom management: A professional decision-making model,* 2d ed. Boston: Allyn & Bacon.

Manning, M. L., and L. G. Baruth. 1995. *Students at risk.* Boston: Allyn & Bacon.

Mendler, A. N. 1997. *Power struggles: Successful techniques for educators.* Rochester, NY: Discipline Associates.

Short, P. M., R. J. Short, and C. Blanton. 1994. *Rethinking student discipline: Alternatives that work.* Thousand Oaks, CA: Corwin Press.

Vaughn, S., C. S. Bos, and J. S. Schumm. 2000. *Teaching exceptional, diverse and at-risk students in the general education classroom,* 2d ed. Boston: Allyn & Bacon.

Six Blackline masters are provided on the pages that follow:
- The Newspaper Model
- Phases of a Power Struggle
- Divided Journal
- Action Plan
- Teacher-Student Conference
- Solving Behavior Problems

The first five are explained in the selection. The last blackline master is provided so that teachers can use any or all of the strategies in this selection to solve a problem with a student. Protégés can use the blacklines with their students when they encounter behavior problems. Mentors can guide their protégés as they use the blacklines and as they devise ways to deal with students' behavior problems.

Students with Behavior Problems

The Newspaper Model

Name:_____ Date:_____

Problem: _____

Who	What	When	Where	Why

Write a paragraph describing your view of what happened.

Signed: _____

Have another group member write a paragraph about the situation.

Signed: _____

Phases of a Power Struggle

Explosion

Causes

1. _____
   _____
2. _____
   _____
3. _____
   _____

Cool Down

1. _____
   _____
2. _____
   _____
3. _____
   _____

What the teacher could have done to prevent the problem:

What the student could have done to prevent the problem:

Resolution to problem:

Teacher:_____ Student:_____ Date:_____

Blackline 12.2

Divided Journal

Student:_____ Date:_____	Upon Reflection Date:_____
Description of What Happened	**What I Would Do Differently**
Student:_____ Date:_____	Upon Reflection Date:_____
Description of What Happened	**What I Would Do Differently**

Blackline 12.3

Action Plan

Students:

Problem:

Quick-Recovery Actions

Next-Step Actions

Long-Term Solutions

Teacher:_____ Date:_____

Students with Behavior Problems

Teacher-Student Conference

Student:_____ Teacher:_____ Date:_____

Teacher's concern:_____

_____

_____

_____

Student's concern:_____

_____

_____

_____

_____

Possible options:

1. _____

_____

2. _____

_____

3. _____

_____

Parent involvement:

Parent's signature:_____

Date of next conference:_____

Blackline 12.5

GUIDEBOOK

Solving Behavior Problems

Directions: Review the strategies in this selection and brainstorm possible solutions to a real problem you have had with a student.

1. Write a brief description of a student you have taught or are currently teaching who has a behavior problem.

Student's First Name:_____ Age:_____ Grade:_____

Description of Problem

---

2. Based upon the strategies reviewed in this selection and your own ideas, brainstorm two possible solutions to the problem.

Solution One:

Students with Behavior Problems

Solution Two:

3. Write a reflection about the insights you have gained about the student and the problem.

My Reflection

Signed:_____ Date:_____

Conclusion

> In our efforts to support new teachers, we need to remember to encourage them to hold on tightly to their original passion for teaching. And those among us who still love to teach can light the way by being positive role models and by showing new teachers how we find our own ways to keep teaching meaningful.—Hurst and Reding 1998, as cited in Scherer (1999)

Just as the Greek teacher Mentor guided the young Telemachus, today's mentor teachers guide new teachers. In addition to helping the protégés develop the organizational skills to succeed, mentors also act as role models. Mentors "walk the talk" and invite new teachers into their classrooms to observe and discuss pedagogy, strategies, and practical tips they learned throughout their careers. Most importantly, mentors share their passion for teaching with their protégés. Despite all the problems faced in the first few years, new teachers can not only survive but also flourish if they are committed to the profession and the students they teach. In this book, *Mentoring Guidebook Level 1: Starting the Journey,* we have attempted to establish the basic foundation of quality teaching. In *Mentoring Guidebook Level 2: Exploring Teaching Strategies,* we expand the process by discussing a higher level of practical brain-compatible learning strategies that help teachers. Integrated lesson designs, teacher-made tests, portfolios, dealing with parents and paraprofessionals and starting the professional growth process are all addressed. In the second book, mentors can select chapters that meet the needs of their protégés as they continue their professional journey.

The most important role a mentor can play is cheerleader—mentors can help keep the love of teaching a major focus throughout the journey. Mentors who share a love of teaching and learning with their protégés can meet and overcome challenges because they work as a team. Together, the mentor/protégé team share a love of teaching and find new ways to keep teaching both meaningful and fulfilling.

REFERENCES

Hurst, B. and G. Reding as cited in Scherer, ed. 1999. "Helping New Teachers Keep the Light in Their Eyes." In *A Better Beginning: Supporting and Mentoring New Teachers*. Alexandria, VA: Association for the Supervision of Curriculum Development.

Resources

by **Barry Sweeny**

The following section offers lists of online as well as audio and video resources that provide further information and support for many of the strategies and ideas discussed in this book.

Induction and Mentoring Web Sites

Best Practice Resources, Inc. (BPR)

http://www.teachermentors.com

This is my own Web site. It has over 300 web pages, 1,100 links, and it is continually growing! The Web site is dedicated to promoting powerful induction and mentoring programs. The research-based materials and assistance are very practical and based on expert information. The information on this site is offered in four ways:

1. Forty-seven categories contain a mix of resources, books, research reports, and Web site links. This section includes links to other organizations that are interested in or support mentoring, as well as a section with Web pages on any of the state-level beginning teacher programs in any of the fifty states.

2. A listing of over 100 BPR staff development publications is provided, most of which are on induction and mentoring. Some of these publications are free and can be accessed right from the Web site. Others are for sale at very reasonable prices. The publications include mentor training manuals, overheads, a training script, mentoring calendars and checklists, information on how to develop an induction program, a summary of the research on mentoring and induction, and information on improving the impact of the mentoring and mentor program.

Adapted from *Leading the Teacher Induction and Mentoring Program* by Barry Sweeny, pp. 159–174. © 2001 Corwin Press. Used with permission.

In addition to mentoring and induction, BPR provides resources for:

- Effective staff development
- School improvement planning
- Peer coaching
- Authentic performance assessment

Each of these sections offers links, information on current events, written materials, and other resources.

3. Free limited assistance and guidance to induction and mentoring programs is offered with leaders through the role of Mentor of Mentors carried out over e-mail and via telephone.

4. Consulting, training, and presentations in induction and mentoring are included. There is a section of the Web site that includes information about the services BPR provides, a client list, and client comments about the work of BPR.

Mentoring Leadership and Resource Network (MLRN)
http://www.mentors.net

Another great mentoring Web site worth visiting and exploring is MLRN. This group is an affiliate of the ASCD. MLRN was started in 1991 by a group of mentoring experts who wanted to help others access the knowledge base about mentoring of teachers. In January 1998, MLRN stopped its paper-based approach to publishing and put all their materials on their Web site. The members of this group (membership fee is $15 a year) can now access all the newsletter articles, papers, and journal articles MLRN has published since 1991. There are currently about seventy-five resources available.

A newer section of the site is designed specifically for mentor program coordinators and there is a membership listing to help coordinators locate and access educators who are interested in mentoring in their area. Most of the resources are in a Member's Only section of the Web site. Non-members can access parts of the site to learn about MLRN and to see a listing of the materials that are available to members to help them decide if they want to join. Program leaders can submit mentoring articles or studies to MLRN for web publication.

Links to Other Mentoring and Induction Resources on the Internet

On my Web site, which is described above (BPR), there are over 1,100 links to mentoring and induction Web sites. The following listing of links are mentoring and induction Web sites that are in addition to those on my Web site. These are arranged by category.

Please keep in mind when checking out the Web sites listed here that some of these links may have changed or become inactive by the time you try them.

Advice for and About Beginning Teachers

Helpful Hints for Beginning Teachers
http://www.positiveparenting.com/jane4.html

Information on School-to-Work
http://www.ncrel.org/sdrs/areas/issues/envrnmnt/stw/
sw5camp.htm

Kappa Delta Pi New Teacher Advocate
http://www.kdp.org/

New Math Teacher Advice
http://ncrtl.msu.edu/

I Love Teaching
http://www.iloveteaching.com/

New Teacher Seminars
http://www.rochester.k12.mn.us/gip/calendar.htm

Been There Done That Seminar
http://www.utofd.com/Teachers/NewTeach/beenther.htm

Dade County New Teacher Web Page
http://www.utofd.com/Teachers/NewTeach/newtchsc.html

Realistic Assignments for New Teachers
http://www.columbiagroup.org/retention3.htm

Survival Kit for New Teachers
http://www.inspiringteachers.com/

The Substitute/Student Teacher's Survival Handbook
http://www.teachergroup.com/

What to Expect Your First Year of Teaching
http://www.ed.gov/pubs/FirstYear/

Web-Based Books and Publications on Mentoring and Induction

Beginning Teacher Handbook
http://www.ccthomas.com/catalog/esped/more/
0-398-05833-4.html

Kappa Delta Pi New Teacher Advocate
http://www.kdp.org/

Mentoring and Peer Coaching Resources
http://www.teachermentors.com/

Characteristics of Effective Mentors

Mentor Characteristics
http://education.lanl.gov/resources/Mentors/character.html

Teacher as Caregiver, Model, and Mentor
http://www.cortland.edu/www/c4n5rs/wheel/12.htm

Descriptions of Mentoring Programs

North Platt, Nebraska
http://www.esu16.k12.ne.us/brochures/entry.html

SmokeyHill
http://www.smokyhill.org/BTMT.htm

Mentoring Program for Science Teachers
http://www.imsa.edu/team/spi/impact2/catalogs.html

University of Dayton: Mentors Help New Teachers Adjust
http://www.udayton.edu/news/nr/012397a.html

Montana
http://www.nsf.gov/od/lpa/news/publicat/frontier/2-97/
2montana.htm

One Year Internship (United States Department of Education) *Education Week* **on the Web**
http://www.edweek.org/ew/vol-16/30cincy.h16

Indiana Beginning Teacher Internship
http://ideanet.doe.state.in.us/super/083096/do1.html

Internship Training Plan
http://ideanet.doe.state.in.us/super/083096/safe2.html

Peer Resources Mentor Programs
http://www.peer.ca/mentorprograms.html

Mentors Forum—Mentoring Guidance and Information
http://www.mentorsforum.co.uk/

The Mentoring Group
http://www.mentoringgroup.com/

Evaluating a Mentoring Program

Evaluation of Professional Development
http://www.ncrel.org/sdrs/areas/issues/educatrs/profdevl/pd500.htm

Program Evaluation
http://www.mentorsforum.co.uk/cOL1/tools/Evaluating.htm

Evaluation of or by Mentors

Evaluating the Relationship by the Protégé
http://www.vcu.edu/teaching/oldteaching/medicine/mgevaluating.html

X-Change for a Day—Program Evaluation
http://www.nnlm.nlm.nih.gov/train/xchange/mentor.html

Grants and Funding for Mentoring

Public Funding and Professional Development
http://www.columbiagroup.org/public.htm

Cost Neutral Induction Program
http://www.rochester.k12.mn.us/gip/isgip.htm

Help for Mentors

The Mentor Teacher Casebook
http://darkwing.uoregon.edu/~ericcem/mentor.html

The National Board of Professional Teaching Standards
http://www.nbpts.org/

Mentoring, Coaching, and Staff Development Resources
http://www.teachermentors.com/

Preparing New Teachers for Bilingual Education
http://www.ed.gov/pubs/ModStrat/pt2d.html

Mentoring the Mentor
http://www.nsdc.org/library/mentoring.html

Mentors and Mentoring
http://www.erlbaum.com/Books/searchintro/BookDetailscvr.cfm
? ISBN=0-8058-9932-4

Incentives and Recognition

Incentives in a Graduate Induction Program
http://www.rochester.k12.mn.us/gip/clinical.htm

Quality Standards and Incentives for Teachers
http://www.columbiagroup.org/quality.htm

International Mentoring

International Mentor Program
http://www.iteachnet.com/teachnet.html

The European Mentoring Centre
http://www.mentoringcentre.org/

How Are Other Countries Preparing Teachers?
http://www.columbiagroup.org/howare.htm

Teacher Induction in Countries Around the Pacific Rim
http://www.ed.gov/pubs/APEC

Mentor Program Coordination

Mentoring the Mentor
http://www.nsdc.org/library/mentoring.html

Induction Program Governance Committee
http://www.rochester.k12.mn.us/gip/coord.htm

Consultants in Mentoring and Induction
http://www.teachermentors.com

National Reforms and Standards

The National Board of Professional Teaching Standards
http://www.nbpts.org/

Organizations that Support Teachers and Technology

Association for the Advancement of Computing Education (AACE)
http://www.aace.org/

Association for Educational Communications and Technology (AECT)
http://www.aect.org/

International Society for Technology in Education (ISTE)
http://www.iste.org/

ASCD Professional Development Online
www.ascd.org/pdi/pd.html

AT& T Learning Network
www.att.com/learningnetwork

The Community Learning Network
www.cln.org

Ed's Oasis
www.edsoasis.org

The Global Schoolhouse
www.globalschoolhouse.org

International Education and Research Network (I*EARN)
www.iearn.org

PBS Mathline
www.pbs.org/teachersource/math

Tapped-In
www.tappedin.org

U.S. Department of Education
www.ed.gov/inits/teachers/teach.html

The Well Connected Educator
www.gsh.org/wce

Orientation of New Teachers

Orientation Schedule
http://www.rochester.k12.mn.us/gip/calendar.htm

Fairfax County, Virginia—New Teacher Orientation
http://www.fcps.k12.va.us/DIS/OSDT/nto.htm

Portfolios/Professional Development Plans

Teacher Portfolio Assessment
http://www.ed.gov/databases/ERIC_Digests/ed385608.html

Preservice Teacher Mentoring

Answers to Student Teacher Problems
http://www.lll.hawaii.edu/esl/crookes/Narita.html

Mentoring Student Teachers
http://www.udayton.edu/news/nr/050696.html

Recruiting and Retaining New Teachers

Preparing New Teachers for Bilingual Education
http://www.ed.gov/pubs/ModStrat/pt2d.html

Recruitment for Induction Program
http://www.rochester.k12.mn.us/gip/app.htm

The Job Market—Teacher Recruitment Agencies
http://www.2teach.govt.nz

South Carolina Center for Teacher Recruitment
http://www.scctr.org/minority.htm

Office of Teacher Recruitment
http://www.firn.edu/doe/bin00023/teachin.htm

About Recruiting New Teachers
http://www.rnt.org/about/index.html

Teacher Recruiting and Retention via Mentoring
http://www.columbiagroup.org/retention2.htm

Recruiting and Retention: Rewarding Teachers
http://www.columbiagroup.org/recruiting6.htm

Recruitment Partner Network Information
http://www.rnt.org/collaborations/index.html

Recruitment of Mentors

Effort To Recruit Mentor Teachers Fails
http://www.edweek.org/ew/vol-16/37guff.h16

Research in Mentoring

Teacher Mentoring: A Critical Review
http://www.ed.gov/databaes/ERIC_Digests/ed397060.html

Research Activities in Europe
http://www.mentoringcentre.org/frames/researchframe.htm

Empowering the Faculty
http://www.ed.gov/databases/ERIC_Digests/ed399888.html

Resources for Mentor Programs

Mentor Teacher Forms
http://www.khsd.k12.ca.us/MENTOR/mentor9798/forms/
index.htm

**American Federation of Teachers Mentor Contract
Language**
http://www.aft.org/research/models/language/tquality/
mentor.htm

Roles, Tasks, and Strategies for Mentors

A Quiver Full: Mentoring Strategies Book
http://home.earthlink.net/~drdelliott/quiverful.html

Components—Induction Programs
http://www.ed.gov/databases/ERIC_Digests/ed269407.html

State Induction Programs

A Survey of State-Mandated Induction Programs in the Fifty States
http://www.teachermentors.com/

Indiana's Beginning Teacher Internship
http://ideanet.doe.state.in.us/super/083096/do1.html

Indiana I-CAN Update
http://www.indianacc.org/tables/3news3.html

Indiana New Teacher Training
http://ideanet.doe.state.in.us/super/083096/safe2.html

Indiana—Requirements
http://www.tc.columbia.edu/~teachcomm/POL-INFO/Indi-ah.htm

Nebraska Entry Year Assistance Program
http://www.esu16.k12.ne.us/brochures/entry.html

North Carolina Web Book—Mentoring New Teachers
http://www.dpi.state.nc.us/mentoring_novice_teachers/

SouthEast USA State Standards for Teachers
http://www.columbiagroup.org/state.htm

Wyoming Mentoring House Bills
http://legisweb.state.wy.us/97sessin/HBILLS/HB0047.htm

Support for Teachers

Designing Internet Projects
http://www.ncsa.uiuc.edu/edu/RSE/RSEviolet/RSEviolet.html

Internet for Girls: World Wide Web Resource List
http://www.sdsc.edu/~woodka/resources.html

Lesson Plan Design and Other Issues
http://www.su.edu/faculty/jcombs/

Technology in Mentoring

Technology in Mentoring—Abstract
http://archives.math.utk.edu/ICTCM/abs/7-FC13.html

The Role of Computers in Mentoring
http://mbhs.bergtraum.k12.ny.us/mentor/what.html#5

Telementoring

Teleapprenticeships in Teaching
http://www.ed.uiuc.edu/projects/tta/design.sup.html

Lessons in Telementoring
http://curry.edschool.virginia.edu/go/mining/96/oct/

Online Innovation Institute for Teacher Development
http://oii.org/

Telementoring Web
http://mbhs.bergtraum.k12.ny.us/mentor/

Examples of Telementoring
http://mbhs.bergtraum.k12.ny.us/mentor/exam.html

Telementoring Guidelines
http://mbhs.bergtraum.k12.ny.us/mentor/guide.html

Hewlett-Packard Mentors for Students
http://www.sfusd.k12.ca.us/resources/hpmentor.html

Telementoring Resources and WWW Links
http://nsn.bbn.com/telementor_wrkshp/tmlink.html

Mighty Mentors—E-mail Mentoring for Teachers
http://www.mightymedia.com/mentors/

EDC/CCT Telementoring Project
http://www.edc.org/CCT/telementoring/docs/pmentoring.html

Bemidji State Virtual Mentorship Program
http://cel.bemidji.msus.edu/virtual/mentor.html

Training and Staff Development for Mentors

Montana State University Mentor Training for Cooperating Teachers
http://www.msubillings.edu/opp/

Mentoring and Peer Coaching Training Materials
http://www.teachermentors.com/

SkyLight Consulting Services—Mentoring
Click on the In-district Training link at http://www.skylightedu.com.

Audio and Video Resources

Videotape Programs

• *High Performance Mentoring: A Multimedia Program for Training Mentors* (1999) by Dr. James Rowley and Dr. Patricia Hart. Includes a Facilitator's Guide, four videotapes, a CD-ROM with visuals, and a participant's notebook. The series provides twenty-five training modules, including two for administrators on confidentiality and how to support a teacher mentor program. $795.00. Published by Corwin Press, 2455 Teller Road, Thousand Oaks, CA 91320-2218, (805) 499-9774.

• *Mentoring to Improve Schools* (1999). Includes a Facilitator's Guide with eight workshops and two videotapes: "Successful Mentoring Programs," and "Effective Mentoring Practices" by Barry Sweeny and Todd Johnson. # 498325H09, $228 (ASCD members), $298 (nonmembers). Association for Supervision and Curriculum Development, 1703 N. Beauregard St., Alexandria, VA 22311-1714. 800-933-2723.

• *Mentoring the New Teacher* (1994) by Dr. James Rowley and Dr. Patricia Hart. Includes nine videotapes, a Facilitator's Guide, and two other ASCD books on mentoring. Focused primarily on the needs of beginning teachers, such as dealing with parents, classroom management, etc. Association for Supervision and Curriculum Development, 1703 N. Beauregard St., Alexandria, VA 22311-1714, 800-933-2723.

• *The New Teacher: Meeting the Challenges* (1999) featuring Linda Darling-Hammond. Order # VTNT-WEB. $99.95. National Professional Resources, Inc., 25 South Regent Street, Port Chester, NY 10573, 800-453-7461.

• *Teacher Induction, Mentoring, and Renewal* (1996) featuring Harry Wong. Order # 505. $355.00. Tape 1 is thirty-five minutes and is on new teacher preparedness through effective induction. Tape 2 is thirty minutes and includes mentoring and teacher renewal. Also includes a guidebook and an audiotape. Published by Video Journal of Education, 8686 South 1300 East, Sandy, UT 84094, 800-572-1153.

• *Mentoring Case Studies* (2002): The Inclusive Classroom, Standards and Assessment, Classroom Management, and Instructional Planning. SkyLight Professional Development. For more information visit the Web site at http://skylightedu.com.

Audiotape Programs

• *How to Mentor in the Midst of Change* (1998). Two audiotapes (# 298181H09) are $24.95 for ASCD members and $29.95 for nonmembers, and the book (# 61192015H09) is $6.95 for ASCD members and $8.95 for nonmembers. Association for Supervision and Curriculum Development, 1703 N. Beauregard St., Alexandria, VA, 22311-1714, 800-933-2723.

Bibliography

Airasian, P., and A. Gullickson. 1996. *Teacher self-evaluation tool kit.* Thousand Oaks, CA: Corwin Press. A Sage Publications Company.

Albert, L. 1989. *A teacher's guide to cooperative discipline: How to manage your classroom and promote self-esteem.* Circle Pines, MN: American Guidance Service.

Barbknecht, A., and C. W. Kieffer. 2001. *Peer coaching: The learning team approach.* Arlington Heights, IL: SkyLight Training and Publishing.

Barkley, S. G. 1999. Time: It's made, not found. *Journal of Staff Development* 20(4): 37–39.

Barell, J. 1998. *Problem-based learning: An inquiry approach.* Thousand Oaks, CA: Corwin Press.

Bellanca, J., and R. Fogarty. 1986. *Catch them thinking: A handbook of classroom strategies.* Palatine, IL: SkyLight Training and Publishing.

———. 1991. *Blueprints for thinking in the cooperative classroom.* Thousand Oaks, CA: Corwin Press.

———. 2002. *Blueprints for achievement in the cooperative classroom,* 3rd ed. Thousand Oaks, CA: Corwin Press.

Bird, T. 1986. *The mentor's dilemma.* San Francisco: Far West Regional Educational Laboratory.

Blase, J., and J. Blase. 1998. *Handbook of instructional leadership: How really good principals promote teaching and learning.* Thousand Oaks, CA: Corwin Press.

Brophy, J. 1999. Perspectives of classroom management: Yesterday, today and tomorrow. In *Beyond behaviorism: Changing the classroom management paradigm,* edited by H. J. Freiberg. Boston: Allyn & Bacon

Burke, K., R. Fogarty, and S. Belgrad. 1995. *The portfolio connection training manual.* Thousand Oaks, CA: Corwin Press.

———. 2002. *The portfolio connection: Student work linked to standards,* 2nd ed. Thousand Oaks, CA: Corwin Press.

Burke, K. 1997. *Designing professional portfolios for change.* Thousand Oaks, CA: Corwin Press.

———. 1999. *How to assess authentic learning,* 3rd ed. Thousand Oaks, CA: Corwin Press.

———. 2000. *What to do with the kid who . . .: Developing coopera-tion, self-discipline, and responsibility in the classroom.* Thousand Oaks, CA: Corwin Press.

Caine, R., and G. Caine. 1994. *Making connections: Teaching and the human brain.* New York: Addison-Wesley/Innovative Publications.

Canning, C. 1991. What teachers say about reflection. *Educational Leadership* 48(6):19. Alexandria, VA: Association for Supervision and Curriculum Development.

Correia, M. P., and J. M. McHenry. 2002. *The mentor's handbook: Practical suggestions for collaborative reflection and analysis.* Norwood, MA: Christopher-Gordon Publishers.

Costa, A. L. 1985. *Developing minds.* Alexandria, VA: Association for Supervision and Curriculum Development.

Costa, A., and R. Garmston. 2002. *Cognitive coaching: A foundation for renaissance schools,* 2nd ed. Norwood, MA: Christopher-Gordon Publishers.

Cummings, C. 1980. *Teaching makes a difference.* Edmonds, WA: Teaching, Inc.

Curwin, R. L., and A. N. Mendler. 1988. *Discipline with dignity.* Alexandria, VA: Association for Supervision and Curriculum Development.

Danielson, C. 1996. *Enhancing professional practice: A framework for teaching.* Alexandria, VA: Association for Supervision and Curriculum Development.

Delgado, M. 1999. Developing competent practitioners. *Educational Leadership* 56(8): 45–48.

Dinkmeyer, D., and L. E. Losoncy. 1980. *The encouragement book. Becoming a positive person.* New York: Prentice-Hall.

Dinkmeyer, D., G. D. McKay, and D. Dinkmeyer, Jr. 1980. *Systematic training for effective teaching.* Circle Pines, MN: American Guidance Service.

Ellis, A. K., and J. T. Fouts. 1997. *Research on educational innova-tions.* Larchmont, NY: Eye on Education.

Evertson, C. M., E. T. Emmer, B. S. Clements, and M. E. Worsham. 1997. *Classroom management for elementary teachers,* 4th ed. Boston: Allyn & Bacon.

Evertson, C., and A. Harris. 1991. *Components of effective classroom management: Materials selected from the NDN-approved class-room organization and management program (COMP).* Nashville, TN: Vanderbilt University.

Feuerstein, R. 1980. *Instrumental enrichment.* Baltimore, MD: University Park Press.

Fogarty, R. 1997. Brain-compatible classrooms. Thousand Oaks, CA: Corwin Press.

Fogarty, R. 2002. *Brain-compatible classrooms,* 2nd ed. Thousand Oaks, CA: Corwin Press.

Freiberg, H. J. 1998. Measuring school climate: Let me count the ways. *Educational Leadership* 56(1): 22–26.

———. ed. 1999. *Beyond behaviorism: Changing the classroom management paradigm.* Boston: Allyn & Bacon.

———. 2002. Essential skills for new teachers. *Educational Leadership* 59(6): 56–60.

Gardner, H. 1981. Do babies sing a universal song? *Psychology Today.*

———. 1982. *Developmental psychology: An introduction.* Boston: Little Brown.

———. 1983. *Frames of mind: The theory of multiple intelligences.* New York: Harper and Row.

———. 1987. Developing the spectrum of human intelligences: Teaching in the eighties, a need to change. *Harvard Educational Review.*

———. 1993. *Frames of mind: The theory of multiple intelligences— Tenth anniversary edition.* NY: Basic Books.

———. 1996. *Are there additional intelligences?* Cambridge, MA: Harvard Graduate School of Education.

Garmston, R. J., and B. M. Wellman. 1999. *The adaptive school: A sourcebook for developing collaborative groups.* Norwood, MA: Christopher-Gordon Publishers.

Glanz, J., and R. F. Neville. 1997. *Educational supervision: Perspectives, issues, and controversies.* Norwood, MA: Christopher-Gordon Publishers.

Glasser, W. 1986. *Control theory in the classroom.* New York: Harper & Row.

———. 1990. *The quality school.* New York: Harper Perennial.

Glickman, C. D. 2002. *Leadership for learning: How to help teachers succeed.* Alexandria, VA: Association of Supervision and Curriculum Development.

Glickman, C. D., S. P. Gordon, and J. M. Ross-Gordon. 2002. *Supervision of instruction and developmental approach,* 4th Ed. Needham Heights, MA: Allyn and Bacon.

Gold, Y., and R. A. Roth. 1999. *The transformational helping professional: A new vision: Mentoring and supervising reconsidered.* Needham Heights, MA: Allyn and Bacon.

Good, T., and J. Brophy. 1997. *Looking in classrooms.* New York: Addison Wesley Longman.

Gough, P. B. 1987. The key to improving schools: An interview with William Glasser. *Phi Delta Kappan* 68(9): 657–658.

Gronlund, N. E. 1998. *Assessment of student achievement,* 6th ed. Boston: Allyn and Bacon.

Gusky, T., and K. D. Peterson. 1996. The road to classroom change. *Educational Leadership* 53(4): 10–14.

Hamilton, C., with C. Parker. 1990. *Communicating for results.* Belmont, CA: Wadsworth.

Hansen, J. M., and J. Childs. 1998. Creating a school where people like to be. *Educational Leadership* 56(1): 14–17.

Harman, W. 1988. *The global mind change.* Indianapolis: Knowledge Systems.

Harman, W., and H. Rheingold. 1985. *Higher creativity.* Los Angeles: J. P. Tarcher.

Harp, B., ed. 1994. *Assessment and evaluation for student learning,* 2nd ed. Norwood, MA: Christopher-Gordon Publishers.

Hayes, C., P. Grippe, and G. Hall. 1999. Firmly planted. *Journal of Staff Development* 20(4): 17–21.

Heidkamp, A., and J. Shapiro. 1999. The elements of a supportive induction program. In *A better beginning: Supporting and mentoring new teachers,* edited by M. Scherer. Alexandria, VA: Association for Supervision and Development.

Herman, J. L., L. Morris, and C. T. Fitz-Gibbon. 1987. *Evaluator's handbook.* Newbury Park, CA: Sage Publications.

Herman, J. L., P. R. Aschbacher, and L. Winters. 1992. *A practical guide to alternative assessment.* Alexandria, VA: Association for Supervision and Development.

Houston, J. 1980. *Lifeforce: The psycho-historical recovery of the self.* New York: Delacourte Press.

———. 1982. *The possible human: A course in extending your physical, mental, and creative abilities.* Los Angeles: J. P. Tarcher.

———. 1987. *The search for the beloved: Journeys in sacred psychology.* Los Angeles: J. P. Tarcher.

Hunter, M. 1984. Knowing, teaching, and supervising. In *Using what we know about teaching and learning,* edited P. Hosford, pp.169-192. Alexandria, VA: Association for Supervision and Curriculum Development.

Jensen, E. 2000. *Brain based learning.* Del Mar, CA: Turning Point Publishing.

Johnson, D., and R. Johnson. 1978. Social interdependence within instruction. *Journal of Research and Development in Education.* (121): 1–152.

———. 1984. *Circles of learning.* Alexandria, VA: Association for Supervision and Curriculum Development.

Jones, V. F., and L. S. Jones. 1998. *Comprehensive classroom management: Creating communities of support and solving problems,* 5th ed. Boston: Allyn & Bacon.

Kauffman, J. M., D. P. Hallahan, M. P. Mostert, S. C. Trent, and D. G. Nuttycombe. 1993. *Managing classroom behavior: A reflective case-based approach.* Needham Heights, MA: Allyn & Bacon.

Kohn, A. 1991. Caring kids: The role of the schools. *Phi Delta Kappan* 72(7): 496–506.

———. 1996. *Beyond discipline: From compliance to community.* Alexandria, VA: Association for Supervision and Curriculum Development.

Lazear, D. 1999. *Eight ways of teaching: The artistry of teaching with multiple intelligences.* Thousand Oaks, CA: Corwin Press.

Levin, J., and J. F. Nolan. 1996. *Principles of classroom management: A professional decision-making model,* 2d ed. Boston: Allyn & Bacon.

Lewin, L., and B. J. Shoemaker. 1998. *Great performances; Creating classroom-based assessment tasks.* Alexandria, VA: Association for Supervision and Development.

Lucas, C. 1999. How a veteran teacher can help a beginner. *Educational Leadership* 56(8): 27–29.

Machado, L. 1980. *The right to be intelligent.* New York: Pergamon Press.

MacLean, P. 1977. On the evolution of the three mentalities. In *New dimensions in psychiatry: A world view* (Vol. 2), edited by S. Arieti and G. Chryanowski. New York: Wiley.

Magee, M. 1999. The curse of the trophy. *Journal of Staff Development* 10(4): 23–26.

Manning, M. L., and L. G. Baruth. 1995. *Students at risk.* Boston: Allyn & Bacon.

Masters, R., and J. Houston. 1972. *Mind games.* New York: Delacourte Press.

———. 1978. *Listening to the body: The psychophysical way to health and awareness.* New York: Delacourte Press.

Mendler, A. N. 1997. *Power struggles: Successful techniques for educators.* Rochester, NY: Discipline Associates.

Mehrens, W. A. 1992. Using performance assessment for accountability purposes. *Educational measurement: Issues and practices* 11 (1): 3–9.

Millman, J., and L. Darling-Hammond, eds. 1990. *The new handbook of teacher evaluation: Assessing elementary and secondary school teachers.* Thousand Oaks, CA: Corwin Press.

Moller, G. 1999. At issue: Teacher leadership. *Journal of Staff Development* 20(4): 11–15.

Pajak, E. 1993. *Approaches to clinical supervision: Alternatives for improving instruction.* Norwood, MA: Christopher-Gordon Publishers.

Peterson, K. D., and T. E. Deal. 1998. How leaders influence the culture of schools. *Educational Leadership* 56(1): 28–30.

Pitton, D. 2000. *Mentoring novice teachers: Fostering a dialogue process.* Thousand Oaks, CA: Corwin Press.

Pribram, K. 1971. *Language of the brain: Experimental paradoxes and principles in neuro-psychology.* Englewood Cliffs, NJ: Prentice Hall.

———. 1974. *Holonomy and structure in the organization of perception.* Stanford, CA: Stanford University Press.

Popham, W. J. 1999. *Classroom assessment: What teachers need to know,* 2nd ed. Boston: Allyn and Bacon.

Rogers, C., and H. J. Freiberg. 1994. *Freedom to learn,* 3rd ed. Upper Saddle River, NJ: Prentice-Hall.

Romer, T. 1999, November. An e-mail message to Barry Sweeney regarding the benefits and results of full-time mentoring.

Samovar, L., R. Porter, and N. Jain. 1981. *Understanding intercultural communication.* Belmont, CA: Wadsworth.

Scherer, M. 1998. A conversation with Herb Kohl. *Educational Leadership* 56(1): 8–13.

Scherer, M., ed. 1999. Helping new teachers keep the light in their eyes. In *A better beginning: Supporting and mentoring new teachers*. Alexandria, VA: Association for Supervision and Curriculum Development.

Seifert, K. L. 1999. *Reflective thinking and professional development*. Boston: Houghton Mifflin.

Short, P. M., R. J. Short, and C. Blanton. 1994. *Rethinking student discipline: Alternatives that work*. Thousand Oaks, CA: Corwin Press.

Skowron, J. 1990. Frameworks for reading instruction. *Illinois Reading Council Journal* 18(1): 15–21.

———. 2001. *Powerful lesson planning models: The art of 1,000 decisions*. Thousand Oaks, CA: Corwin Press.

Solomon, P. G. 1998. *The curriculum bridge: From standards to actual classroom practice*. Thousand Oaks, CA: Corwin Press.

Stronge, J. H. 1997. *Evaluating teaching: A guide to current thinking and best practices*. Thousand Oaks, CA: Corwin Press.

Sullivan, C. G. 1992. *How to mentor in the midst of change*. Alexandria, VA: Association for Supervision and Curriculum Development.

Sweeny, B. W. 1994. *Promoting the growth of new teachers: A mentor training manual*. Wheaton, IL: Resources for Staff and Organization Development.

———. 1998. *A survey of state-mandated mentoring and new teacher induction programs in the 50 United States*. Wheaton, IL: Best Practice Resources. Online at <www.teachermentors.com/MCenter%20Site/StateList.html>.

———. 2001. *Leading the teacher induction and mentoring program*. Thousand Oaks, CA: Corwin Press.

Tannehill, D. 1989. Student teaching: A view from the other side. *Journal of Teaching in Physical Education* 8: 243–253.

Tell, C. 2001. Appreciating teaching: A conversation with Lee Shulman. *Educational Leadership* 58(5): 6–11.

Trager, G. 1958. Paralanguage: A first approximation. *Studies in Linguistics* 13: 1–12.

Vaughn, S., C. S. Bos, and J. S. Schumm. 2000. *Teaching exceptional, diverse and at-risk students in the general education classroom*, 2d ed. Boston: Allyn & Bacon.

Vella, J., P. Berardinelli, and J. Burrow. 1998. *How do they know they know: Evaluating adult learning*. San Francisco: Jossey-Bass.

Villani, S. 2002. *Mentoring programs for new teachers: Models of induction and support*. Thousand Oaks, CA: Corwin Press.

Wiggins, G., and J. McTighe. 1998. *Understanding by design*. Alexandria, VA: Association for Supervision and Curriculum Development.

Zemelman, S., H. Daniels, and A. Hyde. 1993. *Best practice: New standards for teaching and learning in America's schools*. Portsmouth, NH: Heinemann.

Index

MENTORING

Excerpts included in
Mentoring Guidebook Level 1: Starting the Journey
are taken from the following Corwin Press titles.

Kay Burke

How to Assess Authentic Learning,
THIRD EDITION

Debra Eckerman Pitton

Mentoring Novice Teachers: Fostering a Dialogue Process

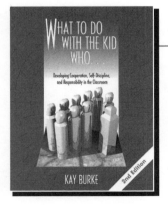

Kay Burke

What to Do With the Kid Who . . . : Developing Cooperation, Self-Discipline, and Responsibility in the Classroom,
SECOND EDITION

Barry Sweeny

Leading the Teacher Induction and Mentoring Program

James Bellanca and Robin Fogarty

Blueprints for Achievement in the Cooperative Classroom

THIRD EDITION

Janice Skowron

Powerful Lesson Planning Models: The Art of 1,000 Decisions

David Lazear

Eight Ways of Teaching: The Artistry of Teaching with Multiple Intelligences

THIRD EDITION

For more information on these titles, videotapes, and conferences please visit Corwin Press's Web site at

www.corwinpress.com